£7–

THE STINGING FLY

NEW WRITERS · NEW WRITING

Issue 43 | Volume Two | Winter 2020-21

THE GALWAY 2020 EDITION

'... God has specially appointed me to this city, so as though it were a large thoroughbred horse which because of its great size is inclined to be lazy and needs the stimulation of some stinging fly...'

—Plato, *The Last Days of Socrates*

The Stinging Fly
new writers, new writing
PO Box 6016, Dublin 1
info@stingingfly.org

Editor: Danny Denton

Publisher	*Poetry Editor*	*Website Editor*
Declan Meade	Cal Doyle	Ian Maleney
Assistant Editor	*Eagarthóir Filíochta*	*Reviews Editor*
Sara O'Rourke	Aifric MacAodha	Lily Ní Dhomhnaill

Contributing Editors
Dan Bolger, Mia Gallagher, Lisa McInerney, Thomas Morris and Sally Rooney

© Copyright remains with authors and artists, 2020

Printed by Walsh Colour Print, County Kerry

ISBN 978-1-906539-85-6   ISSN 1393-5690

The Stinging Fly gratefully acknowledges the support of The Arts Council/
An Chomhairle Ealaíon.

THE GALWAY 2020 EDITION

Guest Editor: Lisa McInerney
Guest Poetry Editor: Elaine Feeney

NEW FICTION

COMHCHEALG

NEW POEMS

ESSAYS

The Stinging Fly was established in 1997 to publish and promote
the best new Irish and international writing.

Published twice a year, we welcome submissions on a regular basis.
Online submissions only. Please read the submission guidelines on our website.

Keep in touch: sign up to our email newsletter, become a fan on Facebook, or follow us on Twitter
for regular updates about our publications, podcasts, workshops and events.

stingingfly.org | facebook.com/StingingFly | @stingingfly

Editorial

The 2016 documentary *Hotel Coolgardie* details the troubles of two Finnish backpackers hired as barmaids in a tiny outback town in Western Australia, where they suffer bad behaviour from hard-drinking locals. *The Guardian* said it had 'a premise right out of (Ted Kotcheff's 1971 thriller) *Wake in Fright*', so naturally I couldn't wait to see it, but it only left me shaken because I didn't think the behaviour of the locals was that notable. There were boors, insecure and petty, and horny young fellas who turned very irritating when drunk, and none of them would have been out of place in the pubs I'd worked in in south County Galway. I'd seen worse: in south County Galway pubs I've been propositioned, shouted at, flashed at, and threatened with bar stools held aloft, and if you're going to sell me a real-life *Wake In Fright*, it better deliver something more disquieting than a typical Saturday night out in a GAA stronghold. Maybe I've been living in some uncouth hellhole and, having been raised in the flames, can't feel the heat and can't hear the howling. Though really, I suspect it's just that documentary film critics are delicate creatures.

I was reminded watching *Hotel Coolgardie* of how disconnected from the common concept of 'culture' many of us are, if we mean culture defined as music and art and literature. Who gets to benefit from culture? Who gets to access it? Who gets to partake? Who, in fact, cares? Galway is a 2020 European Capital of Culture (along with Rijeka, in Croatia), but not every Galway citizen has an interest in contributing, or feels part of it, or gets what all the rírá is about. Galway is Ireland's permanent capital of culture: it's where the tourists go for the music and the pints, it's where the artists end up. I am a Galway artist and I've always been certain Galway artists are not like me: they're into pottery and smocks and drink red wine belligerently in Neachtain's, but never so belligerently that they threaten to throw a stool over the bar.

My editing this special issue of *The Stinging Fly*, celebrating Galway as a European Capital of Culture, might therefore be seen as (a) an attempt at understanding my birth county through culture, the thing we're both supposed to be good at, or (b) a bit cheeky, like. Luckily, what came across in the hundreds of submissions we read for the issue is that discomfort with culture as a packaged product is an invigorating thing. What's especially joyous about this *Fly* line-up is how various it is for an issue based on a defined place: we've got poems about landscape, essays about hell, and stories about all sorts of belligerence, chemically-induced or in the bones. Many of the writers whose work appears in these pages are from Galway, but plenty are not. Other parts represented include Limerick and the Three Sisters— Kilkenny, Waterford and Wexford—who were also in the running to host the 2020 Capital of Culture (given how 2020-the-year turned out, they might have been as well off). All of our contributors are in some way stirred by Galway, in its facets both welcoming and culturally insalubrious.

It's a split common to most places, I imagine. A few years back, I went out in Galway City with family, by which I mean a glut of cousins. A bouncer, young enough himself, performing authority, asked us where we were from. We told him we were from Gort. He asked us which part of Gort. We told him there weren't any parts plural to Gort. He let us in, all of us a bit distracted; we were from only twenty miles down the road, and it was like this lad had never heard of the place. Galway being the second largest county in Ireland, and Gort being only just north of the border with Clare, it might not be such a surprise that a young fella bouncer in Galway City would not be *au fait* with the locales of Gort town. Still, it felt like confirmation that Galway is a place from which it is logical to feel disconnected: an incoherent place, about which others have funny notions.

How I feel about Galway, as a sort-of-Galwegian artist, is not altogether unlike how I feel about those reviews of *Hotel Coolgardie*. Galway is more complex than its popular image, those funny notions people have about it being full of buskers, smock-wearers and transient bartenders. Galway is mad as a box of frogs and not in a way that can be consistently monetised. Galway is a capital of culture and Galway is full of people who couldn't care less. This special issue of *The Stinging Fly* is not a guide to Galway, nor is it a compendium of cautionary tales. But I hope it at least insists that Galway is not the best place for delicate creatures.

Lisa McInerney
November 2020

Faeces In My Airbnb

Gavin Corbett

I had come to the Middle East because I wanted to stop being a 'hippie' and I wanted to start a new phase of my life. Then after some thirty five years I grew to hate the desert and its clear air and the way the blue sky was reflected in the metal tubes and I desired again dampness and dirt under my fingernails and I craved fungal spores in my eyelashes and nostrils and I sought to be cleansed with the remains of fallen life and the very *cac* and the *keich* (Scots) of it but it took until a great personal crisis for all this to come into resolution. It became necessary for me to leave everything behind and start again and requiring such shit and solace I thought naturally of childhood and, being German, of Ireland as a result of my exposure to Heinrich Böll's *Irisches Tagebuch* during my schooling. My dream was to move to the Aran Islands off the Irish western coast or somewhere similarly enshrouded in atmosphere and myth but in order to turn this dream into a reality I needed to experiment for a little time. I arranged to stay for three weeks in the city of Galway which I would use as a station to explore the surrounding territory and take some passenger ferry trips to the islands of fable themselves. Who knew, I might even discover that I enjoyed the city of Galway so much that I would want to live in perpetuity there.

I had not been in my life to Ireland before this adventure and as is the case with many Germans my perceptions of the country were influenced by my reading of the Böll *meisterwerk*. In particular the western portion of Ireland had the most Romantic effect on me such that I realised of course, while choosing to ignore the realisation, that any true experience of the place could only result in anticlimax. Böll depicts western Ireland as the *Heimat* of the last unviolated aboriginal European culture and though I knew surely that Ireland had changed importantly in the sixty plus years since *Irisches Tagebuch* was published I had been certain too that if any such place as Böll portrayed were to exist in Europe if only in the largest remaining vestiges then western Ireland was this place because you simply had to examine a satellite image taken in the night hours of the serrated continent and note how little artificial light there was in western Ireland. It appears in fact on this image, being pale dark blue, as a shallow submarine shelf in the ocean before the dark mountain high depths open up, and amid this ocean blueness only the tiny golden jewel of the city of Galway glitters to offer hope as in that certified by the Queen of Heaven of the title of the Roman Catholic hymn 'Hail, Queen of Heaven': 'Hail, Queen of Heaven, the ocean star/ Guide of the wanderer here below/ Thrown on life's surge we claim thy care/ Save us from peril and from woe/ Mother of Christ, star of the sea/ Pray for the wanderer, pray for me' (Creative Commons attribution) (though perception is dependent of course on the contrast and brightness settings on one's computer monitor). This promise of healing but also the prospect of awe and terror were the twin yet paradoxical attractions for me to western Ireland, as I had developed in my life, possibly independently of Böll, a sentimental idea that the Atlantic waters of Ireland's maritime jurisdiction constituted the vastest example of that rarest phenomenon, a European wilderness, and Europe's only real desert comparable to the Gobi or Kalahari. It was true that Portugal too of the other countries of Europe showed its full face to the ocean but Portugal made its identity by taming the ocean while Irish coastal peoples were famously fearful of the ocean and understanding of their place in the sublimity of its dominion such that if an Irish man goes down in the ocean he accepts that he must sink like a stone.

And so after much excitement and null planning my disembarkation was set for June twenty fourth, Midsummer's Day. I would arrive in the walled settlement of Galway, the 'City of the Tribes', mounted on horseback with a white feather in my *landsknecht* hat as 'Michael of Münster', enjoying the correspondence of the name of my home town with the name of the province to the south of Galway. I would learn the rules of rugby and learn how to play the fiddle. I would catch sea fish and from the rivers, salmon. I would change my given name to Hoireabard (Herbert). I would familiarise myself better with the poems of William Butler Yeats and know the best passages to recite. I might perhaps find another woman, a Deborah Kerr or a Tilda Swinton, this would be the ideal, but yes, you might say I was under no illusions also.

In reality I arrived in the city of Galway by train from Dublin. Irish trains! I must tell you! A detail I had never before seen in any transport I noticed on the rubber of the window frame and this was moss and supporting the moss there was soil, a junior biosphere that came away with my finger like butter. I attempted to recline my 'crown of King Rory' on the headrest of my seat but maybe also there was the swaying motion of the train plus mild anxiety displacing my equilibrium. I was thinking of washing my hands. I got up and there was a man drunk in the threshold of the stall/carriage. I offered him help to resume a stance and now I washed my hands. The toilet was like the mouth of hell. Irish trains! Maybe the sterility of the desert was not so bad! At least there was above my head the window aperture and the fresh fast air. This was even perhaps lulling to me. Perhaps I was thinking also of lifting my face to this small open space.

The prospect from the train carriage as it crossed the island (viewed from back in my seat) was not especially exciting comprising mainly poorly tended and unrelieved flattened pasture. There was something in the landscape though, and this was most acutely true after the train had crossed the Shannon river, that elicited in me a mild emotional response such as that which followed Proust's narrator's sampling of the steeped madeleine and which must have been caused by the similarity to my eye of these struggling fields with the unkempt *geest* of the Lüneburger Heide I remembered from journeys with my parents and sister in my youth. The 'strange familiarity' of the *kopfkino* was nice but the most of my approach to the Atlantic bight was filled with wholly and excitingly alien sensations stimulated by the never before experienced flavour of actually salted air and even the tangible crystallisation of salt on the fine hairs of my cheeks so that I was preserved like Portuguese cod (bacalao)!

I was in need of a sharp and dry drink when the train came to the Galway terminus and I was able to find one immediately at the Hotel Meyrick adjacent. This was where I had organised to receive the keys of my Airbnb accommodation from its owners and it had an excellent bar but it was here I must say also that my illusions of healing and adventure first began to dissolve like the same salt I have mentioned in the clearest water. Sitting at the bar counter in the Irish and American barfly style with my terrific local gin with black pepper and waiting for my hosts to arrive I got into conversation with the owner of several Galway gym facilities. He was friendly and we gave each other our names and telling him my surname was Huberman and expecting him to say that this was the same name of an actress famous in Ireland he said instead that 'Huberman' was an Irish dialect expression for a fart, albeit most commonly spelt 'Hooberman', and that this was why, for example, the Irish actress cannot be taken seriously in any role that is not in the comical seam. He was being truthful and coarse to be companionable, I understand this, and I did not find the coarseness offensive and he could not himself have been aware of the depression he had revitalized in me but with these words I truly was positioned under a cloud for some one hour or more. I knew now that the decision to revoke my married surname, that is, my young Brazilian wife's, Huberman, had been made. A relapse to my original surname was something I had been considering for the eight months since my wife had abandoned our marriage but I suppose that a part of me had been delaying such finality in the hope that my love would understand the waste of her actions, and now with the realisation of the necessity to change my name came also the recognition of how ultimate and profound this split was and all that flowed from it, blackness of mood etcetera.

The owners of my accommodation arrived late to the Hotel Meyrick and I abruptly set under the counter my morose feelings on their appearance. Pearl the woman was nice looking with nice clavicle scapula combination, visible owing to loose fitting and low necked sack cloth like upper wear and pitted redness of skin and delicate pale blue beads drawing attention to this area. She had long crazy but still clean looking hair with much grey in it and approached with a large warm smile on her mouth and pronounced (at least eight millimetre) diastema. The husband, man, Ashley, was bald but had a long beard that was grey also and he wore a Pink Floyd 'Dark Side of the Moon' tee shirt under a brown leather waistcoat and he was more private I would say than Pearl but was still an appealing character. You have to understand how instantly well disposed I felt towards these two people as I recognised fully that they had been 'original' 'hippies' and still lived their lives as such now deep in the twenty first century while I, a good 'hippie' in my adolescence in Germany, had left this life long behind or certainly since the beginning of the thirty five years I had spent subsumed in the fields of science and commerce in the cultural deserts of Saudi Arabia, Jordan, Kuwait and Bahrain building conduits to water the actual deserts. Suddenly the gloom I had put aside just moments before was forgotten entirely and I had thoughts only of the future in this happy place of Galway that was truly a 'hippie' town as I had read in some guidebooks, where the traditional culture of Ireland and the newer permissive lifestyles had blended to make a vivifying admixture.

And – 'You are from Galway yourselves?' I said to them.

'No we are from England but in Galway from 1971,' the woman said.

'And you came because you are "hippies"?' I asked them.

'We came because it was cheap in 1971 but yes it was for a time a "hippie" town but not anymore because the modern world has changed everything including the problem of too many immigrants,' she said.

At some point anybody is wondering why I am meeting these two people for my keys in a hotel beside a train terminus. The answer is simple and I will replicate the dialogue as well as I can to explain this situation.

Pearl: 'We are to board a train to Dublin to apply in persons for passports at the Irish passport offices.'

Michael: 'For Irish passports?'

Ashley: He is nodding.

Michael: 'You are finally Irish, congratulations!'

Pearl: 'We have not got our passports yet and we are still British even if the passport applications are successfully processed. British and Irish is all the same people.'

Ashley: He is lifting his shoulders to say this is indeed the reality.

Michael: 'This is astonishing to me. This is the attitude that Irish persons themselves would hold?'

Pearl: 'They should hold this attitude. In the near future all the native persons of this archipelago will know by the enemies leaned against them that they are a single breed.'

So the owners of my accommodation were fucking racists. Terrible! And surprising! They had not in appearance presented as the kinds of people who might possess such views. I presumed by their attitudes and by their enthusiasm to secure the Irish passports that they were also of the nationalistic 'Brexit' mentality I had read so much about. What would my mother have said?! My mother, who would happily have defected in her life to the DDR from the West, once said on Lüneburger Heide, 'Though it might be only one part corpse of Himmler to several thousand billion parts soil, this is the soil that is poisoned by the corpse of the cur Himmler!' I suppose the irony of such a siting is that the Lüneburger Heide was a British Army training ground in the Cold War period and I remembered that often in our holiday village were the ox like nationalistic British privates singing the Troggs at the extent of their voices and urinating in sidings and punching boys in the stomachs. Now the ride in the taxi taking me to the 'Pearl and Ashley' house felt like some sort of Charonic *catabasis* but with no prospect of the counter directional and heroic *anabasis*. Oh well, as the British themselves say. It was time effectively to 'keep calm and carry on'.

The house faced the Eglinton Canal that makes an arc in the western section of the city and immediately I entered this building I understood it was a typical artists' home. A smell of incense, Middle Eastern or Belo Horizonte in its evocations, mixed with hashish and domestic animals filtrated in the rooms. Emotions fought in me as I thought I am home in my soul as a 'hippie' in this place yet feel disaffected by my knowledge of the assemblers of these inoffensive material signifiers of a life. The walls were painted strong forceful and regulating colours, red Australian earth shade in one room and blue in another, then the downstairs lavatory room like two shades of a cucumber, one the skin and one the flesh. The master bedroom, which I was not permitted to sleep in, was a living pink. On all of the walls were paintings of every thickly textured abstract expressionist variety, some interesting. On every surface that would support them such as mantelpieces and many many shelves were Pearl's sculptures. She had two motifs or obsessions in her work, one the snail and one the Celtic symbol known as the triskel. Impossible to know of course whether the snails and triskels were belonging to Pearl or to Ashley but I guessed they were from Pearl because the feeling I had was that she was the *führer* in the marriage and these were purely expressive objects. Maybe Ashley was the artist of the evasive abstract expressionist paintings. The tin workshop attached to the rear of the house, which I had been advised not to enter, had many snails and triskels also although undoubtedly the triskel was preponderant. Every one of these small sculptures had a date cut into the clay and by the evening I had examined all of the undersides and noted that the evolution of Pearl's work was from snail to triskel, a simpler but more copious design, less perhaps manifest with spirit and more about the unmodified spirit in the wild. Perhaps there was something fascist in this or perhaps nothing at all. I made a promise I would put the politics of these owners out of my mind and live the time here as if I knew nothing about them but the more I emptied my mind of such things the more I exposed it to the tidal bore of *Weltschmerz*.

I was getting anxious in this house and some day I was sitting on the toilet bowl and I was crying about my wife. Fucking hound! I love her! And now I was thinking about items only half thought about and barely previously noticed which was: specks of shit attached in the toilet bowl, only one or two but significant and I have a problem with this really. I find it uncomfortable to be on the toilet seat with someone else's albeit practically microscopic shit breathing up at me but what can you do but sit on the toilet seat and tolerate the thought. You cannot 'shit in your hands'. Another thought arrived though unhappily not to displace this thought but to add to it and this was that women never have this problem of sitting on toilet seats with the skin of their bottoms. It is perhaps a consequence of the woman never having the option of the wall mounted urinal to despatch her waste. Every time the woman enters a public or hotel lavatory facility the biology means that she must use a regular toilet bowl and she does this without any thought or hesitation. I have seen every woman in my life make this lack of performance. Squat and she is on the toilet, skin on plastic! Perhaps with a little whispered 'Hooberman' and it's no problem! The woman has none of these issues. The great buttocks spread open across the whole of the void to remove the flesh as much as possible from the giant pelvic matrix.

For clean air I embarked outwards always intending to cross to the centre of the city. First over the placid Eglinton canal, then the eruptive water courses between the canal and the centre. My life working in the engineering behind the provision and transportation of water makes me respondent to the flow of it to or in urban spaces and I could not for many occasions move with fascination in these complicated channels. The first thing to note on my first time seeing these channels was the force of the water. All day in that journey across the island the weather had been mild and never raining and by the time the train arrived in the Galway terminus the cloud was gone and the sky was bright. Where was this water coming from? Was there some managed weir/sluice system further upstream? I was thinking of the map and its close analysis and I could say no to this question. The second thing to note about the water was the colour. It was dark yellow, the colour of the famed 'peat bogs' or the colour of the 'cryptosporidium' I had read about in the shaded box in my guidebook. I had read too of the volatility of the weather in western Ireland and concluded there was a deluge in the north and out of sight of the city. With the map of the territory clear in my imagination I could envision the huge Corrib lake and the possibility of terrible squalls and the lake almost reaching to the ocean. The city of Galway was the stricture through which the giant bladder must discharge and I was standing among these multiple egresses in the crotch of the woman. While all was otherwise peaceful such as the skies above and the starlings on the banks and in the trees the torrents flowed to dismiss the alien object such as the speck of shit or the blob of troublesome jisolm.

We had agreed among us that I would stay three weeks in the 'Pearl and Ashley' house. During this time Pearl got arrested for violent disturbances of the peace at a hotel in the north of Connacht province and after being charged for this crime she and Ashley fled to the United Kingdom. All of this came to me from astounded gossip. This was another example of a profound and broad federalisation of responsibility of Pearl and Ashley. Now: there might be someone to tell me to leave the house before the agreed time such as an agent of Pearl and Ashley, for example a British family member. What actions does one take in this situation? The gossiping neighbour (his name was also Michael) said: 'Hold tight until.' 'Until what?' I said. He smiled and walked away, he was not listening properly. Ending sentences with 'until' was perhaps in the Irish idiom. I weighed with my hands a large decorative wall slate with sharp edges on the way back to the inside of the house. Come here you British tans! Gah!

Twice I took the passenger ferry to the Aran Islands and through the fault of my own state of mind and not the islands themselves I realised that they were an unsuitable environment to spend my new life, or the remainder of my life thought about another way. I spent some of the time investigating the territory west of the city and because I am still not driving after my sixty five years I hired a bicycle and cycled to the coral beach of Carraroe, the strangest place in Europe, like Samoa. On another occasion I cycled in the rain and acute wind to the cottage of the priest like celibate Patrick Pearse where he went to get away from his 'boys'. I was astounded also by the beauty of Recess and one time I saw in the bog shreds of garbage on a tree. I left my bicycle standing almost upright in the 'chocolate' (peat) and I ventured tenderly across the heathland. Was it neglect, was it a mirage? It was neither, it was the typical Irish 'wishing tree'. Rubber Lance Armstrong cancer battle style bracelets abounded, plus Lindt Bunny neck bells, small colourful trolls, rosary beads, the delicate 'Miraculous Medal' of typical Irish devotion, the fisher's flies embedded by the barbel, candy bar wrappers. White bird shit was everywhere. I gave my own gift: a five riyal Saudi note I had in my wallet and I also took off my wet wool socks and hung them from the tree. In these moments a portion of the clouds above became thin and was coloured a strange brown and also allowed through the strange brown light, like the colour of tough stained bare heels. I walked the penitent's path back to my bicycle with the skin of my feet being abraded from the leather of my shoes. I was in a movie and I could not believe it.

A man I met on the road who was from Dublin and who spent time in the youth hostels said he did not like the 'bitter' people from Connemara especially and the people of the city of Galway too but I did not find enough evidence in my time to agree. In the city I enjoyed walking in the port, local bread, buying juggling equipment and practising juggling for one day and getting to know the swans. I must say that I felt like a stranger in this demonstratively friendly city but this was not an alienating feeling, in fact it was a positive feeling because I am now again the 'outsider' I am most of my life, whether that is the 'hippie' among the 'suits' of Essen or the 'man with the sand coloured moustache' in Bahrain. When all is said about this though I must state that most of all this time I spent hidden in the 'Pearl and Ashley' racist house where I drank from Pearl's cups that were swollen almost like balls and contained the wet coffee in the larder very well.

The most extraordinary events happened entirely in my own mind after I looked in Ashley's pot named the 'Swearing Jar'. Curious to see what might be contained in such a vessel I opened it and found mostly nothing except for a small piece of paper at the very base which I recognised after some moments as a token of LSD. I thought for two days about taking it and then one night after drinking a bottle of wine I did take it. My 'trip' could be summarised as the metamorphosis of myself into a snail! Just like its foolhardy progenitor this snail was also a curious 'fellow' who crawled about the house enquiring with its eyes on stalks after certain substances. Dipping its eyes into one particular pot of slime these eyes became engulfed in ghee. Feeling also hungry the snail decided to suck the ghee off its eyes with its mouth. Becoming even more curious once its eyes were in its mouth the snail pushed its eyes even further into the digestive tract. Pushing and pushing the whole head was soon in the digestive tract and the neck and then the etcetera etcetera until the whole body was turned inside out and appearing gradually outwardly via the anus and had repositioned itself back to front inside its own shell.

The Corrib Great Southern, 2020

It burns again, that behemoth on the hill
where we toasted the glories of the Tiger,
high above the watching, implacable sea.

Snaggle-toothed with fangs of broken glass,
it lies like a great wyrm of old, coiled
around a hoard of scoured-out rooms

and smashed-down ceilings, its hide tattooed
with crude graffiti, bleeding from scales
of rusted iron, splintered wood.

The scavengers come, Egyptian plovers
that pluck debris from between the teeth
of this bloated, stranded reptile,

this grounded giant that bequeathed its wings
as verdigris sails to the building next door.
It has surrendered to waiting for death

by a hundred attempts at arson,
until the inferno that cracks its bones
back down to the rebar marrow.

Ruth Quinlan

Awkward Relations

Kevin Barry

1

The west of Ireland seemed to begin somewhere around Gort. Suddenly the fields were merely attachments to the elaborate networks of drystone walls that gave the realm its distinctive look and apparent purpose—the putting up of walls!—and something even in the voice of the wind seemed to rasp out *Connacht*, a kind of a hoarseness maybe. Invisible tribal lines were crossed as the Bus Éireann motored staunchly northwards. There were rumours down shaded demesne avenues of Horse Protestants. It was 1989 or 1990, and it was the law in Ireland at that time that there would be a nun alongside you on the bus eating Taytos. I would go from Limerick to Galway after work on Friday, weary from another long week of getting threatened outside the District Court not to put someone's brother's case in the newspaper—'or I'll bate the head off ya'—but excited at the smoky prospects of the weekend ahead, and there might even be the chance of a shift in the Warwick if the drunken stars arrayed themselves rightly. At that time in our history on a Friday evening bus to Galway a lot of people would look as if they were out of the Hothouse Flowers. There were acres of terrible paisley for as far as the eye could see. Glance across the aisle of the bus and there was every danger of some little hairball with a Liam Ó Maonlaí fixation and a bum-fluff beard wielding a tin whistle about his cheerful face like a threat. The Germans were martyrs for the place altogether and there was eternally bound for Galway city on that Friday evening bus a Dieter-and-Monika type couple with their backpacks, their rollies and their wispy Atlantic dreams, and, if you weren't careful, they'd nearly lean across and start talking to you. It seems now like a scene from a century past but then of course it is one.

2

The purchase of cannabis resin in Limerick in 1990 involved going to a bar called Buddie's in a laneway off Foxe's Bow at the top of William Street and consulting with members of the local biker community who of an evening gathered there. Their hogs were parked outside the little bar, a collegiate huddle of glistening Harleys basking in the last of the summer evening's sun. I was a rudderless 21-year-old with hazily psychedelic inclinations, an incongrous day job as a newshound cub reporter, and an impressionable nature, and to me the scene felt growlingly urban. I used to do what I could to keep the minor possession cases out of the paper and I had some brownie points in Buddie's for this. The bar was about the size of the small parallelogram on a Gah pitch and as liable to ructions. The walls of the laneway were daubed with sky-high, trippy pictures in vivid, electrified colours. If the late sun held and the light was just so—it's the midsummer I'm thinking of, and all of the mid-western summers were fabulous back then—it might have been a scene from a backstreet of Oakland but for the tin-pan flatness of the Limerick accents clattering out like spilt nails over the pint bottles of Bulmers and the big fat doobies.

The city was depressed as a motherfucker but it had its moments of glow.

3

The purchase of cannabis resin in Galway in 1990 involved going to a premises of ripe repute called the Harbour Bar down on the docks. On one occasion that I visited, two roaring maniacs beached from the local fishing fleet were playing tennis across the bar with an ashtray for a ball. We, the other patrons, took this very much in our stride—it was about half past six in the morning, for the Harbour Bar had a market licence, and the usual niceties relating to social demeanour and clocks did not always make it past the threshold of the place. It was still genuinely a fisherman's pub and many of the regulars lurched dramatically on sea-legs as they crossed the long-suffering floors, and Jesus above on the cross, if that carpet could have talked. There was always some enormous lunatic in from Conemara, the size of a hill and with dangerously emotional eyes. The toilets were from medieval times. A mad auric energy emitted from the Harbour Bar and gave to that entire district of the town its jaunty and gypsyish airs. Galway was very much a town back then—a big country town with ignorant elbows and a pleasant face, like a harmless cousin who maybe has a few notions about himself.

4

Limerick city has never fitted comfortably within the mythology of the west of Ireland. By accident of geography it is indisputably of the west but somehow it seems not to belong to it. The traditional images of the west that are summoned tend to be of an overwhelmingly rural mien, as if drawn by a hand just lately knuckle-deep in the stony soil. But walk the plain-faced mile of O'Connell Street in Limerick of a November Tuesday—the evil estuarine wind snakin' up from the river and into your lungs—and if you're not exactly in Paris, you are indisputably in a city.

It's an islanded one, psychologically. It's a place besieged by the energy of its own antic humours. There is a crazy and surreal cut to the fun of the place—it also has its dour and melancholy days, and it has them in all seasons. It has changed for the good in recent times. It is no longer the mono-ethnic, God-bothered place it was in 1990—the 'Confraternity City', a district of great piety and devotion—and there is no longer the same sense of existential threat to be felt outside hot chicken joints in the roaring hours past midnight.

5

Can a town be said to have a face?

If it does, there is something unknowable in the sly little grin of welcome that Galway bestows on the visitor. The place personified does not seem like an entirely trustworthy character. It looks as if it might drop the hand on you given the slightest flicker of encouragement. . .

6

It is here worth noting that parts one to five of this piece, which petered out at the point directly above, were written in February of this year, when I was in South America, and when the coronavirus was still something that was happening a long, long way away. In the intervening few months, I have returned to the hills of south County Sligo, and I have been rattling around the house in that now universally familiar funk of paranoia spiced with strange little outbursts of joyousness. Concentrated bouts of consecutive thought are as difficult as they're rare but what can be said for a raging global pandemic is that it certainly gives rise to an air of questioning. When all you expected of life and the world is suddenly uncertain, when the veils fall away and the edifice crashes, you begin to question the absolutes and the fundamentals of things.

Turning back to this piece has been difficult—Why bother with writing anything!? Why bother with the fucking world at all!?—but here at my desk now, in the early Maytime, at least that new sense of questioning or interrogation has accompanied me, and I find myself asking what are our cities even for anymore. What should we do with them now? What are we to make of them?

7

For about a third of a century, there has been a kind of booster energy charging the streets of Galway. It was a ragged and vaguely artsy town that mysteriously discovered how to sell itself, how to expertly shill, and it has done so at times in these recent decades quite relentlessly.

A cusp moment seemed to occur around the turning of the century. As a journalist, I was in town in August of 2000 to write some colour pieces for the *Examiner* about the Galway Races. I did so from a room at Jury's Inn overlooking the hysterical rush of the Corrib River as it charged like raw commerce through the town—I couldn't be arsed trying to make my way through the crowds out to the actual racetrack. The town was rabid, barking, infernal. A squadron of helicopters owned by one of the Haugheys took off from Eyre Square to ferry the racegoers out to the course and back, and the place sounded like *Apocalypse Now*. It was a kind of culchie inferno. It must have been around this time of the early century that a friend of mine remarked to me that only the Russians have less class than us when they get their hands on a few pound.

This was the first, initial jet-blast of Tiger energy and Galway was transformed by it, and not in a good way. It was visibly starting to become a victim of its own touristic successes and of its times. You couldn't get a seat for a flea in Neachtain's. It had once been a town of crumbly little nodges of hash, but now everyone was absolutely hammering into the gak and, Jesus Christ lads, it seriously didn't suit us, what with us being garrulous half-eejits anyway, just by cruel nature.

When I used to go for a night out in Limerick, back around 1990, I'd have maybe twenty quid in my hip pocket, and that would be a flush week. This would somehow extend itself to cover a night of pints and Bacardi-and-bitter-lemons and nodges, the price into a disco, a punnet of curry chips from Friar Tuck's, and a taxi home from Economy Cabs. I'm aware that it sounds as distant now as something out of Dickens.

When I'd come back to visit the town, maybe around twelve or thirteen years later, the typical Limerick young fellas seemed be living Tony Soprano lifestyles, flinging grubby fifties at Ukrainian poledancers and heading off to New York the next morning to buy jeans.

But the effect of the Tiger era on the city was, over time, subtly different than its effect on Galway. It was starting from a place of lower expectation; it had been less successful in selling itself, and in a sense it had less to lose. The surge of Tiger money that coursed through the city's veins brought also a seeping of neccessary confidence. It was as if the place had sidled up to itself shyly in the mirror one prosperous morning, raised a fake eyelash, and said—

You know what? Not bad.

The arty crowd stopped leaving Limerick. I think this started to happen somewhere between ten and fifteen years ago. It had cheaper rents than elsewhere and, increasingly, it had the feeling of a scene: its vibrant hip-hop community was transformative in terms of the city's sense of itself.

When I last lived in Limerick, in my early twenties, anyone with a creative or artistic inclination had one thought on their minds, and it was to get out of the place at the earliest opportunity—you wouldn't see our arses for dust. The city lacked any sense of cultural self-confidence then. If if it wasn't for the art college and the Belltable, it would have been a wasteland altogether. We envied Galway its more bohemian airs. We were an hour up and down the road from each other; we were in all essentials closely related, but very awkwardly so. Once backs were turned we'd each badmouth the other.

From 2004 to 2006, I lived in Liverpool, and the relationship between Liverpool and Manchester reminded me very much of the relationship between Limerick and Galway. The English cities were also just an hour apart, but creatively, and in terms of cultural bragging rights, Manchester seemed to suck all the air out of the northwest. It felt as if Lancashire in this era could sustain just one great artistic city, and all the cultural resources tended to be drawn in the direction of Manchester. Liverpool had a bit of an inferiority complex about itself as a result, and being granted the European Capital of Culture designation in 2008 was a significant advance in terms of the city shucking that off. When Limerick competed against Galway for the 2020 designation, I'd hoped that something similiar might occur but of course it didn't work out.

As events have transpired, it might have been as well off. Galway will not suffer any long-term consequences because the 2020 year hasn't worked out as hoped—it has enough going on culturally. In fact, given the size of the place, it conceivably has too much going on culturally—the problem in Galway these days can seem to be one of crowd control. If Limerick had received the designation, and things had gone the way they've gone, I'm not sure the city would ever have recovered from the sense of martyrdom that would have settled on its shoulders. We're martyrs in the place at the best of times.

10

Every essay tends to tilt by its nature in the direction of a lie. An essay is never begun entirely innocently; always it's with a projection, or a thesis, and the succeeding paragraphs work themselves into an unholy froth as the piece attempts to prove itself out. Sometimes one almost has to avert one's gaze from the writerly acrobatics on display. The better essays hold sway against the tilt and manage to land in unexpected places, but these are rare enough.

This essay—if such a ramshackle assemblage of 'observations' can even aspire to the title—began with a particular notion in mind. It was to suggest that Limerick has evolved creatively in recent decades in a more organic way than Galway; that it has had its eye less on the cultural euro, and that, resultingly, it is now the more artistically innovative and vital of the two cities. The aforementioned events have conspired to largely spare you, the fortunate readers, from this piece.

Instead, as I think of the two cities now, I think of nothing so much as their delicacy. So much has been stripped away from us this year, especially the expectation that all will continue much as before. All of that smug certainty has been taken from us. If we are to be optimistic—and really there's no other rational way to proceed right now—this means that we can begin to see our cities as pliable spaces, as places that are still open to change, to positive manipulation, and to artistry. Maybe we need to believe that it's all to play for yet.

Furey Meets The Bishop

Young Furey walked to school,
ambling down Poor Man's Hill
to sit beside Richard Blake,
most battered boy in class,
who, one day, whispered:
*'You never beat me,
you must be my friend.'*

He'd never seen a house so large,
garden walls beyond his highest jump,
windows wider than a cinema screen,
sleek car, resting, behind tall gates.
Blake's mother dressed like Sunday mass,
a sniff, cold eyes, offered milk, cake,
told them to play football *'on the lawn'*,
but not to touch the cherry tree.

And the garden stretched forever,
trimmed hedges, shrubs, burnished wooden seat,
pale statues, draped, mown grass stretching off
to the far wall where Furey set up goals,
taking Richard's best shots easy,
'til one wild kick sailed higher
than the rest, clipped a scanty faun,
nicked the high stone coping, disappeared.

Furey, climbed the cherry tree,
swung into a foreign space,
'We're not allowed,'
Richard fading as Furey dropped to earth.
A place, alien, beating fronds,
plants he'd only seen in books,
great apple trees, fruit-heavy, and far off,
a glasshouse, green-full, glinting in the sun.

He plucked an apple, searched around,
moved deeper, a glade opened out,
where an aged man, artist's brush in hand,
stood at an easel, touching colour to a scene.
Naked, wearing nothing but a black beret,
turning fast to spy young Furey,
apple bit, agape.
A crozier finger beckoned,
as the bishop, spittle-raged, hissed, *'Boy'*.

James Martyn Joyce

In a London Fish Shop

I wore a peach dress and magnetic earrings—
it was later than the time I would usually eat
and I felt very pink between the monochrome tiles.

In my head, he knows the waiter—
who seems to be more than just a waiter
but memories lie every time you remember them.

He orders me cod. And I'm not sure if I believe
it was the best fish I've ever eaten because he told me
it would be so, or if because it actually was.

He questions me about the museum
I tell him, *I liked the blue whale—*
never knew how big they could get.

Bits of squid dance on his fork,
dead legs gripping at the air
I ask for another coke *please*.

I wore a peach dress and magnetic earrings
it was later than the time I would usually eat
and I felt very pink between the monochrome tiles.

Jade Murphy

In the Inn District
Mary O'Donoghue

It was still dim, even at ten in the thinning morning. Twenty years ago I was one of hundreds of recruits. A skinnymalink in 60 denier and big surplus boots, I enlisted in this city. The flats were as scarce as Soviet bread, and the queues to rent them were ruthless. It was the age of tuna from the tin and cider from the tap. Everyone ballooned in winter and got famished by May. Decimation meant the death of every tenth person, and maybe that happened too. Mothers didn't know us off the buses, and fathers asked no questions.

Hans Castorp said the flatlands was the place he left behind to go to the Magic Mountain. One month after being conferred with the knowledge of all of German literature, I said goodbye. I forsook the small bars with their nooks and snugs, the bladderwrack and the trawlers. It was the summer of the pine marten scandal, a vendor in the Saturday market selling the tree cat's secretions as love drugs. It was a city where new-fangled things got contagious then miserable. I was surprised to get out in one piece and unpoisoned.

In London I lived in shabby isolation in a half-transfigured garage. The windows were higher than I could reach to see. In winter the landlady gave me a bedspread. She was an anxious Ealing creature, sphinxlike in her wrinkles, and she smoked in bed. She was afraid she'd set herself, the room, the house ablaze.

But I can't give up my most loyal and beloveds, she said, tapping two Windsor Blues on the table.

She had read unsolved-crime-mysteries where an ashen pair of slippers was the last thing left. Combustion, she said, was a terrible way to go.

Take it! she ordered, and pushed yellow chenille on me. The bedspread undulated eerily, an enchanted fleece shorn from the last of a species. In a deadly house fire, my garage would be the last bit standing and still I wouldn't see a thing, only scudding clouds and a thousand-volt yard light that searched like a prison break.

In America I would learn the word *afire*, which was a better, finer word for the suddenness of women in flames.

If the world were ending in a month. Okay? Let's say a month. Not six, not a year. You might not have that long. A month focuses things. So, a month. And say you had the resources to travel unlimitedly. Where would you want to go?

Someone got this question going at our supper club, supper clubs being what happen when you turn the gate for forty in a country not of your making. I'd been teaching English to the children of German auto-makers in a series of southern United States states. I advanced around the map like a heat rash, following the work where it was. The auto-makers wanted a scholarly register and paid well for the labour.

One time I told Mercedes kids if they didn't pay attention I'd teach them *The Sorrows of Young Werther*. When they heard it took Werther half a day to die after shooting himself in the head, they were transported.

Please! Please, Miss!

I said it would be much too much for their tender hearts, and anyway I'd be fired.

They didn't care if I got fired as long as they heard about Werther.

We negotiated an agreement to build slowly to Werther, to earn him by moving through alienation, isolation, and *Das Intimleben des Adrian Mole*. The children of German auto-makers loved that sebaceous, whiny twerp.

So. Come on now.

The supper club.

Where would you all go for your month?

This was before people came to acknowledge the pain and dying of the world, and answers involved a predictable ravening. Suckling pigs cooked beneath banana leaves, coral reefs in the southwest Pacific. Bali.

David Bowie's ashes had been scattered there. Someone said she still burst into tears at the mention of him, in spite of the time that had passed.

I just can't, she said. I can't believe he's not in this world anymore.

He never was, someone advised. He was always only ever visiting. Goodbye, spaceboy.

The Galapagos. Paris in spring. Yurts that opened onto beach, and *plein air* showers.

Someone said that everyone likes the idea of showering outdoors.

And then you do it. And you can't figure out how to look like the kind of healthy, sexed-up person who showers outdoors. And you forget the fucking towel.

They howled. Someone else was ashamed of not having hiked the Appalachian Trail. She knew it took six months at a good clip.

I felt an old twinge, the same needle that tickled me in the wretched London season, and then on the Upper East Side when I pushed cranky lawyers' crankier children in colossal strollers. It had taken a while to locate me in the southern states, heat lightning and visa disasters spinning it off course. Now that needle found all my rolling veins, and the bruises would be callous and black.

Everybody thinks they're just testing things out, my older cousin in New Zealand once said. Until they're not, because the ground has crumbled behind them, because some brigand cut the rope bridge, because, as the book said, you can't go home again.

She was an eloquent alcoholic, unattached. The kind of wedding guest everyone loved to watch swing their children around the dance floor but who nobody thought would make a good mother. Later she would fail to sing 'Carrickfergus' and beg for a chance at 'The Town I Loved So Well'.

I'm nowhere and nothing and can't hold a fucking note, she wept.

Consoling her was hazardous work, involving pints of water and anterooms to exert her unseemliness and grief. I held her by the shoulders like she was a bloodied boxer and I sending her to the ring to get killed again.

She marshalled herself to try Morrissey. She made a good show of 'Everyday is Like Sunday'.

She always left for New Zealand next day.

I told them Galway. That's where I would fetch up for the month.

Ireland! Someone had been to Ireland. She couldn't understand why the whole country said mixed veg on menus.

Like they don't want to say what the vegetables *are*. Because the knowledge would be too much.

The supper club said they'd scuttle all their ships and itineraries, their exotic islands where rare animals walked up to befriend you, and join me in Galway instead.

Hire a bus, go region by region. So. Much. Fun!

The man who devoted his life to Thomas Bernhard looked round the supper club and said we were crazy. Ireland was low, very low on his list. Its best writers were beer-mats by now, the whole place PTSD'd from the Church.

He had taught a long time at a university and resigned because Thomas Bernhard meant nothing to the narcissistic stresses of Generation Z. We dallied round one another for a time, extracurricular to the supper club. Open mics with unwashed, jilted poets, flat whites and pastries in the park. There were surreptitious promises of astonishing sex and long international films. *The Mysteries of Lisbon* and *Sátántangó*.

He was trying to turn a Bernhard book into a podcast and wanted me to rehearse. He would play the main character, I his disabled wife. I sat for hours on a cushionless chair while he spoke one sentence into my ear.

In the inn district it is still dim.

I told him it was a terrible idea for a podcast. People listened for talk, variety, liveliness. Human interest and the spice of life.

What if I told you he killed her? he said. Do you think they'd all listen then?

I agreed that many podcasts hinged on a dead body and threatened to stop seeing him.

You're declining me with full intentionality, he mourned. You're choosing not to persevere with this journey.

He added he'd always thought I had a paltry imagination, for literature and language, liquors and wines, liquors needing courage, wine a finer palate. Travel, even, and pets.

Everyone says Labrador, *everyone*. The golden friendliness. Please.

When I told the supper club I was sinking my money into a foreclosed guesthouse in Galway, they couldn't compute. Where again? Near a greyhound track? Their own dreams of magical places had died during winter. Now it was all about getting kids into college. It was rankings, athletics and meal plans. Everyone was tight on money.

We had been kind to one another for a time, for years. We scrupulously brought one another to appointments, to follow-ups when the results were dubious. They wanted to but didn't take me out to say goodbye.

Mind how you go, said Thomas Bernhard. Make sure there's no MSG in the mixed veg.

*

There was a pall from coal smoke.

Would you believe it, said the woman who walked off the bus before me. Some people are gone back to bituminous. Renegades!

She said she used to be a college professor and before that an activist. When I looked more closely, she might be a suffragette, one hundred and ten years old.

I think the smoky coal crowd like being part of the cause of the end of the world. This is the west of Ireland. The liminal edge. They think the worst to happen will happen here last.

We walked companionably on the greasy paving stones.

I'm from down in Clare, the woman said. We see things very clearly. It's just a painful curse. Worse times, though, it comes on as a migraine. A bastard behind the eyes, like your man Withnail!

She stopped at the red door of a dark bar.

I don't know if they're doing sandwiches with the soup today. Nor if the sandwich will be made with a roof rat or flakes of foot fungus. But it's worth a try, in the unceasing hope for human decency. Goodbye to you and enjoy your stay!

She was a tonic welcome back to daftness. I should have told her I was here for the duration.

I gained the hill and the morning lifted.

Thomas Bernhard breathed in my ear. I stood at the midpoint of a street of guest houses. Vacancies all the way, and every second name something mystical, Arthurian.

Mine had never had a name, the agent said. It changed hands several times, and nobody made a go of it as a business. The agent blamed the parsimony of the sharing economy.

Shameless carry-on! Unprofessionals. Renting out a utility room and calling it a Room for the Kids. And people stupid enough to pay the night's money.

I didn't want to make a go of it either. I wanted rooms where people might come to gather without my entertaining them. William James smoked a pipe in the library while his wife did social reproduction in the drawing room. I'd come back to this city, this country, to dock, but I'd leave for upstairs when the ground floor turned into the Walls of Limerick.

We all, said Thomas Bernhard, we all crave return to the mother country's bosom.

But when asked, he wouldn't tell where he was from. He sounded Anglo-Australian. One of the supper club said, don't believe it for a second. He's the quintessence of self-invention. That asshole is from the Florida mangroves!

My mother and father lived in an outpost of deepest Cork. Tradition had it that I landed with them each Christmas, and again for two weeks in summer. Everything went kindly and courteously, in the way of familiar strangers. We tried to make the old places new. Beach towns and the bars of hotels. Bingo, even, for silly, screaming laughs, though the bawdy ways of calling numbers had been cleaned up.

You can't say two fat ladies anymore, my mother said. Nor legs-eleven. It's misogynistic. Or do I mean sexist? Which is the worse one? Is it? Really! Anyway. You know what I mean. You just can't say the old things anymore.

Describe your parents, Thomas Bernhard had commanded, as though my answer would determine our forging a life together.

Soft, gentle creatures, I said, after a long time. And persistent all the same.

He said they sounded like snow. I had no gift for depiction, he said, and in that I failed the saints and scholars.

His own were two people he should put in pots, he said.

Like the play. Surely you know Beckett. Mine, they'd want the pot fitted with all the comforts. Electric blankets and Chivas Regal. And USB to charge the phones.

Mine were bamboozled about the B&B.

We don't entirely understand, my mother said. We don't understand at all. After all this time, Galway?

But they supposed I'd make a go of the place because in their estimation I was old enough and had always been independent. They put a hefty amount to the deposit because they said we would all make the money back.

All the tourists in summer. Mighty! And the race crowd. And you can lodge students the rest of the year.

Thomas Bernhard said it was their insurance.

This is how they lure you. Home is so sad. It stays as it was left, shaped to the comfort of the last to go, as if to win them back. They've been reading Philip Larkin.

I said it should be nothing to him. We hadn't bothered one another for months.

I know, he said. It's just I see the bigger picture and have no choice but to inform you. Now go back to that second image of the kitchen. Heathenly fuck.

A guesthouse? More like a transport to Australia.

If this was what the supper club meant by abuse, the nonchalant knowing better and predicting worse, then he was a mastermind.

In any case the place was rock-bottom because the yard for parking was the size of a sock. And the lights and the noise from the greyhound track. And the last owners' mortgage calamity. Their fleeing. Then burst pipes, a hole in the roof, starlings and pigeons and bats.

Poor things, said my mother, in the abstracted tone she had for other people's distant disasters. It's hard to get going these days.

She said I'd always had romantic stirrings for derelict houses.

What I had were colours to paint and plans for distressing the furniture.

The first dog showed up when the builder finally, rancorously, finished his work.

He's taking too long, my father railed. He's taking the piss entirely! Tell him you know what's what.

I did, but the builder was unmoved.

You have to see things my way, the builder said. I do one bit of your job and let it settle, and I move onto my other job, and let that settle, and so on and so forth. And then I come back round to you. Capiche?

A Connemara racketeer, he pinched his dark eyes to unfathomability.

Just when you thought you were out, I drag you back in, is it?

My voice grappled for know-how and menace.

Ah, now. There's no need for that, Miss.

My mother said I shouldn't have been making tea and cutting sandwiches for him.

I bet you did triangles, too. That might be polite in America, but you can't do it here. Not anymore. You'll never see the end of them.

The builder left me a bill I couldn't decipher, every line item a brand-name or compound verb. Bostik and Superquilt. Tear-out, take-down, the argot of gangsters. I sat against a sanded wall and drank half a bottle of dreadful red.

The sulfites and tannins were breakdancing in my chest when the greyhound walking back and forth outside the sliding door stopped and became real. It looked at me mournfully and swung away running.

Come back, I called out. I love you!

In the inn district the evening air was dense and damp. If it hadn't been for paint fumes I would have felt heavy-hearted, utterly mistaken. I had fifteen job applications travelling the SMTP highway. Their embellishments might make a better, finer person blush, but this was the age of self-peddling. You had to talk a thing up, then up.

My cousin in New Zealand would have a mystical or caustic read on the situation. In a hushed moment at a christening, she told a scattering of us she had done unguarded, contaminating things for money. The dark mystery made her our hero. She left for New Zealand next morning.

When Leonard Cohen died my mother renamed the cat, so they had a cat called Ladies' Man.

When the cat went under the wheels of a tractor, my father called it Death of a Ladies' Man.

Because I was going to turn into one or other of them anyway, I called the greyhound David Bowie, and waited and waited for him to come back.

You know he's a serial abuser of women? We think you should know, so we're telling you.

A small splinter group from the supper club had taken me for coffee to talk. They'd known Thomas Bernhard for years, had borne him because he'd never tried to cull from their number.

But you. Of course he's trying it. You're. Young.

I waited and hoped for *and lovely*. Instead they talked about California, where technocrats were paying ten thousand for the blood plasma of younger people.

They say it makes them feel great! See what we're saying?

Thomas Bernhard had bitten me in the stupidest, most bloodless place, my elbow. It hurt because it crunched. I listened to their tracts on a man they'd known but not known for years.

I mean, he can be very charming. He knows all the craft beers, and never brings a dud. And he never overstays his welcome. Like someone else we know.

They moved on to lamenting the disgraced football coach who left his house only to come to the supper club.

Sometimes. Okay, sometimes, I'll say it, sometimes I get the sense he hasn't showered since the last time. Is that awful of me?

We agreed it was, but it wasn't wide of the mark. But he always said the funniest thing on any given evening. And his crime had been embezzlement, not cameras and hot tubs. Thus he was forgiven. And Thomas Bernhard forgotten.

True, it had been hours in that chair, him circling, trying different tones to say that one boneless sentence. No bathroom break, a urinary infection one week on. The doctor asked if there was anything else she needed to know. The elbow, the foot, the wrist. Had I been worried at by a dog?

I told her I hadn't heard the phrase since childhood. A television ad to keep your dogs from killing sheep by night. A cartoon dog ambled out from a house and joined a pack of marauders. They flung themselves to the fields and ripped the bellies of sheep. A lamb nudged its fallen mother, the dog returned to the fireside. At school we enacted the ad. Anyone who got to play the main dog sat back by its owner, with knowing flames in its eyes.

The first dog returned, with a second dog in tow. When they recruited a third they moved in. I was in no position not to yield.

Fine, I said. Let me show you to your rooms. Thank you for booking directly with us.

The fawn hound took the room with the shared blue bathroom, the white one got a sweeping view over the shallow lough. The black hound, my first visitant, took the room with the connecting door to mine. He got bay window, cushions, and a painting by the painter whose name I could never remember, but whose gentle Disney tints and Christmas cottages made me sicken for American years I hadn't had in northeastern places I'd never been.

I trained the hounds to defecate collectively. I shovelled weekly to the back corner of the back lawn. The tumulus stank until it dried out, and nobody came to track my dogs down.

I was there fixing up, painting over, walking dogs for a month before my mother and father showed up, each with a rolling suitcase. I hoped they'd brought wine but they hadn't.

Just the weekend, my mother said. The luggage was on special offer and it's great for not balling up clothes!

They'd left space for shopping to bring back to Cork. My father said there wasn't a lazier name for a commercial district than Shop Street. It was so much worse than Main Street.

The further down you go! At least you got the old joke from that one.

I gave them the vacant room, the en-suite painted Cream of Furze above the wainscoting and Enlightenment below. It took them fully half a day to run into David Bowie, then Heine and Hesse, who by then were inseparable and slept in a figure of eight.

Oh Jesus, they cried! Dogs! Dogs in the house? They'll destroy the place!

I showed them everywhere. No hair, no smell, no trace of a creature at all.

Hounds leave a light mark, I told them. They might as well be wearing slippers and hazmat, that's how clean they are.

They grudged a dog-walk by the lough. My father tried to remember a Van Morrison album.

You know the one. The one where Van and his missus. They're walking greyhounds, I'd swear it.

My mother tried to remember Van's missus's name.

A model. Beyond belief, a woman so good-looking, giving him a look. But you never can tell when it comes to love. They're not still married. Are they?

My father looked out over the lough, said you could never call it a lake, not in a million. Too scrubby round the edges.

Michelle Rocca, I said.

My mother praised my power of recall, said I always remembered inconsequential things.

Michelle Rocca is important, my father contended. She took up with the most significant singer-songwriter of the twentieth century.

David Bowie hauled on the leash, drawn by a figment twitching in the bushes. Heine and Hesse sprang the other way, away from arrant nonsense. I thought I saw the ancient suffragette on the footpath by the railway line, but at wet and windblown distance I couldn't be sure.

When my parents went shopping they got useful plastic items. Pump-action soap dispensers. Tall boxes with holes in the lids, for pouring breakfast cereals. They said no guesthouse could be without them, and reminded me to get at least one gluten-free option. They got bigger boxes still for the greyhounds' foodstuffs. Fleece blankets and a tall stand for bowls.

Think about it, my father said. Bowls on floor, and it's a giraffe reaching down for a daisy. Very bad for digestion, impossible.

Their efforts were generous and exact. I'd never have thought of so many receptacles.

You could, my mother suggested, market this place as dog-friendly. What other guesthouse along here does that? None, I'd venture. There's any amount of biddies and crackpots out there who want to bring Rover on hols!

We parted on good terms and sandwiches packed for their train. There was talk of my going their way for Easter, their coming mine for the races. They might fit a shed with old carpet.

For the hounds! my father said.

My mother took my hand in hers. She said I looked better and fuller than when we used to FaceTime.

If I wasn't looking straight at those dogs inside the window, she said, I'd say they were my imagination.

On one of those FaceTimes Thomas Bernhard said he'd stay out of sight and make no sound. I used earphones to guard the jolly, abrasive voices of my parents.

My father said he had an awful notion there was a control freak nearby, telling me what to say.

I've seen it in films. Mainly American.

He always kept a bead drawn on the depravity of the U.S. I came away blinking from the screen, tight on the cheekbones from performing ease and serenity.

I want to soundproof you from those people, Thomas Bernhard said, moving to me with hands gasping for air. Those horrible, earsplitting people. How did you ever survive, to get away, to me, to try this thing we're about?

We went to the cork-tiled room. The chair was pulled out from the table, the cushion removed. He switched on the recorder and dictated date and time.

The hounds might well be your imagination, I told my mother. But it would take some powerful extra thinking to project them into *his* head.

My father smiled, swept up in the thought experiment.

You'd collapse from the psychic effort, I told her.

I've seen something like that, said my father. Heads imploding in a sci-fi film. Someone trying to think someone else's thoughts. The two of them went kaput.

In the window for all to witness, Heine was kissing Hesse. David Bowie stood to one side, aloof, as all strays and vagabonds must do.

Tearmann

Tá marmar
chomh flúirseach
ar an mbaile seo
go bhfuil na cosáin
déanta den gcloch bhán
timpeall café
atá á riaradh
ag tuairgín mná
ón imigéin.

Ní léir go gcuireann sé
aon bhuairt uirthi féin
ná ar an gcrann
a bhfuil cois eilifint fé
sa chlós lasmuigh
go bhfuil rian na hiasachta
ar an gcanúint thuata
a labhrann sí
ag friotháilt
ar mhuintir na háite.

Siúlann sí chomh mall
is dá mbeadh crúsca lán
á iompar aici
ar a ceann,
a súil stáidiúil
ag taisteal ó dhuine
go duine den slua,
go dtí an fharraige mhór
thar raon na gcnoc úd thall.

Ar an scáileán
os mo chomhair,
tá fear béal faoi
ar bhruach na habhann.
Tá T-léine dhearg air
is bríste gearr,
leathláimh caite aige
thar dhrom a iníne
mar a bheidís sínte
lá samhraidh
cois toinne.

An é nár chualadar
an raidió á rá
nach fada anois
go leáfaidh
an leac oighir
is go dtriomóidh
an talamh,
go leagfar na fallaí
atá tógtha againn
eadrainn
is an drochrud
atá ag teacht?

Tá an pictiúr
chomh beo
go dtabharfá
an leabhar
gurbh fhéidir
do láimh a shíneadh
thar dhrompla
na díleann
is an Rio Grande

gualainn an athar
a chroitheadh
is a rá leis
i gcanúint thuata
do mhéar is do shúl
go bhfuiltear
ag feitheamh leis féin
is a iníon dhonn

i mbaile chomh geal
le marmar
mar a bhfuil bean
ag friotháilt go ciúin
ar gach stróinséir
dá dtagann chuici
ag lorg tearmainn
ón doineann
i gcroí an duine

i bhfad Éireann
ón bhfarraige mhór,
is a deora goirt
gan teorainn.

Uachtar Ard, Meán Fómhair 2019

Louis de Paor

Memorials

Clara Kumagai

The body can translate into any language. A jump, a twist midair, the conviction of feet returning to ground: they are impressive wherever he goes. So it is a simple pleasure to do this, an art that requires both intense concentration and a peaceful emptiness of mind. It is also a way to keep warm in a country where the wind is acrobatic enough to throw rain in every possible and impossible direction.

Djiu Be Fu is popular. He suspects that it's not purely because of his performance, because he could be an attraction while doing nothing at all. People gawp at him like he's a talking animal or gaze as if he is an exotic treasure. Sometimes he forgets and sucks his teeth in case there is food caught there, or touches his head as if he is wearing a strange hat. But it is all of him that is strange: his accent, his eyes, the strong shine of straight hair. However, he is a performer, and performers can't live without eyes on them. A show means freedom, not just of body and mind, but of the consciousness of difference.

He will have to return home sooner or later, but he still doesn't have money to prove it was worth leaving in the first place. He will have to tell stories of the places he has been and the things he has seen, and he rehearses them in his mind the way he rehearses his routines. *When I travelled with the circus...* or *In England, they...* or *Irish people always...* That's what is done when you leave home. You return with money and with stories. The stories are probably the more important of the two.

He always dreamed of the places at the ends of the roads that led out of his small town. He only ever heard gossip about the people who had left the borders of China. *Yuewen went to Taipei to be an actress. Wei left for Japan to become rich.* Whenever he asked where these people were now and if he could meet them, there was always a shrug or a head shake. *He never came back. We never saw her again.* If he asked why, he would be told, *She is too wealthy to be bothered. He is too poor to come back. Her family is dead.* He wanted to go, but he wanted to return, too.

He considered ways to escape. A businessman? But he was bad at math and hated to haggle. A teacher? But he had no knowledge to impart. A soldier? But the battles being fought were within China or at its borders, and that was still too close to home. Besides, he might die.

A circus visited. He loitered after the show to talk to the performers, who told him they had been everywhere and were on their way to go there again. He practised balancing, tumbling, and flourishing, and when the circus returned a year later, he said, *Look what I can do.* And when they left he left with them, and travelled over land and sea.

In a small town by a grey lake in the west of Ireland, the circus performs. After the second performance, a young woman waits by the tent to say that he had been amazing and she had read about China in books and would he like to take a walk with her tomorrow? So he finds himself with a girl with black hair and blue eyes, strolling around the edge of the lake in the softness of the early evening. She's eager to talk and point out what had been a moat and a castle centuries before, the white swans and their grey children, the glowing stained-glass windows of the cathedral.

She is the first audience for his stories and is as rapt for tales about London as she is about Nanjing. He asks if she wants to travel and she says, *Yes, more than anything.* She pauses. *Does the circus need any workers?* He thinks of all the possibilities that could unroll before him: saying no and leaving decently tomorrow, saying yes and stealing her away, remembering her when he is old and married in China, marrying and growing old with her in China, parting ways in some European city or in the next town. He is so engrossed in the envisioning of these futures that he doesn't see the group of men coming their way on the path. One of them calls the young woman by her name and asks her what she's doing, and she replies smartly, *Walking and talking.*

It's only after they are around him that he senses danger. They exhale alcohol and their hands are suddenly pushing him, taking his arms, dragging him toward the end of the pier. Her voice is echoing like a church bell across the water, but they laugh and yell over her. *It'll do him no harm. He needs a wash, look at him. The skin on him.* They are pretending to each other that it is a joke and that they don't mean anything bad to happen, not really. Arms lift and swing and heave him into the air and he flings himself forward on the momentum, diving up and somersaulting. If they throw you then embrace the air. If you fall then do it with grace.

Underwater, everything is hazy and slow. He can skim through the air so easily, but the water is heavy and unforgiving. It is as cold as exile. If they throw her into the water he is ready to catch her as she tumbles down, but there is only him. There are noises, perhaps voices calling to him, distorted by distance and time. How will they find him? This is the farthest from home he has ever been.

Even as a dreamy teenager, I wondered how big of a problem it was that I identified so closely with a gravestone. It's in the graveyard of Loughrea library, a converted church that still houses sacred things, namely books. There's an information sign in front of the church about when it had been built and other historical details, but the final paragraph reads:

> **Perhaps the most unusual headstone in the burial ground is that of Djiu Be Fu who died on August 27th, 1936. A Chinese performer, he lost his life tragically in Loughrea Lake.**

I was a reader of everything as a child—*The Farmers Journal*, ancient magazines, the parish newsletter, countless books—and was instantly impatient once I had finished them. But I read these two sentences over and over, even though I never found the actual grave in that deteriorating cemetery.

It was comforting to know of another Asian in Loughrea history. By the time my younger sister was in first year she had classmates from Poland, the Philippines and Brazil, but for the majority of my secondary school years the foreigners were just me and two girls from England. I had lived in Ireland almost my whole life, a handful of years before it became a place where people immigrated *to* rather than just emigrated *from*. My mother is Irish, so really it was a homecoming as well as an immigration, though the homecoming part is not usually what's picked up on. But here was another exotic foreigner who had been in Ireland long before me and settled here, if not in life, then at least in death.

I thought about that Chinese man in the graveyard because, in a place where everybody seems the same, there is solidarity in any difference.

Djiu Be Fu was rich, an eccentric who had left his wife and child in China to travel westwards across Asia and Europe and Britain. He discovered that the west coast of Ireland was the final piece of land before the ocean and Canada. He was a drinker, and the heat in his face made the cool lake water irresistible. He was prone to panic, and flailed his arms until they were exhausted, and then he slipped beneath the surface, flaming cheeks becoming pale and cool.

I have a memory of a white Irish boy, a cousin or a classmate, saying once, *If you call a Japanese person Chinese, it's like calling them a pig.* I absorbed this and because I was a child I didn't question why he thought this or how he had learned it. I remembered the woman in the Asian food shop who used to give me white rabbit rice sweets; the shopkeeper who yelled at me when I tried on sunglasses and then walked out of the shop to show my mother; my parents' reminiscences about The Pink Pearl's dim sum in Vancouver and the waiter who would usher them to the top of the queue because they were such regular customers. I thought about the goldfish given to us by the owner of a Chinese restaurant in Athlone. He was friendly and chatty—excited, I think, to see other Asian people. My brother and sister and I admired his fish tank, and we were in the car when he rushed out of the restaurant and handed us a 7Up bottle with two little glimmering fish swimming inside.

I thought of my father walking down the street and a man passing by saying to his son, *Chinese, Japanese, dirty knees.* I thought of sitting on a bus and a girl outside pulling the corners of her eyes up and down. They hadn't known the difference between being Japanese or Chinese; they had just known difference, and for them, too, that was similarity enough.

Djiu Be Fu was a poor scholar touring with a book about the history of ceramics in China. He was performing readings to small crowds. He lost his footing and fell into the water and there was nobody nearby to help him. They said later that the copy of his book in his coat was too heavy, and dragged him down. His dying regret was not listening to his editor.

One day, when I was maybe fifteen or sixteen, I went into the library and sat in the back corner, across from the small section of historical non-fiction. A title hooked my eye and I lifted a heavy hardback book from the shelf. It was *The Rape of Nanking*, detailing the Japanese destruction of the Chinese city in the 1930s. I began to read the introduction and very soon felt sick. The man in the graveyard died in 1936, and in 1937 Nanjing was brutalised. I closed the book and felt layers of guilt settle as I returned it to its space on the shelf, about what I didn't know and what I was afraid to learn.

There are miles of difference between people and countries, created by history and culture and language and time. Maybe if that Chinese man had met me and my family, he would have felt no solidarity at all.

Djiu Be Fu had an Irish lover but when he went to her home to meet her family they refused to let him in the door, told him to go back to where he came from, and her pale face at the window only watched. He threw himself into the lake in dramatic despair and his heart was a stone in his pocket.

My Japanese grandfather fought in World War II. We didn't share a language, so could never speak about it. Even if we could, we wouldn't have.

He was my Japanese grandmother's second husband. Her first had died in the war. I don't know how long they were married or how much time they spent together before he died. They had no children. In my grandparents' house there was a photograph of him that I've never seen. This first husband was handsome, according to my mother, who was the one who spotted and asked about the photo. *Very* handsome, she said.

After his death, my grandmother was left with only her husband's name, and this she was made to keep. When my grandmother married again, her new husband—my grandfather—had to take her first husband's surname: Kumagai. My grandmother had become a Kumagai when she married into the family, and now she was the last one who could carry on the name. And her father-in-law insisted that it be carried on, no matter the blood. This is not unheard of in Japan. My grandfather had been the third of four sons in the Sawada family; perhaps he would not have inherited much, perhaps it was better to become the head of a different family, perhaps after the war there were few choices left, perhaps it was love. My grandfather, like his new wife, accepted the conditions of marriage, duty, tradition. If that first husband had survived, what would I be like? My name would be the same, but my blood would be different.

My actual grandfather returned from the war. I don't know where he had been sent or what he had done. My father's family were farmers, and in the house they had silkworms, in the garden they grew vegetables, in the forest they foraged mushrooms. After digging up sweet potatoes, my grandmother showed me how to wash my hands in the rainwater gathered in broad leaves. My grandfather fed his iridescent koi carp and mourned when the herons sometimes plucked them from the pond. Things grew and lived and were consumed and lived again. There are many things I am still afraid to know.

Djiu Be Fu had an Irish lover and when he went to her home her family ushered him in, delighted, and plied him with cake and tea. She put her mouth close to his ear and whispered that he should tell them that they were engaged. He made hasty excuses, avoided her grey eyes, left the table, thought a swim would clear his head. An eel touched his leg in the water and he panicked and drowned. His lover mourned, recovered, and married a Welsh man. It was said she had a taste for foreign men.

On a mountainside in Aichi Prefecture, behind our Japanese family home, there's a graveyard. Japanese gravestones are usually tiers of stone with a pillar on top, as tall as my shoulder or my eye. My grandmother inherited her first husband's house, and his family's graveyard. There are twelve generations of Kumagais, split over two different plots. The first is right beside the house, the gravestones small and rounded and weathered, replaced now by a polished stone to represent the first six generations. The other six are higher up, at the end of a mountainside path. That's where my grandparents are now. We put a pinch of rice on each gravestone and pour water from a kettle over the pillar. Then we bow and clap and bow again.

I wonder if my grandmother's first husband is here, too. Where did he die, and were his remains brought home? Perhaps he is far away and lonely, killed for a cause meaningless to him; maybe he was proud to fight for his nation and ready to do the things that countries at war demand. In Japan, families usually have a simple altar or shrine in their home, small enough to fit into an alcove or on a shelf. They honour household gods and ancestors. Family members who have passed away can be memorialised there, even if their remains are far away. So my could-have-been-grandfather might be remembered in such a way, somewhere. The end of his story is the same, either way: *He left to fight and never came back.*

I was born in Vancouver, which has one of the oldest Chinatowns in North America. People emigrated, lived and worked there, but it's hard to forget home. In the 19th century, some families paid for the bones of their dead to be dug up and returned home to China, where they could rest in true peace. For the man buried in a Loughrea graveyard, there was no such service. In China, Taoist followers have shrines in their homes. Dead are remembered during Ghost Month. Maybe there is a family who also has a story they tell: *Djiu Be Fu left home to become famous and never returned.*

Djiu Be Fu was not a performer at all, simply a quiet, curious man. But somebody said the only Chinese in Ireland were in the circus, and so the rumour spread. He didn't drown at all but had a swift and sudden heart attack at the edge of a grey lake and fell gently into the soft mud.

When I started this, I wrote one story about Djiu Be Fu but realised that telling only one story was wrong, never mind that all of them are fiction. Different versions of Djiu Be Fu's history have wandered through my mind for years, but if any of them are true it's by chance, or coincidence, or something else. Maybe he would be angry at these fantasies, or pleased at remembrance, or amused by speculation. I remembered him as a circus performer, but when I hunted the internet for the exact inscription, I found that there was no mention of a circus at all. I'd presumed it from *Chinese* and *performer* in as reductive an assumption as any I have encountered myself. As simple as, *You're not from here.*

I'm often asked how I've ended up in different places—Tokyo, Vancouver, Galway. I can spin out a handful of stories, versions abridged and unabridged, depending on my mood and the manner of your asking. I can go back as far as my parents meeting in the US almost halfway between Ireland and Japan, or to my birth in Canada, or my neighbourhood in Tokyo, or I can just say, *Ireland*, and see what you dare to question. There are so many paths that lead us to the places we are and as many ways to tell them.

Djiu Be Fu was raised in An Cheathrú Rua and had far more Irish than Mandarin. He had been infatuated with the giddy spin of jigs and reels from a young age. Musicians played with their ears and their hands, so it didn't matter what he looked like. In Loughrea he had so mighty a session that his whole body was dizzy with music. It was the dawning of the day when he and his musician friends left the pub and strolled along by the lake humming bars of music. At the pier, the water rolled a steady beat. *I'm going to swim*, he told his friends. *Mad!* they said, *It's freezing!* But in he jumped, and perhaps it was because he was singing that he choked and inhaled lungfuls of water. His friends jumped in to save him but they were too late. He was buried with his fiddle and the musicians played an Irish lament at his grave.

Differences don't need to be erased and similarity shouldn't equate to sameness. But when we are young or when we don't know any better, it's easy to do because it's simpler and it's comforting. Friends who are also half-Japanese or mixed race—especially if they grew up isolated from a wider community—have told me that they know this feeling: *You're different like me.* I suspect, for myself, this reaction will never go away. But what intrigues me more now are parallels, mirror images, intersections. They're uncanny and marvellous.

Standing in cemeteries, looking at stone and carved characters, all I can do is imagine and remember. I'm the result of names and blood crossing oceans, leaving, returning, living, dying. In a graveyard while remembering another graveyard, I think of two men, both dead long before me, in places they did not suspect they would be, being written about by a person they would never have considered. If they saw me, they would wonder where I came from. They might think: *she is not my blood,* and they would both be correct. Perhaps they would think: *she is a little bit like me,* and they would both be right about that, too.

The First Migration (or Running Away After the First Slap)

Sea Road, Salthill

Gates ticking by like dark shirts on a line, like the blobs of rage in my chest, which fade as I begin counting *one two five eleven* because I am four and know numbers, just like I know that we're nearly at the sea because the wind is blowing us a salt kiss; and daffodils bounce yellowly on their stems like a brass band marching to a silent tune *three seven* and birds follow us, air-surfing from telegraph pole to tree, and I look through the bars of each gate, to strangeness, to a different front door and *this is my foot* I say staring down *and my other foot, one two,* I tell Ivor, who doesn't know how to count yet, because he's only three—and then I look up and the sky is sending messages I can't hear, something to do with the new clouds coming in, eating up the sun, all the high flying blue vanishing, until everything is as dark as the sandpaper road under our bare feet, and I know that green is softer than tar so I cross over, calling Ivor to follow, *see the grass* I say turning around, but my little brother is whimpering and, trotting towards us, long-haired and horned, is a billygoat monster—trip-trap—from our fairytale book, and then I'm running back, dragging my brother's hand, past gate after gate, blundering into a question: *will I ever know my own home again?*

Afric McGlinchey

Bad News

Dean Fee

Marianne sits by the fire and scribbles in her battered notebook while she waits for me to bring her a vodka tonic. She drinks it in three swallows, and I bring her a second. This one she sips while she pets her dog Jack, who is actually a girl, but Marianne has some thing about dogs being boys and cats, girls. It's midway through February and the pub is so quiet I can hear her move her false teeth with her tongue; their slow knock oddly soothes me. Marianne always comes to the bar when she's ready for her third drink. Her notebook put away, she usually takes a seat by the door to watch out the window as she drinks it. Today, though, she sits outside, hacking a cough as she goes through the door.

Through the window I see the back of her head and the curve of her hearing aid. She has her face turned towards the weak sun. I glance at her after half an hour and see she hasn't moved. I go outside. Her face is still turned to the sun. Her eyes are closed. She still has half a vodka. Jack the dog looks at me, tongue lolling, then back to her.

Marianne, I say, but get no answer.

In some way I know she's dead because instead of nudging her, I hold my index finger under her nose. There's no breath. I stand for a moment but no feelings come. I leave Jack to watch her and go inside to phone someone. I don't know who. We are on a narrow street that runs through the city and down to the sea. The street is busy with people and I have no one to ask. It's Rag Week and I'm terrified that the roving gangs of students will land in on top of me. Today's Donegal Tuesday, when students don their GAA jerseys and queue for The Hole in the Wall from eight in the morning. Thankfully they stay away from my bar, something Marianne would comment on, then bless herself. She hates—hated—young people.

I look around for help and Marianne seems to pulse in the corner of my vision. I feel as though every passerby knows she's dead and it's wrong to leave her in this spot of sunlight, as though she's on show. I think that maybe I should close the bar, but Johnny isn't due in for a half hour. Johnny isn't the worst of them, but I don't think he'd appreciate me closing up shop.

May, 2018: On my first day working for Johnny, Marianne stared at me for a long moment before whispering, Vodka tonic, and when I gave it to her she pushed it back at me and said, No ice, no lemon. She spoke like a ghost, like she was out of breath.

August, 2018: Young Paul, Johnny said, pulling me in with an incline of his head.

What's the craic, boss.

I see you're a reader.

And how do you see that?

He pointed a fat finger at the book I'd propped, tent-like, beside the till. Because I seen ya reading that tome, he said.

Fair enough.

Have you ever read any of Marianne there? he goes on.

Marianne where?

There, he said, the finger back out again, pointing to Marianne by the fire. Don't be staring, gasson.

She's a writer?

She is surely. Marianne Farrell. Have you not heard of her?

I've heard of Marianne Farrell, of course, I said. I just didn't know that was her.

Johnny nodded, happy to have served the connection.

She keeps to herself, like. Bit of a recluse, he said. But Jaysus she's some writer. You'll have to read her, boy.

I will.

I went back to my work, trying to equate this grumpy, deaf woman who drank like clockwork with the noted writer Marianne Farrell. On my way home I stopped in Charlie Byrne's and bought all her books.

My housemates were in the kitchen, listening to music and cooking. I read in my room until I heard them go to the sitting room. I ventured to the kitchen with a frozen pizza, and read more as it browned.

I devoured Marianne's novels within the month. They were beautiful and mostly plot-less; they were about the day-to-day, boring routines of humans, about the little things that fill us up and bring us down. Marianne wrote about friendships and lovers, and a lot about family. I was especially taken by *Bad News*. It was a novel written as letters from a daughter to her deceased father, reprimanding him for all the bad he had done while he was alive: the cruel things he had done to her and her mother, and the way he turned truth on its head to manipulate those around him.

January, 2016: And that's the end of it, my father said.

His face had gone purple from the shouting. He turned back to the skirting board, knelt and picked up the paintbrush. My mother tried to normalise the situation by starting on the dishes.

I've no interest in Law and I hate Dublin, I said.

My father stood back up and came at me with the dripping paintbrush. He held it up to my face.

Didn't I just tell you that was the end of it? Didn't I? He waited for me to answer. Well?

Daniel, my mother said, from the sink.

Shut up, you, he said without taking his eyes off me. Well, didn't I say that was the end of it?

Yes, I said, finally.

Ah here, he said, standing back. Fucking crying now.

He went back to his work, asking himself where he'd gone wrong, and hadn't he tried his best?

Into the wall he said, If you want to go to Galway and waste your time trying to become some fancy writer, then away with you. You'll not see a penny from me.

My mother only gave me a shrug of her shoulders. I went upstairs and got my bags and left.

I was on the bus back to Dublin when my mother texted me to say she had put some money in my account and that she'd try to help as best she could. A week later I left Dublin and moved into a student house in Galway. Powered by the desire to prove my father wrong, I locked myself in my room and started typing.

November, 2018: All along the River Corrib you can see Missing Person posters. Some are fresh, but most are weather-worn, yellow from the sun or ripped and wet from the wind and the rain. On a midnight walk around the city I saw one that bore a familiar face. I used to see her in Garvey's when I'd call in for a pint after a nightshift. She was a popular girl, always surrounded by workmates, never alone. I stepped closer to the telephone pole. Her name was Mairéad. There was a number to call if she was spotted.

I crossed the Corrib every day on my way to work. Its churning waters brought me quickly and fully to the present moment. Often I'd stand on its banks and try to imagine what it would feel like to fall in. Not just the sensation of the plunge or the temperature change, but of how the mind might work in that situation. Would I remember the ad I had seen before the movie in the cinema that said it was important to stay calm, to wait until the shock receded? It's panic that kills most people and the Corrib has taken its fair share. As I looked at Mairéad's picture, curved around the lamppost, I realised that the river was in the last three stories I had written.

By the time Johnny arrives, I have pulled Marianne's headscarf down over her eyes. One of them has peeled open and I can't bear to see her looking so unsightly. She always presents herself well and I intend to let her keep that tidy dignity.

Jesus Christ, Johnny says. Are you sure she's dead?

Of course I'm sure, I say. It's been almost an hour.

And no one else has come in?

Not a one. Couple of Americans looking for food and I saw Peader Foley walking past and he gave a wave but that was about it.

He must be away up to Freeney's, says Johnny.

Linda Clarke cycles past on her bike. Mighty weather, Johnny, she says.

Mighty, Linda, he replies, with a big smile, and then turns back to Marianne, his face serious. Jack licks his hanging hand.

Howeyah, Jackie. He bends down to pet her. We'll have to call an ambulance.

But she's dead, Johnny.

I know that, for fuck's sake. It's the ambulance that does take them. With a wave of his hands he consigns Marianne to *them*, to the dead.

February, 2019: A story I have written about the river has been shortlisted for a prize in a national broadsheet and is set to be published in its Sunday edition.

I always brought a broadsheet into work with me since Johnny only ever brought the red tops, and Marianne often made use of them when she moved to the window for her third vodka; I strategically left the Sunday edition open on her table, in the hope that she would read the story, cop that it was me who wrote it and lavish praise upon me. She did indeed read it. I watched her, my heart hammering, as her eyes moved left to right and she picked at the small white hairs over her upper lip. When she finished, she moved on to the next column without any sort of introspective pause, and when she finished that she drained her drink, waved a finger of goodbye at me, and left.

The next day she asked if I wrote the story in the paper, the one about the river and the lad convincing the other lad not to kill himself. I smiled and said I did, that it was me.

Contrived shite, she said.

My stomach sank.

Too much waffle about the river, she went on. Never step in the same river twice, blah blah blah. There's enough cunts going around writing about rivers.

She ran her agitated gaze over the empty pub. The next time you write a story to be published, she said, wagging her finger, bring it to me first. That way you can avoid any more disasters.

Jesus, Marianne. You're not one for tact, are you?

Dear Daddy,

Today was really hot and I sat outside in the sun reading. Do you remember last year when we had the Clerkins over for lunch? They brought Brian and Luke and we sat out in the back garden. I remember very well. I was wearing my favourite dress and it was beautifully sunny out and you and Mam sat with the Clerkins around the wobbly patio table. Do you remember that table? And you were drinking beer. And I was playing with the boys down the bottom of the garden in the shade of the big trees. It was like another world down there when you pushed the low branches back and stepped into the cool dark, the earth underneath crackling from fallen branches. Brian and Luke were boring, though, and they didn't like being in the cold and they left. I stayed and I was happy. But then you came, you stumbled in after me and dragged me out by my arm. I was sulking and you were trying to make me laugh and you picked me up to face you and spun on the spot saying isn't it nice being in the sun with your daddy? I beat at you to let me down. You did, and I sat on the grass with a hump on me. Then your face went dark. You grabbed me by my ankles and though I scrambled to get away you overpowered me. You swung me around. The grass went blurry and my dress rose up and everyone could see my underwear and I screamed for you to let me down but you just laughed. Everyone laughed. It was an age before the looping swing came to a stop and I had wet myself. I was left on the grass, crying, the world still turning, and you knelt over me, laughing, and the sour stink of drink off you as you kissed me sorry.

Your Daughter

Summer, 2004: I was eight and my parents and I were walking along the River Lee in Cork when my father, in a flash of giddiness, picked me up and held me by the ankles over the edge. I smelled alcohol and heard the screams of my mother, begging him to put me down, Jesus Christ, Dan.

The story is told at dinner parties as a funny family memory, and over the years has been altered so that my father hadn't been drinking and the fact that I had wet myself is omitted. Instead it is told as though I had asked to look over the edge of the wall and when my father—with a good firm grip—held me out to see the water, I started crying. My mother then adds that that's probably why I'm so afraid of heights.

April, 2019: I stood on the bridge above the floodgate near the end of the canal, where the smooth roll of the river transitions to its full and fierce flow via a 20-foot drop, where the water plummets, beer yellow, into a vicious gargle. I could feel my dad's grip on my ankles and the surge of blood to my head that followed. I could feel my dress rising over my head, and everyone was laughing.

Magnolia is as regular here as Marianne but because they don't get on, Mags doesn't even look at her as she walks into Johnny's bar. I watch through the glass in the door as Johnny leans forward and tells Mags what's happened. Mags rubs a pendant nestled at her chest before turning towards me. She mouths, Oh God, and blesses herself and when she gets her drink—a glass of Guinness—she comes out and sits beside us, holds Marianne's hand, gives it a tender rub with her thumb.

She wasn't the worst of them, she says. God bless her.

No, I say. I feel tears well in my eyes.

Mags says no more but after a moment she pulls Marianne's headscarf back to where it had been and with the tip of her finger pulls the rogue eye closed.

She looks at her closely before straightening Marianne's blouse and cardigan and wiping with a wetted thumb a stray line of lipstick from the corner of her mouth.

February, 2019: It was just after eight in the morning; Marianne had told me to come early. I hopped off the city bus into sleety rain, shielded my face with a scarf, and checked the exact address on Maps. The house—stately, Georgian—was on the far side of Lough Atalia. There were no curtains on the windows and as I walked up the driveway I could see through the house to the back yard, where there stood an old mobile home. Inside the house I saw the shapes of tables and dressers and shelves, covered in white sheets. There were cobwebs on the door knocker and I was about to break them when I heard tinny music coming from around the back of the house.

I turned the corner and the music got louder. It was a woman singing in a foreign language, opera, I assumed. The lights were on in the mobile home. I knocked, rattling the door. A shadow moved inside and the door opened, revealing Marianne in a bathrobe. She had her hair up in a towel and looked like a 99.

Come in, she said, barely audible over the music. You're soaked.

I stepped in, neck bent so I didn't hit my head. There were books and folders on the worktop, on the table, on shelves, on the L-shaped couch that ran along the walls and ended in an unmade pull-out bed. Sheaves of paper stuck out like tongues from under everything. Past the bed was a kitchenette that had in its sink a steaming and soapy basin of water. Through a door to my left was a small bathroom.

Marianne closed the door behind me and stooped to an old hi-fi system with the record turning on top of it. She turned a dial and the music was reduced to a hum. I asked her what it was.

Some Czech shite my daughter used to play, she said. I like noise in the morning.

The place smelled of mould and of Jack. I asked where she was.

He's out running the fields, said Marianne. He'll be wanting his grub. Sit down there while I throw some out to him.

She grabbed an industrial size bag of dog food from under the sink and with only the robe and towel on, opened the door and went outside. Through the window I watched her Mr Whippy head bob past and out of sight. I pushed aside stacks of slim books and sat on the couch. I flicked through a few short volumes of poetry, but I didn't recognise any of the names, nor did I read any of the poems.

Marianne came back, grumbling about the weather. She washed her hands and sat opposite me, pulling the tangle of towel off her head. She combed her fingers through her hair.

Show us what you've got, then.

She always had her hair in a tight bun. I'd never seen it down like this, so long and not altogether grey.

Are ya awake? she said, and kicked my shin.

I presented the few pages I had printed off for her. It was a story about my uncle, Robert, who brought me to a Russian circus during which an elephant keeled over dead. It was one of my most vibrant memories, and I wrote it like a fiction. I was confident she'd like it. I started to explain but she held up a finger.

The work must speak for itself.

She began reading. I settled back into the couch and looked around. A wonderful calm came on the room. The sleet tapped on the flat roof and the wind rocked the cabin gently; the walls creaked and plates and cutlery in the kitchen clinked. In my mind I narrated the moment as though it were fiction. I pointed out the Sacred Heart on the wall above Marianne's bed, noting that it was at odds with what she had said in the past about God and religion. I noted the scratch of her pen in the margins of my work. I zoomed in on the dog in the fields, her coat wet and mucky. I put myself in Marianne's head as she read my sentences, marvelling at a turn of phrase, maybe the one that ended the second paragraph. I pictured her finishing the piece: eyes glazed, she'd put the paper down and say, Christ, Paul. This is incredible—

This is non-fiction, she said.

She held the papers out to me, but I was too confused to take them. She shook them. Here, she said.

How'd you mean? I said.

She sat back, papers on her lap, and sighed.

This is too real to be fiction, she said. Trust me, I know about turning life into fiction.

I asked what of hers was based on her life.

Not my life, my daughter's. *Bad News* was taken from the letters she wrote to her father. Not word for word, but it was basically them. I just wove a narrative into them and made it so he was dead.

And she didn't mind?

Oh, she did. She hasn't spoken to me in almost twenty years.

I'm sorry to hear that.

Doesn't matter, she said, standing up. It's all in the past. And anyway, that's not what we're talking about. Have the elephant step on someone in the audience. Have the elephant kill your uncle. That'd be good. You don't want to get into the habit of using your own life. Trust me.

She stood over me, holding out my story. She'd made red notes all over it.

Have a look at that and come back again next week, she said. I'll see you in the pub.

I saw her again that day shortly after I started my shift. She had her hair up in its bun and she followed her usual routine, as if we hadn't already met that day. It made my visit feel underhanded, like we had broken some rule of etiquette.

May, 2019: I was on the L-shaped couch and Jack was resting her head on my lap, getting a rub behind the ears. Marianne said, Pascal Moran used to write in second person, too, and he was a cunt.

Yeah, I said. But that doesn't mean I shouldn't use the technique.

It does, she said, and calls the dog over to her.

Jack doesn't move.

Fine, you brat, she said. Be like that.

She turned back to me, And it does, Paul. The man was a scoundrel and he's too well associated with that style. If you wrote like that people would think you were trying to emulate him. Half of them would brand you some ill version of him and the other half would be too angered by the reminder of the man to enjoy the work. Myself included.

He can't have been that bad.

He was. One night in Neachtain's, Maura Whelan's husband ordered a pint of stout. Moran, walking past, thought he had called him a lout and boxed the ears off him. He was as ignorant! He was barred from the pub and because he loved it so much he blamed Paddy Whelan and spent the rest of his life bad-mouthing him around town.

Jesus, I said. That's bad form.

I know, she said. Now, stay away from that second person. It's too easy anyhow.

*

June, 2019: I arrived to find Marianne weepy, oddly sentimental. We looked at no work, nor did we talk about writing. I made us some tea, which she poured brandy into, and she told me about her failed marriage. Told me that her daughter still wouldn't talk to her, and how the letters she sent her came back unopened. They were delivered to the big house, and Marianne left them where they fell, underneath the letterbox. She couldn't handle them, sickened by her own pleading words.

I can't bear to go into that house now, she said.

I asked her did she not think it might be an idea to return to her own work? Maybe if she was writing again, it would work as a form of therapy.

Writing? she said. As therapy? Hardly.

I shrugged and her eyes went from indignation back to watery regret.

I have been writing, she said. I've been working on a novel ever since she left. I keep asking her to read it. I want her permission to publish it, but she won't give it. So I can't really say it's finished.

Is it about her?

Everything I write is about her.

She coughed for a long time and I got her water. After she drank it she wiped her eyes.

Don't take your family for granted, she said. Especially your father. There's none of us beyond forgiving.

We all have our multitudes, I said.

As Mags rubs Marianne's hand, I wonder if her daughter will show up to the funeral. I get a strong impulse to call my father. I actually consider it. Maybe I'll tell him about getting the elephant story published. It's the sort of thing he'd like.

I see the ambulance coming down the cobbled streets, and passersby moving respectfully into the doorways of shops and restaurants, out of its way. I knock on the window to get Johnny's attention. His head appears behind a reflection of the street. I point at the ambulance and he comes out onto the street to flag the paramedics down.

July, 2019: If Marianne's drinking routine was upset, she could become very vexed. It was Race Week and I was doing my best to keep her temper cool, but the pub was wedged and someone had taken her seat by the fireplace and she had to drink her three vodkas at the bar with Jack between her feet. Her shoulders were bumped regularly. With all the noise she found it hard to hear me and I had to shout in her ear.

Are you all right, Marianne? Do you want me to move them away from your seat?

She pulled me close with a curl of her fingers and whispered in my ear, Fuck all these cunts.

My shift finishes at eight. As I'm leaving, Johnny calls me into his office. He's on his swivel chair, squinting at the computer, his glasses perched on his nose. He spins around when I enter and takes the glasses off.

Can you take the dog with you? he says. I've been trying to get through to this Mary Farrell all day, but it's just ringing out.

He hands me a grubby slip of paper with that name and a number on it.

I think it's her sister or something. She gave it to me years ago in case of emergency.

Sound, I say.

She was awful fond of you, lad, he says.

I know she was.

I need a drink so I take Jack and go to the off-licence and buy six cans of Tuborg. I sit down at the Arch, by the water. A dreadlocked girl moons over Jack for a while and gives her water in a collapsible dog dish, but when she sees that I'm not on for talking she returns to her group. I go over the notes Marianne gave me on my most recent story, but I can't concentrate. I just read and re-read her words in that scrawl of red pen. I eventually drink enough to call the number.

Hello?

Hi, I say. Is this Mary?

Yes, she says. Who's this?

This is Paul Sullivan. I know—I knew—Marianne Farrell. I was given your number as a next-of-kin.

There's silence at the end of the line and I say, Hello?

Yes, she says. You said you knew her?

Yeah, that's why I'm calling. I don't know if you know, ah, she. . . I'm sorry, she died earlier today, and I have her dog here and I was wondering do you know what I should do?

She's dead?

God. . . Yeah, I'm very sorry to say. Are you her sister or. . . ?

She was my mother.

Oh, I say. Jesus, I'm sorry. I'm awfully sorry. I can call someone else about the dog, if you want?

Yeah, maybe, she says. I have to go. Thank you for calling.

Just a sec, I say. Just one second, before you go. There's a load of letters meant for you in her house. I know your mother was very sorry for what she did to you. Maybe you should read them.

And what do you know about what she did? Who even are you?

Just a friend of hers. She told me about how she used the letters you wrote to your father as material for her book. I think she was very sorry.

Letters I wrote to my father? That's good. That's very good.

What do you mean?

I see she's fooled you too, Mr Sullivan. I didn't write those letters to my father. I wrote those letters to her. You can keep the dog.

She hangs up. I let the phone drop to the grass and then, unsure what else to do, what thoughts to even pursue, I go to the pub.

That same pale sun that Marianne turned her face to in her last moments rises and stretches out across the Corrib. Jack sits by my feet and my backpack rattles with empty beer cans. I stand on the Salmon Weir Bridge, watching the fishermen. They're wading up to their thighs, flinging fishing line alongside the current, spooling it back behind them. I've watched these lads for over two years but have never witnessed a catch. I'm aware that the early morning drivers might think that because I'm wobbling from the beer and looking towards the water, I'm suicidal. I stare into the river anyway, watch the turmoil, note how oddly uniform it is. The peaks peak at the same spot, every time. I pull my last can out of my backpack, but my cold fingers cannot hold it and it goes over the edge with strange grace, turning slowly in the air before sinking into the water.

Dear Daddy,

You were always a great storyteller. They would gather around you in Granny's when the sun went down, and light the candles as you sat sit in the big chair—the story chair, I called it—and though you'd hold my hand while you spoke, you were always far away. They'd hang on your words and you were held up by them. But they weren't always the truth. You'd embellish. And if confronted afterwards you'd say to never let the truth stand in the way of a good story.

They used to say you were a bit mad, that you were living the lives of a thousand men all at once and who could be sane and whole doing that? They used to be afraid to tell you anything in case you'd twist it into a story. I was never afraid of that. I should have been.

Your daughter.

My head is tight and my eyes find it hard to deal with the sun, as weak as it is. I'm embarrassed when I have to pass someone on their way to work. I keep my head down and hold on to the railing of the canal that will lead me home. Jack is walking slowly, matching my pace. I think of Marianne. I think about her novel, trying my best to imagine her doing all those cruel things, but I can't. I mutter at the dog but she seems to understand. She's been very good the whole night, not a peep out of her as I dragged her from place to place, knocking on windows with closed blinds, pleading to be let in for a late drink.

I'll call my father tomorrow and I'll tell him about the story and he'll get a copy and read it. He'll call me back and ask me was the uncle in the story his brother Michael, and I'll say it was and it wasn't, and my father will laugh. He'll tell me he remembers the story about the elephant. He'll tell me he prefers this version, it's got something else to it. A lie, I'll say and he'll go quiet down the phone for a moment before saying, Yeah, the lie makes it.

I cross the bridge to the other side of the canal and when I look down I spot the can I dropped. It's caught on the rim of the old lock, the current turning it over and over against the barrier. There's a set of steps down to the water and I think I can reach the can from there so I pet Jack and tell her to wait. I make my way down, my feet shuffling for purchase on the slimy stone. The water seems calmer than when seen from above. I crouch at the bottom, reach in and pull the can out. The water is freezing and my chest tightens. I wobble and my vision reels. The water comes closer, but I find my equilibrium and right myself. I realise, as I stand back up and catch my breath, that it's the first time I've ever touched the river.

Island Life

'I don't like too much social life anyway. It is gossip and bad white wine.'—Edna O'Brien.

1

All summer they sit, like cakes
in a cake shop window, dusted
with promise, treats for a cloudless
day, fair-weather destinations,
notional ports in a storm.

2

She backs her life
close to the edge
along a road
that ends in a tidal
cul de sac stitched up
by gannets and terns.

3

No man is an island but
she is no man so perhaps
she'll become one, an island
compact and self-contained,
three waterfalls, an orchard,
a herd of feral goats, sixteen
types of wild orchid to lure
hatted experts in summer
                              then wait
for the season to change, for
the island to empty, the stillness
of salt-splashed winter months.

4

You live in a beautiful part of the world,
so remote.
I do.
You must get such great inspiration.
What do you mean?

5

She'd need to insulate
that roof, double-glaze
her windows, and what about
the seat of her pants? She'll need
a jockey's bollocks to survive
the long nights of doubt, the long
knives of auto-dissection, the
wearisome 'I' in isolation.

6

You think they're following you
then you look back but
there's no one there.

7

Building bridges, burning them,
going a bridge too far—for now
no need to bridge the gap between

island

&

home.

Time enough for tomorrow
tomorrow.

8

When she decides
to leave
there will be nothing
to be afraid of,

nothing that
bounds her front
and back, the nothing
that is everything there is.

Geraldine Mitchell

Ballyphallus — Sex, Magic and Yeats

Rob Doyle

This essay was meant to centre around a visit I intended to make to Thoor Ballylee, the tower near Gort in County Galway where W.B. Yeats lived for much of the 1920s with his wife George Hyde-Lees. The Thoor was to be the magnetic symbol around which I would spin my thoughts regarding the twin currents in Yeats's life that intrigue me most: magic and sex.

The night before I was due to take a train across the country, however, a friend sent me an image grabbed from the evening news. It showed the tower with its lower section completely submerged in water, as if it were rising from a lake, while in the foreground two men in high-vis jackets rowed a boat towards the structure. I hadn't seen any news in the preceding days, so I hadn't been aware that much of Galway was underwater, a result of the storms I'd heard howling day and night from the house in Rosslare Harbour where I'd lately retreated from Dublin rental prices.

While the Galway floods may or may not be related to climate catastrophe—the kind of epochal nightmare whose coming haunted Yeats—Thoor Ballylee does seem generally prone to flooding and dampness. Ezra Pound, a friend of Yeats's who clearly relished mocking him behind his back, referred to the tower as 'Ballyphallus or whatever he calls it with the river on the first floor.' A reader of Freud and Jung, Yeats would not have needed Pound's jibe to notice the sight-gag of a middle-aged poet, increasingly concerned with matters of virility, moving into a (moistly) phallic structure immediately after marrying a woman twenty-seven years his junior. Thoor Ballylee not only provided setting and stimulus for Yeats's and George's occult engagements, it also appears to have quickened Yeats's erotic imagination. In the summer of

1926 he wrote to Olivia Shakespear, the first woman with whom he had ever made love, that he had been flooded with sex dreams since returning to the tower.

Like his horny old-man's appetite for young women and his flirtation with fascism, Yeats's passion for the occult has at times been regarded as an embarrassment, but it's what keeps me coming back to him. Like everyone in Ireland, I read Yeats in school: key poems relating to Maud Gonne, the 1916 rising, myth, and twentieth-century Irish history. After that, he never really goes away: Yeats is diffused in the culture; an ambient, avuncular presence. Every so often I branch out and read some more of his poems but, like a Bob Dylan fan who only listens to the mid-'60s albums, I always revert to my favourites, those poems whose grooves and images are already well-worn in my mind—in particular, the ones charged with eschatological foreboding and sublime visions of upheaval. Besides, Yeats the poet is of slightly lesser interest to me these days than Yeats the randy old goat and Yeats the virtuoso of occult credulity.

The story of Yeats and George's prolonged experiment with automatic writing and automatic speech has been treated sceptically by many commentators. The reigning narrative, established in Brenda Maddox's absorbing 1999 biography *Yeats's Ghosts* and reinforced by Colm Tóibín and others, is that the phenomena, which began a few days into what had initially threatened to be an unhappy marriage (on his and George's wedding night, Yeats was tormented with desire for Iseult Gonne, onto whom he had transferred an attraction formerly felt for her mother), embodied an elaborate dance of seduction between a young wife determined to banish the image of her rivals, and a sexually inexperienced husband for whom the mystical and the erotic were intimately linked. In other words, the automatic script that produced some 3,600 pages of writing over the three years in which it was conducted was an aphrodisiac and a channel of intra-marital communication. During some four hundred 'sittings', Yeats would bombard George with questions, and she, assuming the voice of a shifting array of 'Controls', 'Guides' and 'Instructors' from the beyond, who bore fantasy-novel nomenclature, would tell him either whatever he wanted to hear, or whatever she wanted him to hear. There is no question that George believed in the occult nature of their undertaking. Like Yeats, she had undergone a long prior schooling in esotericism, having been initiated into ascending levels of the Hermetic Order of the Golden Dawn, taken part in seances, and read extensively in Neoplatonist and Rosicrucian literature. If she was having Yeats on, she was having herself on too, in an erotically exciting *folie à deux*.

Even if there was nothing supernatural taking place—no channelling of the spirits out of *anima mundi*—the experiment provided Yeats with a lifetime's worth of images to mine for poetry and plays, along with the intricate details of the cosmological system he would elaborate on in his philosophical work, *A Vision*. Appraised from a pragmatist's whatever-works perspective, Yeats and George were accomplished magicians.[1]

1　There was a time when I would have regarded any dabbling in magic as a sign of desperation. Actually, I'm not sure that time has passed, yet in the last year I myself have made my first attempts at magic—specifically, at chaos magick. My friend Cormac, a musician and Muay Thai fighter who moved to Australia to start a family, told me via WhatsApp about the chaos magick rituals he had learned to perform. You decide what it is you desire most, he explained, and then you perform a ritual intended to bring about the desire's fulfilment. 'It's *scary* how well it works', he said.

I've come to take an agnostic and pragmatic approach to these things: perhaps there's something to them, and perhaps they can help me, and what do I have to lose? Moreover, the question of whether chaos magick amounts to *actual* magic—an overriding of the laws governing the physical universe—is moot. Primarily, chaos magick entails reprogramming one's unconscious mind to harness its energies in a particular direction, rather than letting it be pulled apart in a chaos of warring sub-desires. I studied the PDF that Cormac sent me that detailed the steps involved in performing chaos magick and, heeding his advice to 'be very, very specific about what you wish for', performed a first ritual in Berlin early last summer, followed by a second a couple of months later.

It's best not to divulge what desire a particular chaos magick ritual is intended to fulfil. Suffice it to say that in my case, the desires were worldly—in one case exceedingly so—though not dishonourable. It's too early to say for certain that both rituals have been successful, but they appear to be headed that way. The rituals involve symbols known as sigils, drawn from the disassembled letters that spell out the desire whose fulfilment is being sought. You distil your desire into the image of the sigil, then stare into the sigil while you 'engineer a break in consciousness'. According to the instructions I read:

The simplest way to do this is sexual overload, either alone or with a partner.

For my first ritual, I achieved 'overload' alone. For the second, I did it with a partner (herself a practitioner of chaos magick).

At the moment of orgasm, stare unflinchingly at your sigil, imprinting it deep into your mind.

Now destroy the physical basis of the sigil, go do something else and forget anything ever happened.

I burned my sigils, enjoying the heightened sense of ceremony as paper curled in flame in the stove at my flat in Friedrichshain.

At some point in the twentieth century, biographers began to consider it first acceptable, then imperative to recount their subjects' sexual and onanistic experiences. Actually, Yeats divulged plenty of such information in his work. His first orgasm took him by surprise on a Sligo beach at age fifteen. 'At first I did not know what the strange, growing sensation was,' he later recalled. After he learned to repeat the experience, his life became a perpetual struggle not to do so. 'It filled me with loathing of myself,' he admitted. His biographer Brenda Maddox seems to regard masturbation as a theme in Yeats's life, rather than something that just happened in it. She describes him as a 'solitary masturbator', consumed with lifelong regret for his 'onanistic youth'.

Indeed, sexual regret *is* the compelling theme of Yeats's later life, but of course it was not the jerking off he regretted, it was the missed sexual enjoyment for which the jerking off was a substitute. Yeats didn't make love with a woman until he was thirty, when he succumbed to the beautiful Olivia Shakespear (no doubt enchanted by that provocatively missing 'e'). After their year-long affair fizzled out, he enjoyed no further sexual relations for seven years. Famously, he spent most of that period yearning, in a dreamy and ethereal way, for Maud Gonne's fiery classical beauty, whilst being repeatedly rejected by Gonne in his proposals of marriage. (Gonne instead married John MacBride, the volatile, drunken revolutionary who died a martyr in 1916. If we were to be crude in our speculations, we might suppose that the warrior MacBride could satisfy Gonne in a way she knew delicate Yeats never would.)

Rather than harden into a sexually envious late-life reactionary, Yeats determined to make up for lost time, no matter how ridiculous it made him to incarnate that stock comic figure of humankind, the geriatric lecher. 'I shall be a sinful man to the end, and think upon my death-bed of all the nights wasted in my youth,' he wrote to Shakespear, who remained his lifelong confidant. Late-period Yeats is horny-period Yeats, even if his frantic philandering coincided with anxiety over his flagging potency. He made himself the object of enduring mockery for undergoing, in his late sixties, the 'Steinach operation'—basically a vasectomy—in an effort at rejuvenation and increased sexual power. Remaining married to George, he cultivated a harem of much younger lovers, his sexual market-value enhanced by the Nobel prize he was awarded in 1923. The glossy photographs grouped towards the end of the biographies portray what can only be described as a series of babes: the novelist Ethel Mannin; the actress Margot Ruddock (who threw herself out a window in Barcelona after a visit to Yeats); the poet Dorothy Wellesley; and Yeats's favourite mistress, the journalist Edith Shackleton Heald (who was considerably older than the others, in her fifties).

While Yeats's rage against the dying of the erotic light was commensurately successful with his career, the basic predicament is of course far from rare. From my reading of twentieth-century male writers, I sometimes suppose that sexual regret is a universal affliction of men as they grow old. The novels and biographies seem to attest that no matter how much or how good it was, it was never enough, and that each generation must discover this melancholy truth anew. Even baby boomers who made the most of the sexual revolution were to find, around late middle-age (the period when Yeats was seized by erotic urgency), that the young were inventing apps to facilitate ease of sexual congress, and exploring porn-generated desires the lascivious boomers had not thought to indulge. Every country in time becomes no country for old men, and the young in each other's arms perennially set the dying animal dreaming of Byzantine consolations.

Taking advantage of the reduced obligation to shame and tact that is the prerogative of the elderly, Yeats introduced ribald elements into his poems. Perhaps anxious at being made to seem prudish by the sexually frank and scatological modernists, he even included what looks to me like a reference to anal sex in his late poem 'Crazy Jane Talks with the Bishop':

> A woman can be proud and stiff
> When on love intent;
> But Love has pitched his mansion in
> The place of excrement;
> For nothing can be sole or whole
> That has not been rent.

The moralists of each successive generation take a stab at cancelling Yeats over his enthusiasm for eugenics and Mussolini, but his not very fanatical late-life priorities are made clear in the lovely 'Politics' which, although not strictly the final poem Yeats wrote, appears last in volumes of his collected poetry. While listening distractedly to a 'travelled man' and a politician discuss contemporary upheavals in Italy, Russia and Spain, the poet admires a girl standing nearby:

> And maybe what they say is true
> Of war and war's alarms,

But O that I were young again
And held her in my arms.[2]

Yeats's philosophically questing *oeuvre* thus ends in a near-audible erotic sigh (But *O…*).

By the time he wrote 'Politics', a year before his death in 1939, the 'Controls' who communicated with him through George had long fallen silent, having served their purpose in the Yeats's marriage and his creative life. Among its other functions, automatic writing had aided the couple as a kind of sex coach, indicating how frequently they should engage in intercourse, and even badgering Yeats to make sure his wife was sexually satisfied. The 'Controls' also elaborated on the links between sexuality and Yeats's metaphysical system as laid out in *A Vision*. For instance, when Yeats asked the spirit known as 'Aymor' why some children died young, 'Aymor' explained that such deaths were caused by weak sexual desire at the moment of conception; conversely, healthy babies were engendered by powerful orgasms and strong desire during procreative sex. (In this detail, 'Aymor' accords with the vitalist, pseudo-mystical doctrine Norman Mailer would propagate amid marijuana fumes and pulsing testosterone decades later, which included the belief that 'good fucks make good babies'.)

A friend of mine recalls being made to learn by heart and recite 'Politics' at school. It's a curious image: dozens of adolescents chanting in unison an old man's lament for not having screwed around more when he was young. After I left school, I didn't read Yeats again until my mid-twenties, at which time my interest was revived from two directions. The permanent exhibition 'The Life and Work of William Butler Yeats' opened at Dublin's National Library in 2006, and it included an intriguing display exploring Yeats's occult concerns. The following year, the band Bright Eyes, fronted by Omaha-born Conor Oberst ('the real deal, a boy genius', according to embittered indie rocker Richard Katz in Jonathan Franzen's novel *Freedom*), released their seventh studio album *Cassadaga*. Idle speculation: perhaps Oberst had wandered into the National Library whilst touring Europe with

---

2   In an echo that suggests the enduring nature of poetry's themes, the Yeatsian demotion of political commitment in favour of the erotic manifests in a couplet from Irish rap-group Versatile's 2019 track 'Escape Wagon':
I never gave a bollocks about politics
'Cause all I ever wanted was me bollocks licked.

Bright Eyes, and the aforementioned exhibition sparked a fascination with Yeatsian esoterica. Wherever the passion originated, *Cassadaga* is steeped in Yeats, in particular the apocalyptic prophesying of *A Vision* and 'The Second Coming'. The album takes its title from the town in Florida that Oberst visited upon learning of its reputation as 'the psychic capital of the world', populated by mediums adept at seances and tarot-readings such as Yeats had studied a century prior. Allusions to Yeats abound, with mentions of automatic writing, the phases of the moon, telekinesis, reincarnation, vortexes and 'centres of energy', and a spiral that unwinds 'knocking over fences, crossing property lines'. While Oberst may or may not have read *A Vision*, he was familiar with Yeats's confusing belief (more recently promulgated by Steve Bannon) that human history unfolds in a cycle of spirals, or gyres. *Cassadaga*'s most stirring song, 'Four Winds', could almost be regarded as a cross-genre cover version of 'A Second Coming', with Oberst directly quoting the poem ('slouching towards Bethlehem') while channelling Yeats's vision of a world hurtling into eschatological disarray. Whereas Yeats brooded over a generalised cataclysm, Oberst foretells a specifically American reckoning with imperial decadence and aggression:

> But when Great Satan's gone, the whore of Babylon
> She just can't sustain the pressure where it's placed
> She caves

In a wounding critique of Joan Didion's work published in *The London Review of Books* in 1980, Martin Amis took issue with Didion's adoption of the closing image of 'A Second Coming' for the title of her jangled collection of essays about California in the 1960s, *Slouching Towards Bethlehem*. Yeats had written that poem half a century earlier, Amis pointed out; Didion's allusion suggested she was the latest in a continuity of writers who believe they are the first to live and work after things have fallen apart. To Amis, the centre never *had* held and never *would* hold; Didion's apocalyptic fallacy placed her within a literary continuity that assimilates and domesticates the evils that present themselves to each successive generation.

Amis's takedown of Didion is itself four decades old. Writers who today demonstrate a Yeatsian conviction of chronicling the End Times can less confidently be accused of succumbing to a timeless fallacy. An apocalypse *is* happening, and it's the scientists, not the poets, who are telling us so. The question tagged to the end of one of the gentler images of cataclysm on

Cassadaga might have been addressed to Amis:

> First snowman built at the end of June
> He slicks his hair for the interview
> His fifteen-minute fame
> Would you agree times have changed?

So, when the end does come—the *end* of the end, rather than the beginning of the end, which is what we currently seem to be in—how will it go down? Fire? Viruses and wars? Floods? Four winds levelling the pines?

I'm looking again at the screen grab of the partially submerged Thoor Ballylee. The waterlogged photo recalls the original cover design of Yeats's collection *The Tower*, which Yeats commissioned from the poet and artist Thomas Sturge Moore. In a gold and green wood-cut style, the image depicts Thoor Ballylee in double: on the top half the tower rises towards the sky, while underneath it is mirrored in a river. In esoteric terms, the design is very on-message ('As above, so below'). A century later, alongside all that quaint rural mysticism, the tower remains a picturesque symbol of all men who, as the light declines, want to go out with a bang. With my trip to a drowned Galway cancelled, I don't know if I will ever make it out west to see Thoor Ballylee for myself. Motivation and opportunity might not again converge to lure me to the damp inner shaft of Ballyphallus, I mean Ballylee, where I could read the site-specific verse 'To Be Carved On a Stone at Thoor Ballylee', whose final couplet bears a broader, a global resonance in our nightmare-vexed millennium[3]:

> I, the poet William Yeats,
> With old mill-boards and sea-green slates,
> And smithy work from the Gort forge,
> Restored this tower for my wife George;
> And may these characters remain
> When all is ruin once again.

---

3   I wrote this essay in early March, and finished it days before it became clear that we were collectively entering what the Taoiseach described on the evening news as 'events that are unprecedented in modern times'. In an era already saturated with apocalyptic white noise, here was an out-of-the-blue emergency that rapidly changed everything—including the context in which the forebodings that end this essay will be read.

Madame Helena on the Prom

A move, a change and a challenge,
says Helena over crystals after I've parted with my cash.

At Salthill Prom at mid-tide on a sunblushed Tuesday,
I spot her tacking a dayglo poster on the windscreen,
she calls to me, a siren song in plush velvet,
Let Madame Helena tell you your future.

I count my steps back to the Avensis,
pledge to whatever power I am now praying,
if I've cash in the car, I'll go back, what harm?

Tell your mother not to worry, she says, not specifically like,
but in synonym, the way she smacks my hand, sucks her teeth.

Helena has a booster pack for the mobile phone
that could carry her voice all the way to the sky above,
but she's soft with me, *it won't always be like this,* she promises,

like she can see my wedding ring moved from finger
to car-dash ashtray. *A move, a change and a challenge,*
she says, after I've parted with my cash.

I was *young.* (I'm still young.) I will have *no more children.*
The two I have *were born lucky, not rich,*
lucky, not rich. (She says this twice, no flies on Helena.)
High honours, a settled bed by the water
and there I will find peace (and there I will find peace).
Her hand on mine around the crystal which keeps
my money where her mouth is; *no more pain,* she says,
no death and I ask her if sense can come from nonsense?

Good news will come in the post. Good news will spill in the waves.
She says I am strong and I will rise (I nearly believe her)
to a height that will surprise friends and family.
(I say feck anyone who is surprised.)

The good friends I have around me, I'll keep.
She sees regret *across the aisle* but the days of that love
are past. My daughters *will wear uniforms*, my eldest girl,
will she truly be a nurse, or is the youngest off to Templemore?

Will I pass them all I have like a draw rope,
latch, pulley, lever, strength, discipline.
And I'll *be happy*, she says. An abstract notion—
mid-half-disaster, no matter how the sun shines in Salthill.

And I know Happy. It's books, my daughters.
Happy is tea shared with my father the last time
I saw him living. Helena wants to know my questions
and all my mind can utter: 'What's next? Is it her? Is it her?

Is it her?' *Be brave*, says Helena, *be brave, sure, what have you* (left) *to lose?*

Liz Quirke

Ode to the Marriage and the Divorce

I don't want to feel the pain
    like the morning after
I retched all morning
    and you piled me into the car
careening down
    you had to stop three times
and get sick
    We were married
When the ferry pulled in
    its bright white and red
I rested my head on the salty rail
    as we knocked along
I convinced myself
    that was why you didn't try.
grey sky grey-beaked gannets
    crazed missiles plummeting
if I could join them then
    Dive you said

but it comes
    I had nine pints in The Quays
after retching all night
    drove like a lunatic
to the ferry at Cleggan pier
    so I could swing the door open
on the side of the road.
    one year by then.
freshly painted
    I walked straight to the bow
my stomach inverting
    in the North Atlantic
you couldn't console me and
    I looked up
everywhere
    into the sea I thought
I could save us both.
    so in I dove.

Carolann Caviglia Madden

She Taught Me To See Unicorns
Fred Johnston

: for Joaquin Roncero del Pino :
Η κυρία και ο μονόκερος. . .

If I were to tell you, Diodorus, that she taught me to see unicorns, you would not believe me. So I remain dumb. I listen to you, see your thin fragile fingers wear the thin gold-and-silver rings more gracelessly, and am reminded of my own advanced age. I have heard you outline the history of your gentle sins and their parallel guilts a thousand times. But today is sunny, a late summery kindness of climate; and the waters of the bay are calm and bathers plunge and dip and scream as if it were much earlier in the year, and generally speaking there is a charming air of vitality and renewal about everything. So I am in form for you and the dead inevitability of our weekend meeting and our *gestelzt* conversing.

We are left in the world, Diodorus, like half-forgotten elements of a long-dissipated dream. Everyone has awakened from us. The world has assumed a new face. But still, as if to remind ourselves that we once lived, that we once plunged into the sea too, we regale each other with reminiscences of what was, what might have been, and some of it we recall clearly and the rest we make up and no one, least of all you and I, cares.

In between the sounds our elderly voices make in the light sea breeze, the silences are filled with the shouts of children and the scream of motorcycles and the laughter of girls; for this is a new age, my friend, and we must spectate and nothing more. We have been allotted no positions of strength here, and we cannot take our heart's nobility for granted. Our glasses are filled with dark brown beer and carried out to us by a waitress who might have been a daughter; of you, of me, it hardly matters. Of neither of us, as things turned out.

You were an ambitious man of law who married well and discovered his wife to be quite unable to have children. That was unfortunate, but rather call it a pure act of caprice by the gods. Nothing malicious. For me, there were books, many of them, some of which I wrote myself and for which I was given applause and money. Now and then I knew peace of mind; but only once, love. You were more fortunate, Diodorus. Daphnis was a lovely girl, and some said she could foretell the future. Didn't you once come upon her, sitting cross-legged on a cushion in front of the fireplace, eyes closed, humming something suitably Easternish? I could almost swear you told me something, once, like that. In any case, she was a lovely girl and a firm, smart, hard-headed mature woman. Cancer. Broke the heart of many a man. Lump in the breast. I was dreadfully sorry. But I probably said all that at the time.

Daphnis on her cushion, prophesying. You and I, Diodorus, sipping beer outside a bar opposite the promenade, not a cloud in the sky. You are smoking; not like you. Not like me either, but I'll have one.

Did I ever tell you about the monkey-garden? No? My name for it. Could have sworn I did. In any case, it was one of the few times in my life with Antiope that I was happy. You will recall that we were never in love as such, more in need, and we strove to satisfy that need for about five years, before falling apart in a scuffle of unfortunate recriminations. The monkey-garden was adjacent to a café not far outside Algiers, can't quite recall the name of the place, but it had a railway station and a hill with fir trees climbing upwards. The café specialised in fish. Very good, too. White local wine that burned the tongue and the cracking feeling in your fingers of shrimp being un-armoured, if there is such a word. Awkward. Never mind. The place was blown up when everything went mad.

The monkeys played about outside the café and jumped up on the wire fencing and had faces, I swear to you, as human as you can imagine. The resemblances to people we've both known were remarkable. Downright frightening. That raucous *raffage*. Antiope thought enough of the monkeys to throw them, uselessly, the cracked pink armour of the pathetic shrimp. But when I see monkeys, and I don't often nowadays as you might understand, this town not possessing a zoo, I am reminded of that sun-dusted African monkey-afternoon-with-shrimp, and even the harsher memory of what

Antiope and I ended up doing to each other doesn't peek through.

'Funny thing, Lycus, the damned ring Daphnis gave me for our wedding won't come off. I've tried everything. Even resorted to prayer. Nothing works.'

I've heard this plaint before, too. Now you twist at the ring and screw up your face and look appealingly to me out of eyes far too tired with the world, far too tired. You resume your beer-sipping and the world of which you have long ago become jaded, just, I think, at the point when the first shovelfuls of earth bounced and scattered along the wooden lid of her coffin, barks on past both of us in the form, this time, of another motorcycle with the baffles removed from the exhausts.

Do you secretly fear, old hypochondriacal blood-mate, that your finger will turn blue and you will die of some odd clotting procedure? That poor prophetic Daphnis will bring you into darkness with her gift of love?

'One size too bloody small to begin with, Lycus. I always said that. She knew best, of course. Said it was better than having the damned thing slip off.'

And at this point the salted wind brings tiny tears to the corners of your old eyes. It is always the wind, of course. For we have grown too hardy, too rugged with age, to allow nostalgia to aggravate us like grit in the eye. We have lived successful lives, what with one thing and another, and we can't complain. If I had had a son I would have called him Sisyphus.

'What?'

So I try to remember why I said that, about having a son, and realise that I have said it before, and have been almost drowsing in the unseasonal heat, and with the beer. Diodorus watches me, waiting for an answer. He tells me, before any answer is forthcoming, that Sisyphus was not a very nice person and the gods punished him. He rolled a stone up a hill and it rolled back on him and he had to roll it up again forever. I say, as I've said a hundred times before, that Sisyphus is actually rolling the sun back and forth across the Heavens and Diodorus clears his throat, tosses the butt of his cigarette into the air where it forms an arc not dissimilar to that described by the sun as it traverses the globe of the sky. He doesn't want to explore my theories about Sisyphus or anyone else.

'Sisyphus is a decidedly unreliable name, Lycus.'

He would seem to think that rolling the sun across the sky is not a manly thing to do. So our conversation on the subject of what I would have named a son had I ever married and had one, dies. Not a grubby syllable remains.

Then I start remembering the one thing I need to remember and which hurts me most to remember. Diodorus always notices the cloud passing over my face. He says my face is a mirror, and it was as if someone had blown the breath of memory across it, and clouded it. It was not a dark clouding, but misty. I finish my cigarette and stare out into the glaring cracked concrete of the promenade. Young parents with their excited children; ice-cream vendors; girls coquetting idly; old men like ourselves with scampering noisy dogs; young men with trousers rolled up to the knees and shirts opened to the waist. Newspapers folding in angry hands against the playfulness of the breeze. Sisyphus pushing the sun another millimetre across the sky.

Diodorus once showed me a ticket stub from a Greek theatre. He told me he had come across it lying in the pages of a book he'd bought in a second-hand bookshop. 'Now,' he'd said, making me inspect the Greek lettering carefully as if in the hope of deciphering some clue to its past life, 'Can you imagine, we know nothing of the people who bought this, who watched the performance in that theatre; maybe they're dead, maybe they are murderers. Can you imagine, Lycus? Perhaps the ticket gives off emanations, and if we close our eyes and concentrate we can see into the past of the ticket and learn something about the owner.' The ticket stub was, to him, imaginable as being endowed with properties of Delphic mystery or divination of some amateur sort. He was capable of elevating the most commonplace objects to realms of the arcane or imagined possibility. It was easy to chide him. He invited scepticism. It made him appear charming or, perhaps more deviously, open and quaintly liberal of spirit. An advantage for a man of law.

I must tell you that Diodorus is my brother and my friend. The elder by two and a half years. Above, or perhaps under, the bells, the voice of my brother remade possibilities for the stub of the ticket. He concluded that we knew nothing, either of us, of the world, or of God, or of Fate, that we were leaves tossed about by the winds of Chance; years later I grew to understand that these words did not, perhaps, deserve the capital letters accorded them so readily. Diodorus was happily married to Daphnis at the time and everything seemed possible.

So you will know that this man became a man of law, charged with defending people most of his life in the narcoleptic halls of justice; and he believed that everything was a clue to something else. Similarly, he used to describe to me his mortal terror, on bad days, of posting a letter into the unrelenting mouth of a postbox. He would feel certain that the irretrievability of the letter was somehow an indication that the posting of the thing was the first act in a great and unspeakable disaster. Edging away from the postbox—and I have witnessed this—he would be wide-eyed with momentary terror. When it passed, of course, he would think no more about it. For Diodorus the Lawgiver—I know that's not quite correct, a misnomer—terror might be inspired by a quite trivial thing. I found my terror in words. I unearthed the possibilities of words, their rhymes and rhythms, their thunder and snigger and scream, and I spent many sleepless nights trying to soothe their musical clamour. But in vain. I became well-known, then quite famous. Diodorus and I met rarely in those growing days. Which was a pity, looking back. People appealed to him to save them from the wrath of the State; they—though not necessarily the same people—appealed to me to save them from the indifferent spitefulness of tedium and spiritlessness.

We made money and we earned the thanks of many. Diodorus telephoned me late one night. I had not heard from him in almost a year.

'She's prophesying her own death,' he said, and hung up.

Twelve months later, almost to the day, Daphnis was dead. It rained the day of the funeral. He had wanted her cremated. Her family objected. He complied. The next time he rang me in the middle of the night was when Castor, a local lad and a twin, filled his pockets with rocks and walked calmly into the river, and stayed there. He had not been in the best of mental health for years. The newspapers were polite and obedient; the body was dragged out of the water and the word 'accident' gratefully surfaced along with it. The autopsy suggested that the pocketsful of stones were the result of the body having dragged for a time along the gravelly bottom of the river, gathering the stones into the yawning pockets. Diodorus was almost weeping now over the phone as he outlined the nightmarish daftness of the proposition.

Castor was buried without further ado. At night it was said that a shout echoed over the river at the place where he had disappeared for good from the sight of living man; the shout contained an obscene word and a hearty guttural laugh, some said. That's the sort of yarn you can believe if you want to; but my brother was dreadfully upset by the ludicrousness of the proposition that the poor boy had drowned by accident. And it would be understandable if the Shade of the boy had decided to guffaw nightly at the joke. It was a long time before my brother allowed life to distress him to the point where he felt it necessary that he should call me in the middle of the night.

'Look at that!'

I look over the road, and Diodorus, ever watchful, has spied two lovers embracing on a grassy space. The girl, turning over in her lover's arms, displays her underwear.

'That's not on,' Diodorus says. 'If I had any say in it, I'd pass a law! What do you think? Tell me honestly. Obscene behaviour, is it not?'

Now you will understand that my brother has acquired the stiff language and mode of speech of most lawyers, and furthermore, like most lawyers, he has come to see life as an illegal act or a legal one. It is a series of things actionable or things innocent. He knows quite well that I, a poet, argue that I know love for what it is, and now, at this fragile stage of life, know only too well that it is more dangerous than an open blade and more inviting than a brothel; if you'll excuse the awkward pun, but you no doubt can see what I'm driving at. I don't see anything actionable in love or love's sillinesses, but I believe all lovers are condemned from the off, as it were. From the outset, by virtue of the excruciating weight of their love. I have written of this. And I have experienced it. Once. With that girl who enabled me to see a unicorn. Did I say unicorns? Well, it was only one.

I reassure Diodorus that love is not a criminal offence and he accuses me of being a poet. Above us, clouds gather in from the sea and an evening bell clangs monotonously over the main gate of the town. Swans will start to rise now over the mediæval garden. Beyond the garden, a high wall and a crumbling squat tower. The last place we walked. Where she showed me a unicorn. It had started out a very ordinary day.

There will be no more beer-drinking. Diodorus, wisely, fears the evening dampness, and I'm not too sure of it myself. I watch him falter to his feet and realise that I probably falter to mine; standing up, I take his thin arm and we walk off slowly. Behind us the promenade begins to empty. Radios blare, somewhere behind the gates of the town an ambulance whines and squeals. We are too old, Diodorus and I. We could sit all day reminiscing and still not have touched one hundredth of our lives. But no one would want to listen; to the young, old people are notorious bores.

'Lycus,' he says, as he always says about now; 'You don't have to see me home, you know. It's quite unnecessary and puts twice the journey on you.'

I love this man Diodorus, my brother. We love each other as they love who know the approaching intimacy of the grave and have lost fear in the dark tunnel of life. If we are blessed we will see many more afternoons sipping beer on the promenade. But one does not wish for this with anguish and fear.

If it comes it comes. Look what happened with Daphnis. And she was young then. And so was I. She had prophesied her own death; probably seated on a cushion in that overly decorated front room. In the mediæval garden she had planted an odd and startling variety of flowers. Her favourite was the wild rose. There was a wild pear tree by the cracking stony gate. I remember that. She pruned it carefully, that wild tree. As if it were special to her.

Diodorus goes to visit her grave quite regularly. I never do. He brings flowers and sits for a while looking at the headstone and thinking, no doubt, that he did not love her enough. That's the usual thought, I believe. He becomes obsessed, now and then, by the belief that she has not really died; more correctly, that the best part of her—the spirit—lives on, and hovers around him. This belief has become more virulent with increasing age, and it worries me. What bothers me most is the new idea of his that he can hear her speaking to him. Vaguely; but a voice of sorts seems to break the silence of his sleepless nights: and what terrifies me is what that voice might tell him. Old age is resurrecting our childhood fears of spooks and ghosts. Perhaps we never quite rid ourselves of a conditional belief that such things exist. A jealous ghost would no doubt be spiteful, just like a living being.

We go carefully, desperately, over the tarmac road and there in front of us is the bridge into the town and the bell sings on, enticingly. There are the swans, flying in triad, honking impatiently, living omens. Sacred birds, she said. But I knew that already from my poetical researches. Diodorus had no time for such things. He thought his wife timid and over-imaginative. He told her once that she ought to find herself a job. She tried her hand, to please him, at baking cakes for a little restaurant off the public square. But the work was seasonal, which the logical Diodorus didn't seem to understand; and when she told him she had no more work and the restaurant was closed for winter, he didn't believe her. My brother had a dark side; he believed only the truth, and the truth was a personal thing. It could not possibly be the property of anyone else. Not even Daphnis, his wife. That was his undoing. A man should believe his wife, if only occasionally. At the very least he should pretend to. But I, on the other hand, believed every word she uttered. Hopelessly.

Now, here is a funny thing; do you see that odd building over there, just partly obscured by a fish-and-chip van? That was once a dancehall, much more elaborately painted than the peeling paintwork would make you think. It was a palace when we were young. Daphnis and her sisters were forbidden the place. She would ignore it, consequently, with a distasteful grimace; typically the property of very religious or devout people for whom dancing is a sin. She was not religious in any sense ordinary people understand, but she was devout. She was devoted to the wishes of her parents. Diodorus enticed her, after they'd both had a little too much to drink—drinking didn't come under her parents' rigid prohibitions, oddly—to dance with him in that dance-palace one night and it was that same night that he proposed to her. So you might say that she married him out of gratitude for having broken a taboo for her—an act akin to taking her virginity—and he married her in return for her act of bravery in going there. In other words, motives completely misunderstood from the first, they married in anticipation of happiness. Such cheek!

Diodorus told me that she had forced him against a wall inside the dancehall and said, `Marry me now, or I'll tell my parents you got me drunk and seduced me in this filthy place and you know what they'll do.' He knew. They'd come round to our home and raise a great fuss, claiming all sorts of things. Daphnis was no fool. I am trying to say that their marriage was a damned one from the start because Daphnis wanted my brother for security and possibly prestige and made no bones about it; Diodorus wanted her body and her silence and compliance socially, and found out too late that he loved her, too. He hadn't foreseen that. I must explain; in our day—has it changed much?—one married for a variety of reasons, few of which had much to do with love. It was probably due to trepidation of some kind. That my brother and Daphnis should marry without love was quite acceptable. What happened next was rather unfortunate.

Daphnis did not want Diodorus to love her. She had other men. He never knew. He will, I trust, go to his grave not knowing. Daphnis cried on my shoulder the day Diodorus informed her of his love for her. We were sitting on a stone bench in the mediæval garden. She wished me to advise her— what was best? What did one do, what attitude of soul did one assume, when someone declared his love? She wanted to run away. And what will I do then, I wanted to know? You, Lycus? Don't bewilder me further.

Diodorus, I remember that conversation well. Soft rain began to fall. She dried her eyes, as if the sky might cry for her. Diodorus was entrapping her with his love. She did not love him. I begged her, traitor that I was, to tell him so. I wanted her to destroy him, my own brother. I was quite blind. She was silent for a long time. Idly, I noticed, her hand touched against her left breast. She looked up at me. It's raining, she said; let's go in.

Diodorus, my brother; you will never be told by mortal mouth what happened next. There is a word for it that has something to do with a cuckoo. But enough word play. Let's get you home. The breeze is coming up and if you catch cold—if either one of us catches cold—it's pneumonia and that's an end of it.

It rained passionately in the little garden, a steady drumming rhythmic rain, and we dressed and stared out into the darkening green sweeps of grass. Daphnis, your wife, Diodorus, had her long fingers on my shoulders, and she kissed my ears from behind me as I stood there, longing for death, longing for her embrace again, longing for her death, for yours. The odour of fresh wet grass came in through the open window. She grew excited, her hot breath against my ear.

'Look!' she said suddenly; 'Look there! Beside the wild pear tree! A unicorn!'

I looked, Diodorus, and sure enough, there he was, white as a sheet, one horn raised up towards the depressing grey vault of Heaven; about the size of a mule, one foreleg tilted. He seemed shy, his head down. I'd never seen one before. I suddenly felt very sad, as if I knew at that moment that Daphnis would die. She was, to me, full of miracles. But immortality was not one of them. The unicorn vanished and the rain stopped. Would you believe any of this if I told you?

She could make me see unicorns, Diodorus; and what did she make you see? Or was it that you were blind to each other, possessed of a deep attractive loneliness in one another's presence of which it was impossible to speak?

She climbed the stairs to adulterous liaisons, while you climbed the ladder of success. Damned rough clichés, Diodorus, but you get the idea. Loved her? I'm almost certain I did. It was a long time ago. Unicorns were possible in those days. Mind that step.

Nestling, green

And so, hardly noticing,
we've entered the lengthening
white nights of Connemara summer

and though it's late
we walk out through the long lingering
reflected in the bay.

Beyond Inishturk,
the slow sun seems
to take its time

as we follow the water's edge
to the sea wall and the field
where the smell of grass

cropped by two ponies and their foals
fills the air. We breathe it
all in. How to slow

life to a saunter,
so we can take in the changes
all around, the nestling green

on the reedy cliff,
the waving yellow flags of June.
Even the spiky plant

whose name
I can't recall has sent forth
its tall, speared furl.

More than once, love, you've said
this is paradise, and if paradise keeps
changing, you might be right.

A pair of oystercatchers
dib and whistle, then lift to circle
the low flat tides of light.

Each sharp note a fractal
of this shared life. Each green change
containing the whole.

Annie Deppe

Creativity, Community, Poetry: Women Writing In Late-Twentieth-Century Galway

Megan Buckley

In her 1995 memoir, *Object Lessons,* the poet Eavan Boland charts her efforts to integrate her poetic selfhood with that of her role as wife and mother in mid-to late-twentieth-century Dublin. 'A woman's life was not honoured,' she writes. 'At least no one I knew suggested that it was exemplary in the way a poet's was.' Boland succinctly illustrates two deeply ingrained notions about the production of poetry: first, that the life of a poet is, by its very nature, elevated or 'exemplary', or in some way exists in a place far removed from the ordinariness of daily life; and second, that this sanctified, transcendent life and 'normal' womanhood are ultimately incompatible and even mutually exclusive.

Other women recognised the disconnect Boland describes. A writing workshop Boland held in the early 1980s on the outskirts of Dublin attracted several women who were new to writing, and to writing workshops. One especially talented, articulate woman, who was married with children, came from a town in the west of Ireland, and Boland never forgot one wry comment this woman made: '"If I said I was a poet in that town," [she] said to me, "people would think I didn't wash my windows."' Boland calls this attitude towards the woman writer 'bleak, desperate and resonant of all the isolation women can suffer in a society where the words poet and woman were—until recently perhaps—almost magnetic opposites.'

But by the late 1970s and 1980s, writing workshops were taking place around Ireland with increasing frequency, and they presented a valuable way for emerging writers—particularly emerging women writers—to remedy isolation and discouragement. When the Galway Writers' Workshop held its first meeting in October 1981 in the Ladies' Club at University College Galway (now NUI Galway), its members quickly decided to produce a publication, or 'little magazine', showcasing their work. Named *poetry:galway*, the first four issues of the mimeographed magazine had simple stapled bindings and hand-designed covers. By the fifth issue, however, its name had undergone a significant change: now known as *The Salmon*, it would go on to have a lifespan of ten years, publishing the early work of dozens of Irish writers who would become well known. It would also become the progenitor of the poetry publisher Salmon, which continues to make vibrant contributions to the world of Irish poetry nearly forty years after the first issue of *poetry:galway* was published.

Although *The Salmon* and, in turn, Salmon Publishing, would become best known for the support they gave to emerging women writers, neither ever published women poets exclusively. Between 1985 and 2007, Salmon Publishing released 197 books by 122 authors: 56 per cent of these authors were male, while 44 per cent were female. But since the four main publishers of poetry in late-twentieth-century Ireland—Dolmen Press, New Writers' Press, Gallery Press, and Dedalus—published only a small number of collections by women writers, Salmon published a strikingly high number of titles by women writers. Despite this nearly fifty-fifty gender balance, the voices of the female poets who were (originally) published by Salmon have become, arguably, the most memorable.

Rita Ann Higgins was in her late twenties when she began to attend meetings of the Galway Writers' Workshop, and her first published poem, 'Dog is Dog is Dog', appeared in the fifth, transitional issue of *poetry:galway/The Salmon*. In it, her trademark sharp wit and black humour are already audible: the titular 'Dog', incongruously named 'Xadore' (possibly from the French for 'I love'?), is unashamed by the calls of nature, and has no patience with his owner, whom he has nicknamed 'Failure-face'. 'If that heap of failure/,' the dog snaps, 'with the varicose face thinks/ that us canines have/ the same urinary tract/ as those two leggers/ she's got another thing coming,/ on her ankle.' Varicose veins, other physical infirmities, and the messy demands of the body recur frequently in Higgins's work, as do her challenges to organs (pun intended!) of authority—typically, then, the poem ends with a reversal of the positions of authority of owner and pet. The mysteriously named Xadore simply abandons his owner, 'exit[ing] to greener lamp-poles.' *Goddess on the Mervue Bus*, Higgins's first book, was published in 1986 ('Dog is Dog is Dog' appeared in her second collection, *Witch in the Bushes*). Three more books—*Goddess and*

Witch (1990), *Philomena's Revenge* (1992), and *Higher Purchase* (1996)—followed from Salmon, and by the late 1990s and early 2000s, critical reception of her work was placing her firmly in the position of being a 'working-class' poet, praising her unsentimental 'social observation, humour, and controlled anger'. Altought this position is perfectly valid, for this reader one of the most interesting, and indeed subversive, elements of Higgins's work is the way in which it reckons with the idea of the suffering body, or the body in pain. Her wry, darkly funny poetic speakers rarely, if ever, speak about their own physical suffering (or incapacitation) directly: instead, it often creeps into poems right at the point at which the speaker's relationship to language is also undergoing a breakdown, offering readers an insight into the nature of the imaginative expression of pain, and of the complicated relationship of pain to speech and language. Take, for instance, the terrifying 'Secrets' (*Goddess on the Mervue Bus*), where the (female) speaker's advice is that secrets must be buried deep *within* the body, in its most tender, vulnerable areas: if secrets are to be safe, they must be pressed deep into the body itself, beyond speech, into the realm of physical anguish and the pre-verbal:

Secrets are for keeping,
not for hiding,
the spines of wardrobes
will talk, sooner or later.

Keep your secrets in your heart,
in hip joints,
between folds of flesh,
or under rotting ulcers.

Never tell best friends,
in time their minds will leak
from old age or too much whiskey.

          ...

As for keeping a diary,
when you're gone
for entertainment, on wet days,
and after funerals,
your nearest and dearest
will read it with relish.

Try blushing with clay between your teeth.

Other Galway-based women poets, too, were making their mark on the Irish poetry scene in the mid-1980s and early 1990s, including Salmon publishing director Jessie Lendennie (she is both a poet and a publisher), Eva Bourke, Moya Cannon and Mary O'Malley. Far from being a 'school' of poets, however, each writer engaged with different subjects, worked with different forms, and made distinctly individual contributions to twentieth-century Irish writing. For instance, much of the work of Eva Bourke—whose debut collection, *Gonella* (1985), was Salmon Publishing's first-ever title—draws inspiration from visual art. The act of responding verbally to a work of visual art is called 'ekphrasis', in which the (male) writer gazes at and 'envoices' a still, silent (female) work of art. But Bourke's work demonstrates that the act of ekphrasis looks very different (and, perhaps, is more complicated) when the writer is female: her ekphrastic poems embrace disorder and the disjointed; they challenge the idea of a single 'gaze' reaching from poet to art object, and suggest that poems about paintings must also take into account the poet's— and the artwork's—surroundings.

Moya Cannon, who was a regular contributor to *The Salmon* magazine during its lifetime, published her first collection, *Oar*, with Salmon in 1990. Cannon has been called an ecopoet, and her work is indeed finely attuned to the environment and the way in which humans interact with it and dwell within it. In her essay, 'The Poetry of What Happens' (2001), she writes, 'Almost from the start the metaphors available to me related to landscape, language, and place-names.' For Cannon, word and landscape, the human and non-human, are inseparable, and this is particularly visible in her poems which deal with the way in which houses and other human dwelling-spaces exist alongside, and are often broken down or deconstructed by, non-human nature, as in her poem 'Foundations' (*Oar*), in which builders discover a midden of clam shells as they dig the foundations for a new house's kitchen. But the clams are given voice to warn their evictors that human lives are no less precarious than theirs:

> Dig us out if you need to,
> position the steel,
> raise the concrete walls,
> but, when your shell is complete,
> remember that your life,
> no less than ours,
> is measured by the tides of the sea
> and is unspeakably fragile.

Cannon, Bourke, and Higgins are by no means the only writers whose voices contributed to the flourishing of creativity in Galway in the late-twentieth century (nourished, in no small part, by writing workshops, *The Salmon* magazine, and Salmon Publishing), but they are some of the best-known. Their careers, and the presence of Salmon, helped to pave the way for the valuable opportunities and cultural space for emerging writers that exist in twenty-first-century Galway: the Over the Edge poetry reading series; the Cúirt International Festival of Literature, with its Cúirt New Writing Prize and Over The Edge Showcase; the NUI Galway Writers' Group Soc; the Masters in Writing course at NUI Galway; and the range of writing courses available at the Galway Arts Centre, to name but a few. Happily, the direct result of the efflorescence of creativity in twentieth-century Galway, which produced original, diverse contributions to Irish literature, has been a continuous blossoming into the twenty-first.

Deadman's Beach

The ground is white where the sun has yet to reach it. The best-looking horse of the neighbourhood bunch pulls rain-slick ivy from a fallen tree with marble teeth. Passing through Renmore, I come across a dead blackbird, suspended upside down at eye level in a metal construction fence. Its orange beak is open. Its street-side wing is splayed outward; its tail points the direction I am going.

I always swim at Deadman's beach. It's empty, except for the two men who used to live there, *till they gave us a place to live*. Both still return. I spoke with one a couple of weeks ago. He asked me was the water cold. *You've bigger balls than me anyway*. As I left I turned to him. Our silhouettes saluted each other. Last week I graduated from the university. Late afternoon with the sun setting, the mounds of beached seaweed made gold, we meet the second man, a camera over his shoulder. He doesn't condemn those coming here to drink, just what they leave behind for him to clean up. The 'fire water' has given him nothing in twelve years. 'Now I just love *taking photos* and *meeting people*.' He waves. He found the body here last year, *awful good-lookin' fella*. We talk swimming, and running up and down the length of shore afterwards to get the heat back into your blood. He says he knew that we'd come here for a dip by the pace of us rounding the head of the docks. He reassures me that the seals would do me no harm.

Today my head feels like wood. Walking alongside Lough Atalia is like being under a blanket; the swan plumes above gunmetal grey. When I reach the beach I sit on a rock with my face in my knees and listen to the *sssshhh* of the water. It's crystal clear, the sky above high and white. I untie my shoelaces. I will not resist. Less cold than some days and seal-less as far as my eye can see. I crash through to warm myself. There's exertion in moving. I lie so the freezing holds the back of my neck like a hand and I watch a train pull across the bridge towards the station. I wave; stretch my feet out before me. I swim across, turn, sprint back. The world is mine.

I relish the rapid activity post-dunk of scratching my bare skin all over with the thin towel then pulling on layers. Boots cling to my feet. Once they are tightly re-laced I feel the cold for the first time in my toes. Thawing is a reminder of feelings.

I explore the men's former dwellings; sink through seaweed and climb stone steps of beach rocks to a sheltered vegetable garden. Massive healthy leaves, fishing cage of a makeshift grill. Behind me is a sculpture, bits drifted ashore; shoes, wood, sunglasses, colander, gloves, lobster cage, thin coloured rope stretched between the pieces, a man-made web. The sign highlighting the Wild Atlantic Way wears a little black rimmed cap, skinny scarecrow.

Coming through the docks, I pass a woman feeding a baby from a bottle in the driver seat of a car, an old man in the passenger seat, the car is at an odd angle on the bridge. A man is fishing from the pier. I stand and watch the enormous Corrib Fisher nose out of the harbour, scattering birds. Brave ones return on the swirls of air and settle in its wake. A smaller boat carves out to meet it. I imagine one of the fishermen leaving his jacket ashore, his mother hot-footing it in a speedboat after the vessel to bring it to him, saying, *it's awful nippy*, the other men laughing.

Ella Gaynor

Blowing In and Blowing Out
Nuala O'Connor

My fingers smell green. My husband has brought me flowers, the weedy, thistly kind I like best—leafy branches, splashes of pink, sprigs of yellow. I strip the end leaves and arrange them in the green glass jug—called the Portumna jug, because we bought it there—and, now, I'm enjoying green fingers, an old, elemental scent. I put the green jug on the table we bought together, in the warm, bright kitchen we built together, and let the bouquet flood me with the curbed giddiness that I recognise as joy, the happiness that only the cocoon of home brings. My day, up to now, has been hard: I'm weary from a medley of pain from chronic illness and a mild wine hangover. But the pleasure of leaves and flowers has raised me from the stuck feeling—the buzz in my brain for several years—whose clamour grows louder as time passes. For a few moments I'm free of the urgent need to move on—to crawl, trot or gallop out of this rut I've become mired in—that I know means leaving where I am to find the place where I really belong.

What does it mean to be of one place but to live in another? Like most people I know, I'm misplaced—in my case, by choice. I'm from the east but I live in the west; the spot I live in is not the one I was born into, or grew up in, so it's not my home and, yet, it most definitely is. Still, even after more than twenty years, my face, my body and my heart, are all turned eastwards. I've never settled in Galway, the county I chose as home—I've never let myself be truly rooted, despite marrying and having children here. I don't belong to Galway and it doesn't belong to me. Partially this is because, as a blow-in, Galway won't let me fully in but, also, I think, it's because I've never really wanted to be let in. Edward Hoagland says that 'to feel at home is the essence of adulthood' and maybe it's brattish to still feel like a blow-in after twenty-four years in one county, or maybe it's just the way I'm formed—I can't fit in because I refuse to.

My friend, the English writer Paul Kingsnorth who, like me, lives in East Galway, writes in his book *Savage Gods*: 'I thought I wanted to belong. I thought I needed to have a place, a people. But every time I find a place, I don't fit into it. . . Every time I could belong, I push it away.' And I wondered, when I read that, whether this is not just about home-seeking, but if it's tied up with being a person who creates, with being inward-looking and a natural loner. Maybe it's the artist's destiny to be constantly on a road, looking forward and pushing on, never quite arriving. Maybe we have to live like that because it's the only way that art can be produced. If you arrive, perhaps you're finished.

I grew up in a Dublin valley, a place of many trees and particular sounds—the rush of the River Liffey over Glorney's Weir, the comforting buzz of chainsaws, the rumbly clod of cattle through the fields. The sun shadowed our row of eight houses in Mill Lane early in the day, even in summer, and my mother and the other women would move their deck-chairs to follow the bright patch of sunlight and continue their cryptic conversations about who had the Big C and who paid what for a second-hand car. I was a sensitive child, a thinker and a watcher, and I liked the company of adults—the symbols and signs of their talk were a fascination to me, I was always trying to unpick their code. And I loved my homeplace fiercely. The fields, the quarry, the graveyard, the old linen mills, and the river were our playground, and I never thought I'd live anywhere else.

When I was four years old, we moved house. My ma, pregnant with her sixth baby, needed more than our rented two-bedroom cottage with no bathroom. So negotiations were negotiated and we moved a whole four doors down, to rent a larger house that dated to 1704, a place rather grandly called Iveagh Cottage. Our new house seemed vast to me and I loved its airy capaciousness when I went there with my da to watch him plaster walls and instal fire surrounds.

One December evening, before we moved, I took the key to the new house and a tiny chair I owned, trotted up the street, and let myself into Iveagh Cottage. I walked its pacific, unlit, high-ceilinged spaces—scullery, kitchen, dining room, creaky stairs, warren of bedrooms—and the house flowed amiably around me. It welcomed me. I trotted home again with my chair and the key, satisfied now to move the full fifty metres to our new house. I wasn't missed until I got back, and my father just gave a pragmatic 'OK' when I said where I'd been.

My feet have itched since my first trip to Europe as a sixteen-year-old Venturer Scout. I'd been to the UK, but visiting the Continent set the travel need ticking in me and over the next few years I lived and worked in Germany, Switzerland and Scotland—I liked the freshness, discomfort, and wonder of new places, but I also wanted to find a welcome in them, test their embrace. *Can I fit in here? Am I welcome here?* In 1996, I moved to Galway with my baby son, with all the energy and enthusiasm of a twenty-something, ready for life to *really* begin. I had a job in a theatre company in the artiest city in Ireland, I was writing a little, and on the hunt for like-minded people, and I was happy. Maybe this is the way the young always enter somewhere new—buffed with hope and enthusiasm, feeling a bit invincible. I was serious about making a good life for my son, yes, but I had yet to fully recognise my innate restlessness, the searcher in me that would always be seeking a true home—a destination that seems to elude me. (We would move house seven times in Galway until my children finally said, 'Enough!')

In my mid-twenties I was a little frantic for a future that would be productive and proper, the life I could settle into for good. I foolishly thought that people became adults around the age of twenty-five and it was my time to do just that. But, despite a wish to settle, I know that I moved west to Galway in a romantic haze. I had been living in a fishing village in the Scottish Highlands and was a couple of years returned to a Dublin that seemed dark and oppressive; I wanted a greener, brighter life for my young son. I'd loved Galway since childhood holidays to Spiddal and Carraroe and student summers spent in the city. I knew well I was moving to a city but, really, I was entertaining notions of an Ireland of Aran jumpers and thatched cottages, of long-haired, wildish men called Oisín and Fiach, of crashing Atlantic waves; of poets and thinkers—people, like me, who liked to travel through words.

Disappointing then to end up, finally, in that most practical and grey of places, a suburban housing estate that abutted more estates of its kind and yet more. As the years passed, I felt myself withering under the leaden uniformity of everything in my immediate radius. I didn't like when I was bitten by a neighbour's Rottweiler and the owner laughed. I didn't like, either, when one neighbour murdered another at a party in his house. These kinds of things can happen everywhere and do, but they unsettled me and made me determined to move on. Untoward events aside, I missed being surrounded by nature; I craved the homely swish-swash of big trees in leaf, the lullaby of water, the echoes of a valley. Constant traffic noise, the lack of green space, and curtain-invading sodium lights agitated me and I longed, suddenly, to go home.

When my sister Nessa got cancer, I was pregnant and working in a Galway library. I felt useless living two hundred kilometres away from her—I couldn't be with her enough, to sit with her when she was immobile, to talk and laugh, to listen and offer comfort. My longing for home was amplified by Nessa's illness and I asked my then husband if we could move to Dublin, so I could be near my sister. But my Clare-born husband—rather reasonably, I think now—didn't want to live surrounded by my people, he worried about being isolated among us. I was devastated and disappointed by this at the time— the pull east was enormous—but I felt my loyalties to my western family too. We stayed in Galway but, by the time Nessa died seven months later, *all* I wanted to do was move home; I craved the familiarities it offered.

Colm Keegan, in his powerful essay-poem on the housing crisis in Ireland, writes '. . . home is more than just a word. It's a feeling. And feelings live in us. In the heart, the great furnace of change.' This is what home, and thoughts of it, does—it provokes longing for belonging. Even homes, perhaps, that we haven't occupied yet. And, when my sister died, I yearned to be back in the only place I'd ever felt rooted, though I knew it was impossible to go there.

When people view potential new properties, they talk about the feeling they give and they mean, I suppose, something like the encompassing warmth that flowed around the four-year-old me on my clandestine visit to Iveagh Cottage. I went there to ask a question of that house, I wanted to know if it was a trustworthy place and, because the house welcomed me, I had faith in it to carry me through my childhood. I felt that too in rural Loughrea when my first husband and I moved there, keen to get out of the city where I'd had a troubling time in a new arts job and was still actively grieving my sister. If I couldn't go home to the Liffey Valley, I wanted some sort of tree-filled oasis for my two young sons as much as for myself and, if it had to be in Galway, well that would do.

I got the feeling—the furnace in the heart—from the field opposite our new house in Loughrea. I called it The Perfect Field and imagined it would help me through the grief of Nessa's death and the emotional fall-out from the bullying endured in the arts job I'd left. But I hadn't reckoned on the vast loneliness of living in a place where I was the solo boreen walker, a blow-in, unneeded as a friend by the other young mothers in the area, who had the ready company of their own sisters and mothers. My husband worked nights and I was often alone with my young sons, and no amount of perfect fields or shushing trees could quell my heartache. I had a nice house in a nice place, but I was catastrophically lonely there, forlorn to my core, and I didn't—or couldn't—ask for outside help.

And so, by and by, I behaved very badly. I began an affair with a childhood friend, a man of ease I'd always liked. Can it be accidental that, while feeling misplaced and isolated, I ended up in the arms of a man from my hometown, someone who shared a history with me, a certain land- and people-knowledge? There was an undoubtable comfort in being with him and though I certainly agonised over my betrayal, I may not have thought enough about consequences or the future. I got caught up in the heady madness of new love.

It's not easy to yank yourself back into an overwhelming past, as Mary Karr would have it, and to examine what went on at that time. I admit my actions back then were lousy, I was selfish and callous, towards my then-husband, towards my children. But those self-serving actions did propel me—as the sad/bad times often do—into a happier part of my adulthood. And, inevitably, onward to yet another homeplace to blow into.

I left my first husband. My partner—now husband—and I chose Ballinasloe in East Galway as our new home. We wanted to be near my ex-, for the sake of the boys, of family life. The 1930s house that we found, backed by woodland, flowed around me the second I stepped onto its honeyed floorboards. I felt instantly welcome; I got and gave trust.

Originally part of the maternity wing of Portiuncula Hospital, our house had been rented by a friend before we bought it. She was haunted in our house by a small, sobbing child. I never encountered that little one, but I found a ghost when we first moved in too, a benign old man whose fag smoke lingered upstairs and who liked to hover by our bed at night. I often wonder what had disordered this man, caused him to be in our house. He was most likely a former resident but maybe he just wandered into our home, a traveller looking for repose. Eventually, I asked him in a polite, firm way to stop his antics and he went quietly away.

Like everywhere I've lived in Galway, I found it easy to write in Ballinasloe. I didn't know many people and, being shy, it was hard to burrow in, so I had—and still have—plenty of time to devote to writing. When I write, I often explore the experiences of strangers in strange places. I've written a novel based on my time in Scotland; another novel about a young Irish immigrant who lives and works in the Massachusetts home of Emily Dickinson; also a bio-fictional novel about Belle Bilton, a music-hall performer from London who blew into the life of a nineteenth-century aristocrat from Ballinasloe and, eventually, moved here to live and die. My next novel is about another Galway girl, the wondrous Nora Barnacle who lived a peripatetic life, all over Europe, with James Joyce. When I examine these novels as a piece, I see a common thread: all of these women are in search of one thing—home. All of them need to break out of one life to find the life that they feel they should be living. Maybe these are the stories that occupy me because, as a writer, I'm always on a treadmill, taking step after step, never quite arriving.

In her poem 'Indian Boarding School: The Runaways', Louis Erdrich writes that 'home's the place we head for in our sleep' and this is certainly true for me in the sense that I often end up in my childhood home in my dreams. Edna O'Brien says she dreams of her beloved childhood home, Drewsboro in County Clare, every night. Not owning it, as she once might have hoped to, is actually the better deal: '. . . being banished from it I can go on filling it with stories for as long as I like,' she says.

For a long time, I held on to a sentimentally serious version of Iveagh Cottage in Mill Lane and its valley setting: I believed it was a place I could return to and occupy. In her memoir, Lorna Sage writes about the pleasure of returning to her grandmother's girlhood home in Wales, the 'smothering, spongy womb' of it. She had reasons for describing it like that—the heat of the place, the sweet foods eaten there, the emphasis on leisure—but for years my thoughts of my childhood home had that cushiony, uterine-like feel. Mill Lane was a place of safety and freedom, a place with its own eccentricities, but eccentricities I understood: the differing whistle-blasts my mother and our friends' mother gave to call us home at twilight from our river-and-field playground; the lack of plumbing in most houses and the resistance by many residents to modernity, such as the neighbours who hadn't been into Dublin city for fifty years or more and saw no reason to go; the rivalries and shifting loyalties between neighbours. But Mill Lane no longer has that halo around it; years and maturity, I suppose, have quashed nostalgia and I see my birthplace more as a house in a nice valley, rather than as a place that insistently calls me back.

Is there a reason why people with static, safe childhoods like mine often become nomads in later life and vice versa? Is the very settled-ness of growing up in one place, as I did, a spur to trying on new places? I have friends who were the children of bankers and gardaí, who moved house constantly as kids and want only fixed, deep roots for their own children. James Joyce, in opposition to that tendency, followed the pattern of his night-flit childhood and couldn't seem to settle in any one place for long—he and Nora lived at nineteen different addresses in their twenty years in Paris alone. Nora, though, always longed for a home of her own, a place to settle in.

I also dream of a particular kind of house, one with enormous rooms and large, old windows: the one I eventually hope to live (and die) in. I dream obsessively, lucidly, and in Technicolor of that house and I'm always, always happy inside its walls. It's truly the stuff of dreams: a secret house with secret rooms on a secret road, that exists in some surreal space between one real street and another.

Maybe the search for what writer Lisa Knopp calls a 'belonging-place' is something that comes with the forties—I've spent most of mine on that mission, though I'm bound by the needs and wants of my children, and by financial necessity, to stay where I am for now. Knopp talks about entering a 'committed, faithful relationship' with the belonging-place she eventually found and I have yet to do that because I haven't found it. I sometimes fret that when the time comes to choose my own belonging-place, I'll foul it up. I know that this thinking goes against Eckhart Tolle's teachings about the now, that I study and try to implement. I'm aware that squandering the now, while obsessively planning for future events, is a form of life-poverty but, still, I persist with my search for the right home, despite the fact that I haven't yet narrowed down where my 'belonging-place' actually is.

In an attempt to locate that place, I like to analyse when I'm happiest and where. I am happy in my Ballinasloe home, I love our road and our house, and I love when my husband and three children are all home too. But I am also happy on visits to Iveagh Cottage, surrounded by my parents and siblings. I am happy, too, with friends who live in a small, sweet house in wild Galway countryside and with other friends who live in a huge Georgian house in a nearby midlands town. I'm happy near water and surrounded by trees. So, happiness equals people and nature and certain kinds of houses. But I'm beginning to understand, as I age, that this belonging-place has to be hugely about people rather than places. It's about being surrounded by those who get you and are happy to co-opt you into their tribe and won't constantly remind you of your blow-in status. It is about being allowed to belong, by others and by myself.

In an essay about writing, Maggie Nelson talks about the fact that humans remain dependent on each other all their lives. She says attempts to will away our dependence on others 'in service of a fantasy of. . . independence' has an inevitable fallout. I feel this keenly each time I land in a new place. As an introvert and loner, I always prefer my own company above that of others. But every time I arrive somewhere new, I seek out like-minded people. Sometimes I find them and sometimes I don't, so I continue to dream of that settle-spot that holds not just the house I want, but the people I long to have around me too. Maybe each stage of life requires a set of four fresh walls that stand in a welcoming community and what I'm searching for now is that final place. I feel ready for the last stage, for the right band of people to populate my life as I move into the next part of it. I have some of them already—my kinfolk, my tribe—but always I wonder is there somewhere out there that's filled with them, some green oasis, a welcoming cocoon? And is there a house there too that will claim me, that will tell me I'm home?

The Next of the Last

Emer Rogers

There was nothing Tessa could do as she sat in the jeep except fantasise about driving off. Her father-in-law was dawdling inside the cottage. Everyone called him by their surname, Nash, which made it feel strange to her, like she was infringing on his trademark. She looked again at her phone in her lap, and then at the dashboard's clock. Still a minute out of sync; she'd given up trying to align them. Her foot tapped on and off the accelerator, revving it.

What was Nash doing? Like, he knew she'd hidden both the spare key to the jeep and his key to his work van a month ago, when she'd figured out that he wasn't ignoring her as she blew on her porridge at the kitchen table, but rather wasn't seeing her. To be sure, she had performed a test of his vision by sticking out her tongue at him.

The appointment with the ophthalmologist—a cancellation that she had managed to nab—was in Galway city, an hour and twenty minutes away if she flaked it and didn't brake on the bends. Aloy was supposed to take his father, but Aloy had other places to be and money to earn.

She put the handbrake down to do a lap of the two-bedroom cottage that she had moved into two years ago. Nash only had one stipulation: 'So long as ye are married.' Perpetually on every landlord's blacklist and as deeply in love as she was, moving in made truly wonderful sense, being after all only temporary.

The cottage was turf shaped, basically a sagging cuboid. It had all the widower accessories—coiled hose, blue rainwater barrel, half a bog, cut and stacked—but was otherwise too bare to be charming. No flowers or leisurely grass, aka lawns, not even a supermarket potted basil was allowed on the kitchen sill. That would be pure clutter. Nash would never say it, but he thought it. They were all thought and no fucking action, these never-say-a-bad-word-about-anything Nashes. Like father like son. They should have updated the side of their bloody van to:

John Nash & Son: Never Say a Bad Word.
(Need A Bad Word Said? Call Son's Wife.)

It was an admirable thing most of the time, that ability to refrain; a joy to behold and a reason to murder them.

She ended her little lap at the front door, braking hard so that the tyres skidded across the mix of gravel and shells. There was still no movement from within. With her wrists crossed on top of the steering wheel, she looked out the windscreen, down the driveway, across the grass-striped lane, all the way out to the tidal island. Bearing down on it, with imperceptible motion and inevitability all at once, was a congregation of black clouds. The sun had just been trapped. But soon, and yet endless frames later, the clouds morphed and stretched over the island and as they thinned, holes appeared through which golden shafts of light shone; it was a beginning and an end of all days in one view.

She sighed and opened the mindfulness app that she had seen on a poster a few hours ago—first thing—in the GP's office. The app's name appealed to her: Headspace. Head. Space. As did its logo. Although just an orange circle, it was smiling at her. She smiled back. It was in no rush. It took up whatever space it needed. Calmly. Even though Nash was going blind, Tessa and Aloy had no space; he listened to them when they were alone in their room.

She looked at her stomach fastened under the seatbelt. 'He heard us make you.'

The GP had confirmed it, Tessa was six weeks gone. She concentrated on the be-calmer app—she had to try, at least—and closed her eyes. A man's voice instructed her to 'Notice any thoughts without trying to alter them'.

She frowned, opened her eyes and saw Elliot on the lane. He was building the Grand Designs monstrosity further up with his wife Aifric, whom Tessa had only seen zooming around in her Audi, staring straight ahead, never a salute and always talking handsfree. Tessa followed her once, to see if she went left or right to Galway or Westport.

Elliot was picking the green nubby blackberries with their baby, Ezra, strapped to his chest. He was probably telling Ezra that he was dropping them on the road for the tweety birdies.

'No, for the rats, Elliot,' Tessa said.

As per usual he was looking proper pluckable himself. Tessa wouldn't mind throwing him on the ground. She'd then begin by examining those clean cuffs of his peeking out from under the Aran jumper, and that thick leather watchstrap, which he would confess was just his casual one, for rustic walks, for flings. He had the time for a fling now that he'd started working remotely. He was so in love with his new way of life. She'd whisper to him that they could do sex remotely too, if he wanted.

'Is it the same?' he'd say.

'Oh, just imagine the efficiency of it,' she'd say, and mean it too, for she'd only be doing it to negotiate a better contract for Aloy. He was working all hours with Nash decommissioned. Nash said nothing; he had his boy and his boy's wife where he wanted them, in his debt, which was amassing second by second like the rain pinging the bucket in their bedroom. Nash paid Aloy minimum wage and then *helped them* out with the big grocery shops, their cut of the ESB, tanks and tanks of petrol, even her bloody haircuts.

'It's okay, Aifric is exposing me on social media and waiving her fee,' was what Aloy had said when Tessa emptied her shoebox of Nash IOUs onto their bed.

'Waving her little finger more like,' she said, holding up her own.

'What?' Aloy said.

'Waving it and watching you wrapped around it.'

Tessa had first met Aloy in Horan's pub on the pier, and within five minutes he was quoting his dead mam; on and on he went about how you should only say nice things. Tessa should have known then, but instead she had just asked him, 'How is what I just said not nice?'

'Look-it, talk like that gets people in trouble sooner or later, right?' Aloy said, nodding at the barman who shrugged while shining a glass. Tessa liked the look of Aloy, long limbed, but with density, a mass of a man with eyes that simply wanted to do right by you.

'So you don't think it's nice to talk about sex?' she said.

'Is that what you heard? That's not what I said.'

'So can I undo this trouble that's coming my way?' she said, munching a chip.

'You can't.'

'Oh great then, so you wanna go fuck?'

Aloy winced.

'Did you ever hear about the priest and the feathers?' he said.

'A joke?'

He shook his head as he took a sup of his creamy pint, and when he was finished sucking the last of it off his top lip he said, 'There is a girl who goes to confession.'

She rolled her eyes and licked ketchup off her finger. He did not continue. 'What?' she said. 'Okay, Jesus, sorry—G'on then.'

'The priest tells the girl—who is very pretty by the way—that once you say something, it's out there and you can't undo that, in the same way you can't empty a bag of feathers out on the pier there and then expect to just collect them all again.'

'I didn't think people our age were still religious,' she said.

'I'm not,' he said. 'I just think that words mean things.'

Elliot and Ezra had reached the cottage's gate. Elliot waved first and then waved Ezra's mini Michelin-man arm over and back. Tessa only gave a cursory nod, but Ezra, an itsy-bitsy ruler transported by his servant Elliot, had already begun his parade down the driveway. Ezra was a wide-mouthed baby whose eyes were black like a fish's. His father operated at a fidgety pace, like he was sidestepping pedestrians that weren't there. She'd seen him a few times out the back of Horan's, like now with Ezra, chatting amongst the throng of tourists waiting to board the ferry, but when it departed he was still on dry land.

'Jesus Nash, c'mon,' Tessa said, before buzzing down the window.

'Not working today, Tess?' Elliot said. 'Tess' sounded too clean out of his mouth, unearned, like his baseball cap. And Aloy had well told him that she had no work—she knew this because she was well pissed off when Aloy let it slip. She did get an offer of a few Junior Cert maths and science classes yesterday—wasn't it funny how things fell together? It was in the Midlands, 200 kilometres away. She immediately googled places she could stay for the two nights, telling Aloy the rates after his dinner, but he wouldn't say much about it. He squinted at her.

'Sorry,' he said.

'Aw Aloy, for Christ's sake,' she said.

She knew that he couldn't help himself, it happened whenever he held in a thought—he farted. She banged the front door; off to do another bar shift that she'd had to blag, all because Aloy wouldn't leave Nash, and Nash wouldn't leave the cottage with its bloody view of his late Annie's island. It was the impossible equation on a blackboard. No logic would solve it.

She answered Elliot's enquiry by picking moss from the window's cracked seal.

'Aloy is working hard,' he said, nodding west towards his house, hands perched on his hips.

The jeep's engine roared as the rev counter soared. 'He is,' she said.

'Surprised he was working today, to be honest.'

'Why's that?'

'Oh, the day that's in it.'

'What day is that?'

'Annie's anniversary.'

'Is it?'

She said it before she could stop herself. Aloy had never told her the date of his mother's death and now she'd have to listen to Elliot enjoying his upper hand.

'Twenty-five years today,' he said. 'Tragedy.'

'Yes.'

'Mother and son paddling together one minute and then…' He kissed the top of Ezra's head. 'And of course, Aloy shouldn't blame himself.'

'What do you mean?' she said.

'Oh, just that no one thinks it was his fault she drowned. He was just a boy.'

Tessa turned off the engine—she didn't want the exhaust fumes to disturb the baby from its gurgling, in case the baby might disturb Elliot from the rest of his story.

Aloy Nash got up to give his seat to an elderly woman in the ophthalmology clinic's small waiting room. He placed his shoulder and his weight apologetically against the scuffed wall, right between the frosted door to the hallway and the white one to Exam Room 2. There were five doors off the waiting room and three tiny box windows almost at ceiling height. They were wide open, but the air was far too thick to fit through. Aloy started to sweat; a drip ran down the length of his back. His T-shirt and work trousers held curls of sawdust from Aifric and Elliot's reclaimed herringbone floor. Aifric wanted it done by the weekend—tomorrow. She didn't care that there was no one to help him. Nor did Tessa. When they booked the job, she hadn't noticed his father's eyes yet and she just refused to understand that Nash could tell everything about a piece of wood from its weight in his hand and its grain against his thumb.

'And what about the saw? If he feels that up, he's dead,' Tessa replied to them both, every time. Aloy, in turn, had nothing to say to that, which was not unusual. What had started as a habit of murmuring as a child had been nurtured into silence.

The door to the hallway opened and Aloy stood out of its way into the middle of the room and knocked his ankle against the low coffee table.

'I'm not totally blind,' a man said—it was Nash.

'I was getting worried,' Aloy said to Tessa.

She had the look of a woman who, disturbed in the midst of murdering you, was trying to remember why she even started. Being around Nash did that to people.

She took a deep breath; she had to swallow it down. 'We're here now.'

Aloy raised his eyebrows, but she just rubbed his elbow, a movement she had never done before. The nurse who told everyone when they arrived that she was called Dervla disappeared from behind a sliding glass window and reappeared in an open doorway. Moving out of her way, Aloy banged his ankle again. Christ. He had twenty-twenty vision and yet he couldn't see this bloody table. He smiled at Dervla. She was about Tessa's age but nowhere near as pretty. He knew that those in the seats would be looking at Tessa and thinking did he not smother her in bed? He remembered that most of them were nearly blind with cataracts and reached out for Tessa's hand. She could only wrap it around two of his big fingers.

'Are you alright to fill it in?' the nurse said to Nash.

'Sure,' Nash said, handing the clipboard with its swinging pen to Tessa.

Nash had three inches on Aloy but was comfortable enough with his size to stand tall in the centre of the room. He was indifferent to time in his short-sleeved checkered shirt and 90s pleated slacks. That was his peak, and he was not stepping down. It was how he'd looked when his Annie was alive—she was the one who'd gotten him into those heel taps on his boots. Nash followed Dervla into Exam Room 3, click-clack click-clack, a cowboy in a flat cap. Tessa and Aloy said nothing until the soft-close door to Exam Room 3 pushed shut. *Clunk.*

'Are you not too busy to be here?' Tessa said, in an unnaturally calm tone that forced her up high on her tippy toes.

'Was in town anyway, I ran out of the oak that Aifric wants.'

'That Aifric wants.' Her feet were back flat on the floor.

Aloy looked away, taking in the horse-chestnut leaves swaying outside one of the high windows. 'It'd be good if Nash could get back working.'

'Oh yeah, good for *him* to have a job to do,' she said.

He nodded. 'It'd be great.'

'Maybe I'll start keeping her husband busy,' she said.

'Who?'

'Elliot.'

'Oh yeah? And how would you be doing that?' The sweat was now snowballing down his back, arriving as a melted avalanche at his arse.

She smiled. 'I get lonely; the nights are only getting longer.'

'It's great, Tess, how you find work for everyone.'

She shrugged at his smirk. 'Doing me is hardly work, is it?'

He noticed that due to the lack of a television himself and Tessa had become the entertainment for the row of eavesdropping outpatients. Could they see him blush as Tessa, still laughing, kissed his cheek?

'Doing Elliot would hardly solve your problems,' he whispered.

'*My* problems?' she said.

'Yeah, you'd still be stuck in the middle of nowhere, just in a nicer house.'

'Would Nash be there?'

'No.'

'Then it'd be a good start.'

'And then what?'

'I'd leave and Elliot would come with me.'

The waiting room was quiet. Outside a lorry was reversing. Beep. Beep. Beep. Aloy saw the elderly woman in the corner bless herself. Leaning down, with his lips by Tessa's ear, Aloy asked, 'How much do you think they heard?'

'Enough,' she said. 'I need some air and a sit down.'

As he moved out of the door's way again, he thought about it and yes, he was fairly sure that she did just tut at all those blind people in seats.

As soon as Nash and Tessa landed back at the cottage, Nash resumed his search, not for a spare key to any vehicle—although he habitually looked for those—but for that photograph of Annie. Nash swayed on his feet in the kitchen, which was wood-clad and narrow, like they lived on a sailboat. The table was pushed flush against the wall. It was too tight to sit all three of them at once; the boy stood, while the wife sat.

Nash remembered Annie in that red swimsuit, the one with the halter neck, her long legs all sandy. A pure natural, she walked a naked baby Aloy towards the waves. But she was fading and he needed to see her again, before the inevitable, before this irreversible fucking thing, retineyetis pig-something, cut him off from everything.

'Best to test your son,' the doctor had said.

'Is there a cure?' Nash asked.

'No.'

'Then best not to bother him.'

Nash thought he knew where the photograph was—in an old diary, yes, the 1998 green pocket one, which he found under the landline. But Annie was not tucked into the first week of August or anywhere else. Tessa and her tidying to be sure. Leaning on the table, he remembered a drawer in its side. He lifted up the oil cloth so as to root around and came away with a tin of cracked shoe polish—brown, he reckoned. Next, he found a thistle-bristle brush, sheathed in a cloth crisp from dried polish. It fit well in his hand.

The night was emerging as he felt around the cottage for shoes to shine. He caught glimpses of Tessa leaving whatever room he entered, and eventually he heard the bathroom door's latch and the splutter of the shower. He settled on Tessa's walking boots that he tripped on by the back door, and Aloy's brown brogues that he wore to his wedding. Black shoes boyo for a navy suit, he had told Aloy, but he hadn't listened. Nash was not sure if he would get to his own black work boots tonight, but if he did, he was prepared to risk the brown polish. What harm was there now?

He put the boots and shoes on the wooden bench outside the front door, which opened out directly from the kitchen. He sat down. He could smell the rain in the air and it had nothing to do with going blind, he could always smell it, he knew he had about half an hour. The moon he still recognised; it was full, even with the clouds. He picked up one of Tessa's boots, pulled the laces patiently out of their holes and applied the dried-out polish onto the boot's tongue, deep into the grain of the leather. The kitchen light switch was flicked—she was out of the shower—and anything that could flither was now flithering inside. He heard them go by his ear.

With his hand in her boot, he could feel the shape of her foot. He liked Tessa. She was the type to save the first fly that flew into a room, devote herself to it, as long as it took to coax it free, uninjured out the window, but she was also the type that when the second fly crossed her path, she'd just wallop it dead. No time for it. She was loved equally for rescuing the fly and killing the fly, because for the boy it was unconditional. Aloy was even tempted to leave for the *city* with her; the girl saw that too. But it was all moot, it wouldn't last; they moved at different speeds those two. She'd be long gone, halfway to that bloody moon before that fella could even bring himself to shout out her name to stop her. For now, the place needed minding and that kept her idle highness busy.

'Did he tell you when he'd be home?' Tessa shouted out to him.

She was cooking one of her smelly spicy yokes and it nearly ten o'clock. They ate so late at night.

'No. . . that floor, it's a two-man job,' he said.

He had stopped with the brush in mid-air to remember his thoughts: Flies! The fly was a gift, a tiny, living, breathing thing that could be murdered with no consequence, so as to provide a release that saved ordinary people from murdering each other. Especially out here in the bogs. He hoped that Tessa would learn the usefulness of flies.

'Nash, is it Annie's anniversary today?'

She'd come out to stand in the doorway. A heavy breather, but nonetheless a beautiful girl—pity about the lack of a chest, but that would come too, with children. Aloy wouldn't have been the one to get her if it hadn't been for that hint of a tinker, especially in her mouth. And the constant borrowing for food and petrol was not his fault, or hers really; her people were shite with money.

'It is,' Nash said.

'Sorry.'

He worked on bringing out the shine on her boot with the brush.

'Is Aloy alright?' she said.

'The job is a two—'

'Okay, okay.'

Around them the night fliers danced through the air, queuing to get in the door. A lonely bit of wind—the herald—lifted the polish cloth, but Nash caught it. The rain was circling above them. He had overheard Elliot telling her about Annie that morning. Would that city prick ever stop rooting for gossip?

'It was Aloy,' Elliot had said, over that ugly baby's head.

'Aloy, what?' Tessa said.

'It was Aloy that Mrs Nash drowned saving.'

Inside in the kitchen, something was sticking to the bottom of the pot, there was smoke coming out the door to them, but Tessa didn't move. Nash unlaced the second boot.

'About Aloy. . . ' she said. His name caught in her throat. 'I didn't know.'

'You see now why he'd need to stay here?'

Her breathing got louder. Nash continued to buff and buff the leather as the raindrops thickened. He only stopped when Tessa took her boot off him. He handed her the other polished one, which she also took, but did not thank him for.

Aloy had finally finished the floor, and he'd even managed to get Elliot to agree to some steep extras after the idiot brought up his mother's anniversary. It was clear that Aifric asked too much of Elliot, staying at home alone all day with that queer-looking babby.

Instead of going home, Aloy drove on down the lane, turning right at its end and then straight on until he got to Mac's petrol station. It was eleven minutes before eleven but the ENTRANCE door was already locked. He could see wee Mac and his big fists inside by the till. There was little point in trying to convince him to sell Aloy a carton of low-fat milk for Tessa's morning tea. But Aloy stayed by the door; what else could he do other than wave in? Mac smiled back and shuffled out from behind the counter before veering abruptly towards the back room. The shop and forecourt lights went out all at once. Aloy inhaled a blend of petrol fumes and evaporating rainwater.

From the far side of the road the sound of the sea reached him. He walked to the edge of the canopy. There was no distinguishing the sea's blackness from the sky's. The moon, exposed now and then by the whirling clouds, was waning, while the tide, he could tell by the slurp and burp, was high. There was no traffic, and this somehow was enough of an excuse for a man who long ago stopped crossing country roads to see the sea to do just that. In need of a torch, he dug his phone out of his coat pocket. The photograph of himself as a baby with his mother was still tucked away in there; he hadn't wanted Nash to stumble across it. He'd only found it that morning in the kitchen, when he had tripped on the landline's cord and sent it and all the shite under it flying. He must remember to put it in the van's glove compartment. It seemed as good a place as any now that John Nash wouldn't be coming back to work.

After Annie died, with Aloy just gone eight, Nash went back to running marathons. He ran backwards into the decade of his youth while Aloy floated forwards through his, each night worrying that he would wake up and walk into the kitchen the same age as Nash. Every day began with, 'Good lad, I'm off for a run.' Nash became thinner and hairier, all banter and no back-up as a parent, as a person. Aloy had found him when he ran too far into the bog, screaming at the Milky Way as the peat ate him up to his waist. Aloy pulled him free and led him home via the sea below the cottage. The waves rinsed the black soil from Nash's clothes and when he began to shiver, he beckoned to Aloy to come nearer, to hug him. Now Aloy, once again standing in the dark by the sea and all grown up, lit a smoke. As sure as he felt the crisp air hit his tight throat, he could still feel the shuddering of his father's flesh and bones against his own.

Aloy had always known that his mother had killed herself. He'd never forget that she left the cottage that morning while he slept and how awkward the auld Northern priest had been about burying her. Aloy had learnt by rote every line of Nash's lie about how his Annie had rescued their boy, the last of her island people. It was a title that Aloy associated with the day of her funeral, and with shaking hands. Nash was from much further inland, but he kept Aloy by this stretch of sea and told him to call him Nash. It was his gift, he claimed, a liberation. He would not ask things of him, burden him like a son, but rather treat him as a mate and Aloy should do the same in return. It was their bond; to question it would be to break it.

'Tessa questions it all the time,' Aloy said to no one, only the sea.

The road was slick, the next bout of rain was just around the bend and the sea, similar to the company of a dutiful dog, was lapping against the rocky shore alongside Aloy.

Throw us a stick, said the sea.

He pointed the torch towards the grassy verge. He squished his fag butt with his foot.

'How about a stone?' he said.

That'll do, said the sea.

He flung a stone and stopped to listen for the plop. He stayed with it, imagining it sinking to the bottom. He thought of Tessa sinking back at the cottage, waiting for him to say, 'Let's go.' He farted loudly, like a belch, and checked to see if she had heard before remembering he was alone.

That first day he had met Tessa, she was new to working in Horan's. She didn't have the uniform purple polo shirt yet and she was wearing denim shorts, regardless of the misty rain. Her skin was as brown as bog water. On her break, she shifted and sighed so much on her bar stool beside Aloy that he gave in. 'Are you alright?'

'Fucking tampon, literally been a little dick teasing me all day. I'm good to go, like right now,' she said.

This small girl-woman just up and says this to him. He looked around the thinning post-lunch pub and then back to the rerun of a soccer game on the TV, but it was gone half-time and the shouty ads had been muted by the barman. Aloy kept watching the screen in the corner, over her head.

'You'll have to take care of it for me, but after my chips though,' she said.

Aloy stepped through a gap in the stone wall to sit on a flat rock bordering the high-water mark. The rain returned without any scuttery prelude, hopping off of everything, flattening his dark, long hair and the blades of grass, but not the sea, which was bubbling. He looked out to where he knew the island lay—he was not the last of her people.

'Shite,' Aloy said, twigging why Tessa had needed a seat in the clinic. They hadn't had a chance to chat about the baby since that morning.

'Congratulations,' the GP had said, shaking Aloy's hand.

'And you're sure?' Aloy had replied.

Tessa had rolled her eyes, but he knew that she got what he meant. He wanted to make sure she didn't get her hopes up unnecessarily. She was a dinger for doing that. He took in the pitch-black view and couldn't imagine living somewhere closer to the city with street corners and without the shifts of the tide to break up his day.

'So,' he said tuning in to the pure rain. It so rarely had the stage to itself without the wind.

Go, you must leave here, the sea said to him.

'But my father?'

Then stay, said the sea.

'But my wife?'

So, do nothing, said the sea.

'But our child,' Aloy said.

A wave broke and the sea shrugged.

Two headlight beams appeared up the road from Aloy, revealing splinters of rain and three canoodling sheep in the ditch across from him. It was the jeep and it was crawling forward, herding without a herd. Aloy stood back out onto the side of the road and when the jeep went by, he banged twice on its rear with the flat of his palm. It stopped and Aloy popped the door. 'Nash?'

'Aloy?'

'Yeah.'

'Good boy.'

'Aren't you blind or something?' Aloy said.

'I could do these roads blindfolded.'

Aloy sat in out of the rain. 'Where are you going?'

Nash waved his hand to deflect the question. 'She's pregnant, did you know that?'

'I did, we talk you know,' Aloy said.

Nash gave him a sideways glance.

'Surprised she told you,' Aloy said.

'She got a bit upset over brogues and I surmised as much.'

'Did you share such surmising with her?'

'I did,' Nash said.

'And?'

'I thought it best to get out of the house.'

'Are you going to let me drive?' Aloy said.

'No.'

'Pull into Mac's.'

'Why?'

'She's out of petrol,' Aloy said.

'Mac's is closed.'

'It's not.'

Nash had no trouble getting the jeep close to what he thought was a petrol pump, but was actually the pay as you go vacuum, and when he did, Aloy took the keys out of the ignition. 'Get out and into the van, would ya.'

'Who'll drive the jeep back up?' Nash asked.

'I'll get it tomorrow.'

'Mac'll have it stripped for parts by tomorrow.'

'Get out.'

They skipped across the puddles to the van. Aloy put on the demister. The wipers thunked over and back, each time barely clearing the windscreen of rain. He let the van crawl towards the road.

'You can build on a room at the back,' Nash said.

'For what?'

'The baby.'

It sounded so simple. 'Ah, but we'd have to borrow from you to do it.'

'Ach sure, I don't care about money, Aloy.'

Aloy checked left and right before pulling out onto the road, but as he did Nash put his hand on the wheel.

'Let's drive the long way around,' he said.

What Nash really meant was, Take me to the beach where we used to pick cockles with your mother, my Annie. Remember she'd eat them raw.

Aloy pulled the handbrake back up. 'Ah, it's too dark.'

'It's always dark for me,' Nash said.

Aloy looked left towards the cottage.

'She's asleep by now anyway,' Nash said to him.

Aloy turned the jeep and drove a lap around the forecourt to face the road again. He hoped it might be enough to disorientate Nash. It wasn't.

'Go right now,' he told Aloy.

Aloy reversed and turned to do a second lap and then another and another, each one faster than the last. The shop and forecourt lights came back on and inside the ENTRANCE door there was Mac, staring out in pure wonder. On the final lap Aloy nearly clipped a petrol pump, the wheel bouncing over the curb. He pulled up sharply.

'Boy?'

Aloy stared ahead into the blackness and tried to blink free of it. He let up the clutch.

'Sure, she'll still be there when we get back,' one said, and the other nodded.

On The M6 Towards Galway

It should have been summer, but all day
the clouds chucked rain down over
Kilbeggan, Athlone and Ballinasloe
and quilted fields that would be pastel
if the sun could only reach them, until
fifteen minutes from Galway the sluices
relented enough to plug up their tears
but kept hovering so low over us that
we could pick out each strand of cloud
like smoke from a raging peatbog fire.
You tilted your face to the window
so I only saw the curve of your chin
and you could have been looking
over the lattice towers that hold up lines
linking communities to a modernity that
knows enough to forecast unending rain
yet can conjure up no better shamanism
than to stare at the sky, with arms cast
out as at the moment of releasing a net,
shrieking: the raincloud, the raincloud!

Toh Hsien Min

Silver Bream

We saw the catch land, knew the fish was fresh.
So I watched you dissect your silver bream,
your knife expertly lifting bone from flesh,
unarmouring the belly's oil-tinged gleam.
You said how fisher-folk would never flip
the fish the way that I had upturned mine,
as that presaged the capsize of a ship,
yet you were forced to flip the bony spine
to turn the other firm yet juicy cheek,
which in turn brought to mind the deluged week
we spent surveying rocks on Inis Oírr
and how the Aran islanders believed
that one should not take to the sea with fear
as its violence meant capsize was soon relieved.

Toh Hsien Min

A Stranger Rides Into Town, A Man Goes On A Journey
Colin Walsh

To be truly home is to be simply here, and most of us are never simply here.

Ian Sansom

1

One of those slow melt summer days where Galway slips around you like the swoon that pulls a wave into the sea. I'm fifteen when I leave the house to walk into town, Discman in hand, earphones in, daydreaming already. (Galway's a cradle for dreaming.) Make it out of the estate unbruised, having avoided certain corners, and the horizon pours into the Atlantic below where Salthill's a shimmering bowl and tiny people freckle the distant prom where I'm eleven and myself and Andrew White stand at the roundabout at Seapoint, each armed with a litre of Yazoo strawberry milk which we've decided to chug down in one. We make a fairly decent go of it till Andrew splutters and vomits a pillar of bright milkshake and Supermacs onto the pavement. It horrifies the power-walkers and we run giddy down the prom past the car park where I'm seventeen, sitting next to Ciara Jordan in her smoke-filled car at dusk with Sonia Sweeney and Paddy and Brendan, chatting about what we're all gonna do when we leave Galway, when we're eighteen, when we're famous. I'm uphill from all that at thirteen, traipsing past posh houses with mad driveways on Taylor's Hill. 'Pure rich people live in them houses,' Brendan mutters beneath trees that spatter light on the cigarette skins crackling in his coarse drummer fingers. I close my eyes and watch the sun riot beneath my eyelids and he catches me and calls me a pure hippy, away with the fairies. Galway turns beneath our feet, the pavement rolls with the sky, and it guides us wherever we need to be. We walk over the galloping shoulders of the Corrib into town and we know these days will last forever, and that we will too.

2

If reality is a ceaseless stream of impressions and affects, stories provide symbolic coordinates to help us navigate the storm. These stories range from learned truths we internalise as infants to narratives we consciously interrogate about the world. There's no human way of living outside story. Escape from one story always comes in the form of another.

3

I was born in Dublin but we moved to Galway when I was three. That's the story I tell to anyone willing to hear it. Tourists trying to have a pint in Barna. Lifeguards on Silver Strand. Women working the check-out in Roches Stores. Strangers looking at the Christmas display in the Eyre Square shopping centre. I'm four, and I've done this sort of thing from the moment I could talk. I stand, hands clasped at the base of my back, body tilted upwards, telling people stories about Kinderworld, my playschool. I'm in love with all the women who work there. They have names like Assumpta. Tracey. I want to marry all of them. I've memorised several Ladybird fairy tales from the cassettes that come with the books and I like to recite them word-for-word for Assumpta. *Hansel and Gretel. The Billy Goats Gruff. Jack and the Beanstalk.* I'm story-mad. When Mam takes me to the pictures for the first time—*Robin Hood: Prince of Thieves* at the Palace Cinema, down the Crescent—it's an overwhelming experience. The worlds of story and real life are entirely meshed for me and I live through whatever book, movie or cartoon I've just devoured. My parents' photo albums are stuffed with pictures of me dressed up. Me as Santa wearing a beard made out of a bag of cotton wool. Me as a Ghostbuster wearing Mam's swimming goggles. Me as Robin Hood, Peter Pan, the Artful Dodger. When I want to be D'Artagnan, Mam draws a curly French moustache on my cheeks with her eyeliner. Dad folds pieces of kitchen roll into rectangles and staples them to the shoulders of my jumper to make epaulettes. I march up and down our unpaved road like that, waving a sword and talking to myself. Mam's brown boots are way too big for me; they reach all the way up my legs and the toes curl back at me like elf shoes. I think I look brilliant.

4

John Gardner said there are only two kinds of story: A stranger rides into town, and A man goes on a journey. In the former, reality gets disrupted by some outsider element (think westerns, detective stories, love stories, horror, etc.), while in the latter someone has to leave their established reality and become an outsider to discover another way of being (coming-of-age stories, adventures, sci-fi, fantasy, and so on).

Whether a story is about the stranger's arrival, the hero's departure, or some comingling of both, all stories hold this in common: *the world cannot remain stable and reconciled to itself.* Stories are predicated on some sort of disruption, an event or character that tears a wound in the world. Whether or not the wound can be closed within the telling of a particular story, it's always the wound that allows for the existence of the story itself.

5

Dad pretends to be a horse and crawls around the house with me on his back. Every night before bedtime, he heats me up a saucer of milk with sugar. He calls it 'hero milk'. I'm convinced that I'm a hero. Mam takes photos of me ruddy-faced and unconscious in bed, with an illustrated book of *Tyrone the Horrible* or *Fred Under the Bed* still clutched in my hand. From these stories I've learned that I'm on an adventure. Life is a sort of heroic quest. I approach my first day in primary school like this. Most of the kids are in hysterics, clinging to their mothers' legs. Mam is worried that I will get upset too. But I seem to be floating somewhere over the entire experience. Mam tells this story often, even now. 'You walked into the classroom in Taylor's Hill,' she says, 'and you sat down with a big smile on you, like you'd been there all your life.' Mam burst into tears for me, that day, but I was so wrapped up in my own heroic adventure I didn't notice her being upset.

School is where I learn how to put letters together. The first story I ever write, a mad scrawl veering diagonally across the page, is about Santa being kidnapped by an evil reindeer named Hornhead Brown. Only Rudolph, the lonely outsider, can rescue him.

6

Outsiders make for good storytellers. Ishmael can narrate Moby Dick because he is not Ahab. Lena can narrate Ferrante's Neapolitan novels because she is not Lila. It's far easier to describe the world's contours if you're hovering somewhere slightly outside it.

7

Every friend I make when I start primary school—Philip O'Connell, Brian Halpin, Sheena Murphy, Cian O'Donohue—has to move away within a year or two because of their parents' work. (Galway's a place that people leave.) At the same time, there are several deaths in the family, in quick succession. Each time someone leaves I want to cry, but I've learned from stories that this is something boys don't do so I chew on my cheeks till they bleed in my mouth. I'm still the cheerful hero, chatty, eager to impress. But the constant vanishing of people, the faces that disappear from one year to the next, have convinced me that my Real Life, the one where I'm a hero triumphing over all adversity, must be happening somewhere else. I realise that this Galway existence is all preparation; one day I will be elsewhere, elevated. I spend more and more time inhaling the exotic plots of movies, TV and books. If I'm too young to watch a film, I read everything there is to know about it in my *Encyclopaedia of Cinema* and write a version of the film for myself. I memorise dialogue from movies I've never seen, words spoken by voices I've never heard. I know I will see them one day, because I know I'll do everything one day, because one day I will be out in the world, living my Real Life, like a character in a story. For now, stories are my trapdoors out of flat Galway Tuesdays in the rain. (Galway's full of dreamers floating outside life, biding their time.) I sit on my bed, reading and writing adventures, preparing for existence.

8

A recurrent theme in writers' interviews is the admission of being a control freak, the sort of person who withdraws from the relentlessness of the outside world to sit alone in a room for hours on end, incrementally reworking isolated moments into narrative, orchestrating reality while holding themselves outside its flow. Such sovereignty is always confined to the page, of course. Beyond the desk, life roars on.

9

I read almost no fiction during my teenage years; Galway has suddenly opened itself to me with a wink and I'm at large in the city with Brendan, Paddy and the gang. It's the rush of being in town with them in summer. It's making hot chocolates last for hours in the nocturnal vibe of Java's. It's having my first shift at the Bish disco, bushing Buckfast and Dutch Gold down the Spanish Arch, Brendan smoking his first ever cigarette in Café de Paris to try and look cool for the sexy eyebrow waitress. It's flicking through the CDs and posters in Zhivago's, walking next to Brendan and Paddy through Eyre Square shopping centre, hands dug in our pockets. It's thumbing at the book boxes outside Charlie Byrne's, getting spat at, kicked and headbutted weekly by shams for being a mosher faggot. It's the belly purr feeling of *did you hear who fancies you?*, falling in love for the first time, losing my virginity under the stars at Galway Bay, getting my heart broken, getting drunk, getting lost. It's coming up against the limits of myself and realising I've internalised loads of hateful shit about what it is to be a boy, a man, narratives I've passively absorbed in playgrounds and boys-only schoolyards, at churches and cinemas, from sitcoms and music videos. It's realising I need to dig the prejudice out of myself, only to discover there are actually multiple selves jostling inside me and none of them particularly like one another. It's developing a sort of self-loathing that translates into an urge to escape every irreconcilable thing in my mind.

10

By my twenties I'm frantically looking for some sort of overarching narrative that will fix the world, hold its contradictions in place. I travel a lot. I live and work abroad a lot. Everywhere I go, I'm reading mystics, religious texts, comparative mythology, history, philosophy, psychology, schematic novels of ideas. I go on silent retreats. I spend time in a Sivananda ashram in the mountains. I fast. I drink very heavily. I practise the shaking meditations of the Bhagwan. I comb my way through the narcotic throb of hot limbs on the Áras na nGael dancefloor. I get into several near-death situations in different countries, out of the thirst for any form of liminal experience. I am hoping that, if I push far enough, something epiphanic will reveal itself and I will finally arrive in my own story. I move from place to place, job to job, belief system to belief system. From the outside, to my parents, this looks like adventure, even freedom. But in truth, my flitting around is more about escape than exploration. I am trying to dodge all irreconcilabilities. I am trying to find a trapdoor in reality. I am trying to outrun time.

During a quick visit to Ireland, I get into a discussion with a guru who's crashing at a friend's flat on Merchant's Road. We talk about the idea of the bodhisattva—the person who knows immortality but chooses, out of compassion, to participate in the suffering of time. The guru offers to read my astrological birth chart. Throughout the discussion, he repeatedly points to a pattern of lines on my birth chart and asks: 'Have you ever felt like you belonged anywhere?' Later, as we step out of Neachtain's into an unexpected Macnas parade (Galway is a place where this sort of thing actually happens), he asks me the question again. As the parade blares past, he shouts 'You know, your chart reminds me of that quote from Groucho Marx, about belonging to a club. D'you know it?' I actually do know the quote. I first read it in my Film Encyclopaedia when I was a child. *I could never be part of any club that would accept me as a member.* When I shout the line to the guru over the chaos of the parade, he turns. The lights flare across his eyes, like I have given him something. He points at me, and smiles.

11

Around this time, whenever people ask where I'm from, I still say, 'I was born in Dublin but we moved to Galway when I was three.' Fifteen addresses later and my adult life could be condensed into a smash-cut video edit of me saying 'I was born in Dublin but we moved to Galway when I was three' as various backgrounds blitz behind me, a storm of languages, faces, climates and countries with my spiel remaining insistent at the centre of the frame, a symbolic compass point. A story I'm telling myself.

During one of my visits back to Galway, I make a passing remark about this quirk to my mam. She laughs. 'Well, you were so lost when we moved from Dublin. I don't know if you ever fully settled. When you were a toddler it was the same. You were always going on about Galway not being your real home.' Mam tells me that for the first year of living in Galway, I screamed whenever we entered our estate. 'I'd pick you up from Kinderworld and as soon as you realised we weren't going back to the house in Dublin, you'd start struggling against the straps of your baby seat. *I don't like this road! I don't like this road!*' Hearing this is disorienting. This isn't the story I've told myself about the chatty toddler talking to strangers in pubs, the kid completely at ease in the classroom, the cheerful hero who recited fairy tales at Kinderworld all day. Mam frowns and shakes her head. 'Half the time I'd come to collect you from Kinderworld and Assumpta would tell me you'd spent the whole day alone in the corner of the playroom, staring at the floor. They couldn't bring you out of yourself. Unless you were reciting one of your Ladybird stories.' I ask her what was wrong with me. 'Ara… you didn't like being uprooted, I suppose. I think you couldn't get used to being where you were. You always wanted to be somewhere else.'

12

In 2008, the day before I took my final unthinking steps off a Shannon Airport runway into the future, Bertie Ahern appeared on TV to make the surprise announcement of his resignation. Within weeks the floor had fallen out of the economy, the country and Galway city. It took almost everyone I knew in Galway with it. They went to Vancouver, Toronto, Montreal, Melbourne, Perth, Dublin, London, Norwich, Birmingham, Edinburgh, Valencia, Barcelona, Castellón, Buenos Aires, Chicago, Orlando, Berlin. None of them have come back. When I see friends now, old friends, people like Brendan with whom I navigated almost every possible emotional extremity growing up, we don't know how to talk to one another. Time howls like a gale between us, blocking out our voices. We can occasionally meet eyes and there's an acknowledgement of an intimacy that distance cannot quite erase. But our conversations stutter and cul de sac, and nothing we say is adequate.

Last Christmas, I met some old college friends for dinner in a new restaurant near the Blue Note. I had to keep leaving the restaurant and ducking down a laneway because it felt like someone was laying bricks on my chest. I thought I was having a heart attack. I stood baffled on Dominic Street, and later on Shop Street, stupefied at how the particularity of these places—the way they are today, with their new shops, different moods—did not match up with the cinematic versions of them that I still carry in my chest. I could not let their reality in.

13

I usually don't tell people when I visit. I stay at my parents' house, and I don't go into town. I visit the woods, Spiddal, and Connemara, because being in nature allows me to pretend that there are things about Galway that remain unchanged. This is cowardice. I am afraid to see old friends, afraid to see the city, because I am afraid of time. Despite myself, I've made an Eden out of my Galway life. This place, which I once saw as a mere prologue to the story of my real life, has now become an ideal to which I can never return. My Galway does not exist anywhere but inside myself, and the notion that I alone am the measure of all that experience is a knot in my chest. I never feel more homesick for Galway than when I'm there. I arrive at the bus station and immediately long to get away so I can miss the place again from the safety of some distance.

14

I started writing fiction while living in Belgium in 2016. I had spent years trying to dissolve the contradictions of life by burying them within various metaphysical architectures. Fiction is a space that actively invokes the irreconcilable, welcomes it in, and after years of running from one totalising Big Idea to another, it felt like writing might be the one way in which I could actually meet the plurality of life.

But making a fetish of writing is just me erecting another Eden towards which the flow of my actual life is subordinated. The act of writing already threatens to become a trapdoor allowing me to escape a world from which I feel increasingly disconnected, a daydream that gives me a simulacrum of communication with others but actually preserves me in my solitude.

There's always the threat that the identity of 'being a writer' will trump the real work of just being a person. I see myself wobbling on that ledge all the time now. I worry that I'm failing as a man, friend, son, boyfriend, brother, colleague, cousin, nephew, neighbour, citizen, person, and that I'm looking to writing (writing!) as some sort of redemptive act that will justify how locked outside of life I actually am. The fact is, I'm deeply lonely much of the time. Often I just want to lie on the floor and not get up. I don't allow myself to do that, because I still believe that writing may somehow deliver me into life. This is one of the symbolic fictions that structures my existence. Nowhere is this clearer to me than in my relationship to Galway.

15

My humiliating hope is that somehow writing this essay will earn me a place in the collective dreamscape of the city where I grew up and tether me to the flesh and clay of the world instead of the isolated sphere of my imagination, where I spend most of my time.

I'm not a complete eejit, though. I know this hope is absurd. But there's knowing on the level of the intellect, and there's knowing of the guts. And my guts remember the first time I got from one end of Shop Street to another without seeing a single familiar face.

16

The constitutive wound in stories is that which knocks the world off balance and enables the narrative to happen. The constitutive wound in life, though, is time itself: it both feeds and eats away at everything, enabling life while sundering it slowly. I write in order to manage the time-wound in some way, and I can talk a big game about how my experience of the act of writing is one of being truly 'home', about how writing now creates a space for me where life's irreconcilabilities do not need to be neutered, where contradiction can be explored as a fertile— blah, blah, blah. This is all just brittle intellectualism when confronted with the visceral panic I feel whenever I'm in Galway, the closest thing to an actual home I'll ever have. Galway forces me to look into the wound and I always blink.

When I was younger, I arrogantly assumed that my story was 'A man goes on a journey'. There is a brutal irony to realising that it's always been 'A stranger rides into town'.

I don't have a way out of this. This essay cannot resolve things with a neat ending. It's not fiction.

17

The day after my panicked episode at the restaurant with my college friends, I met Brendan and Paddy for lunch. We hadn't seen each other in years. We went to Java's, which is no longer nocturnal and seductive. Now it's painted in bright, inviting colours. I was still shook from the night before but I grinned my way through the conversation, heart thudding. We warmed to the moment awkwardly, the way my Dublin cousins and I used to feel out the air between us before clicking into our familiar groove. There's still a deep familiarity between Paddy and Brendan, despite the fact that Paddy now lives in Cork. They communicate in slags, like family. As we left Java's I felt my belly drop, because I'd held myself back from the experience, afraid to just relax and be there with them. We walked up to the crossway at Lynch's Castle to say goodbye, when Brendan said, 'Here, will we take a look at what's happening in the shopping centre?'

18

One of the things the guru said to me the day he read my birth chart was: 'You have an eye for things, I think. And you can put words on the things that you see. This is a gift, but gifts are something to use very carefully. A person like you would find it very easy to… try and freeze things. To stop them from moving as they want to. Does any of this resonate with you?'

I actually laughed.

19

We walked through Eyre Square shopping centre, scraps of noise and laughter moving all around us. The shop that used to be the Zhivago's where Paddy worked. The spot where Mam used to bring me to see Santa. Brendan raised his eyebrows at giddy children clutching toys they'd gotten for Christmas, kids whose parents may not have even met one another the last time I lived in Galway. (Galway is like every place; it is always young, always new.) We wandered in the Christmas music, making chit-chat. I don't know what was happening in that moment, even now. But I felt a sudden, wild love at how Paddy still walks with his hands dug so deep into his pockets, at Brendan's silhouette in the corner of my eye, striding against the glare of milky light. The feeling flooded across the tiled floor of the shopping centre and along the knuckled remains of the medieval city walls where a group of toddlers stood, pointing open-mouthed at the Christmas display. I looked over at Brendan and he winked at me, and it felt like a fissure was opening in the world, and I was being invited into something, and I knew I would remember how, in the surge of that moment, I was so happy.

wanna be

1996

i imagine you at the sportsground
sixteen hair sodden with july rain
green leather jacket corduroy flares
doc martens cider pocket naggin

those videos were too weird for me
dancers a chained dog child smashed windows
i was waiting for blur oasis
puberty teenage angst to kick in

2017

i'm not optimistic when you ask
whether they'll play *the bends* in glasgow
the decades old rebuke of britpop
a rarity on recent set lists

but deep into the second encore
our fingers entwine in your pockets
those opening chords strike at the sky
we cry out *where do we go from here*

Cian Murphy

Keen

You might assume that the scent would
drift out onto the street, like the chemical
bread smell of Subway, even when tucked
in the back of Londis, but the perfume shop
exists with its own ecosystem of smells
contained within a cave-room, bottles
and candles arranged upon cave-shelves,
smells withheld beneath glass cloches.
You might assume that the bottle
labelled 'Róisín Dubh' might contain
spilled beers and smoke constrained
illegally by more than three walls, but
instead it has a musky sweetness.
'Lúnasa'—not named for the moon, but
for the month of August and the harvest
festival—is citrusy and (I am told) has a
tendency to smell acrid on the cold
dampness of Irish skin. Having taken
observations on the prices, I thank the
perfumer, promise with acknowledged
duplicity to come back again and she sprays
my wrist to allow 'Sybarite' to mellow
and greet me through the rest of my day.

Emily S. Cooper

Letter to my 13-year-old self

Listen.

You're so obsessed with not telling anyone anything that when you do it's always the wrong person, at the wrong time.

Your instincts are polished with good reason; do not let doubt get in the way.

You have no trouble spotting falseness, though its aftermath is still a problem. Has it not clicked not to care about people who do not care about you?

The glory of going up in flames is empty and though you are drawn to the fire you have yet to be burned.

Be careful.

You can't resent people for bending just because you confuse being rigid with being unbroken.

Loosen up some. You might be more patient if you just relax.

Pride is a siren call you will have to learn to ignore.

Don't allow a fast foot off the clutch pressure on your heart to drive you into forward motion.

Just slow down. Breathe more.

Yes, that moment in Geography where you fully realised your own mortality for the first time was horrible, why dwell on it?

You can fight everything but death so please stop looking for a way and go to sleep.

Maybe that's not very fair. God knows I don't properly remember what it was like to be you.

You're in the trenches now but the results are (maybe) worth it, for the time you put in.

You think too much. I still do the same.

This isn't funny—you were never in the mood for jokes. I forget how serious we were then.

You grow out of that because you stop being afraid of looking stupid. Everyone looks stupid. That's just life.

On that note, I have four little words that will change yours: who gives a *fuck*. Welcome to working-class existentialism.

I've been ignoring you for a long time. Talking over you to delegate tasks to Future-Katelyn, then blocking out Paranoid-Katelyn's diatribe against us.

Like I said, we still think too much.

There are people you think are important who I wish you did not waste your time on.

If you could see where they'd end up, you'd be laughing.

There are people who were important who I wish did not waste away on us through time, but even now I must admit there are always two of us in it.

Some good news: the day will come where letting people drift away is easy.

In learning to unclench your jealous fingers sooner you might save us damage, but life is a process, I suppose, and though everything hurt more when I was you the good things felt stronger, too.

It's more than okay to love your own company.

You can't equate love and novelty, then think it's The End when you fall out of that onset-infatuation. Don't be dramatic.

Although we do tend to get bored by people after a time and I still don't know why.

The shelf-life of dopamine is Future-Katelyn's problem.

Speaking of shelf-life, don't use vegetables going off quickly as an excuse not to eat any at all. You're only tricking yourself.

Be less sarcastic. It'll come easy enough. Turns out that for someone who hates people you quite like humanity.

I know I said earlier that you had avoided the flames but the years are blurred gunk to me now so in retrospect you're probably not completely unscathed.

To the me of the past if you're already burning, don't wait.

Sometimes it's less about the cliff and more about the jumping.

Katelyn O'Neill

Liz's Kitchen

Why did you become vegan?
To avoid Battenberg on my birthday,
a leg of turkey at Christmas.

But I say
I can't remember
what a ladybird looks like.

She adds so much butter
to her toast, glides the knife
along her tongue.

Says she had a daughter like me,
watched her run suicide drills
with a fractured hip.

Found fists of her hair
in the washing machine,
a tooth in the sink.

Here, she throws me her phone,
a red ladybird
like a clot of blood.

Molly Twomey

Glass To Sand

Kathleen Murray

A misty rain started around Enfield and seemed to move up a gear as soon as they reached the outskirts of Galway. Chrissie thought it looked much the same as any English town: all fast food outlets, bed-and-bath superstores in front of red-bricked apartments with tiny balconies. A tangle of roads and roundabouts dragged the journey out, right when they were nearly there.

'Miserable weather, as per usual,' she said to Greg. 'I'm as well out of it, right?'

No answer. In the rear-view mirror, she saw him hanging out of the booster seat at a strange angle, fast asleep. That reminded her of the car rental guy at the airport, lecturing her about booster seats and the law. Patronising her as if she were a foreigner.

Hemmed in by traffic, she passed the time trying to imagine meeting them. Brenda first. Chrissie was sure she'd mentioned that she was bringing Greg, but Brenda hadn't acknowledged this. She tried to picture Brenda's front door opening, the very moment. No, her mind skittered away.

She imagined going to the hospital instead. She'd visited loads of hospitals over the years so no problem there: automatic doors opening into a bright reception area, visitors and patients and nurses crisscrossing; a bank of lifts, long corridors; bright strips of light overhead leading to the ICU, beeping and humming machinery. Maybe she'd spot Daddy before he recognised her: in the coffee shop, his back turned, holding a mug of tea in his fist, or sitting on a chair outside a closed door, tapping the floor with his stick. She might ignore him, take Greg by the hand and walk straight past. Or she'd say… what would she say? Her mind flipped back to the car rental guy. She knew exactly what she'd say to him. When he heard they were going to Galway, he had a story about some sunken forest that got uncovered by recent storms. Once he saw Greg was interested he hyped it up, said to watch out for treasure floating to the surface. And dead bodies. Stupid joke that frightened the child. She'd take that fella down a notch or two if he was there tomorrow.

She missed the turn the first time; it was nearly impossible to see the sign, *Sea View B&B*. Plus it didn't look a bit like the website. Four B&Bs right next door to each other, each house stepped back slightly. All colonnades and froufrou crap, four bridesmaids on a short pew.

'Greg, wake up,' she said. 'This is ours.'

The child stirred. 'How is it ours?' he asked, stretching and scratching.

'It's your Aunty Brenda's, where we're staying.'

Gathering up the McDonald's containers into a paper bag, she said, 'She'll think you've changed so much. They haven't seen you since you were a little baby.'

'Did they visit us in Ipswich?'

'No. We came back to see them. Once.'

'I like hotels.'

'This isn't a hotel.'

'They always have biscuits in the bedroom,' he said. 'Chocolate ones. You can watch TV in bed.'

She lifted him onto the wall so he could look across the bay. Stretching up to touch the *Sea View* sign, he managed to push a little board, changing it from *Vacancies* to *No Vacancies*. She pushed it back.

Her suitcase ground a noisy channel through the wet gravel. Before she'd her hand up to ring the bell, the front door half-opened. A thin woman whisked them in.

'Just trying to keep the heat in,' she said.

'Brenda, it's me, Chrissie. And Greg.'

'Of course it's you. The boy is so small. I thought he'd be taller.'

Although it was seven years since Chrissie'd seen her, her sister hadn't aged as much as changed. She was wearing lipstick and heavy eyeliner, her hair dyed a much darker brown than her natural colour ever was.

'The house is lovely.'

'These are all guest rooms. We're at the back.'

Chrissie asked her how the business was going.

'Here four years now. You do your best. But we're hammered by NAMA. They're giving away hotel rooms.'

'How's Liam?'

'His back is constant. Crucified with it. The doctor says cut down the long haul, but it's the only way to make a half-decent wage.'

Greg had slipped past to check out a stack of leaflets on a side table: flyers for tourist attractions and maps of Connemara. He picked up one for a water park, children and adults on a big mat hurtling down into a sparkling splash of water.

'You're number three,' Brenda said. 'Top of the stairs to your left.'

'You don't have to use a guest room for us.'

'It's as easy,' she said, pulling a key from a box fashioned as a treasure chest.

'Are Michael and Saibh around?' Chrissie asked. 'Greg'd love to meet them.'

'No. Mike'll often stay in college till the library closes. Or he might be at something. Saibh's on an Erasmus year, in France. She came back last weekend to see Mammy.'

Greg tugged at Chrissie's hand.

'What is it?'

He pointed to an old map on the wall. 'Is that the sea outside?'

'He can hardly read maps, can he?' Brenda's hand lifted as she spoke. People were always looking for an excuse to touch Greg's skin, the even darkness of it.

'A bit,' Chrissie answered.

The boy looked from one to the other.

'How's Mammy?' Chrissie asked.

'She's having an awful time letting go. It's killing Daddy to watch.'

'Is she conscious?'

'The doctors say she might be able to recognise voices.'

Brenda used the key to indicate the lounge across the hall although, she said, everything they'd need was in their own bedroom. Then she pointed out the dining room. For breakfast. They all looked over at the closed door. So they weren't even going to eat with the family.

'Who owns the ducks?' Greg asked.

He was making big eyes at a duck-shaped Easter egg, tucked in beside an enormous geranium. Three baby ducks in gold paper were arranged around it.

'That's mine. First time in my life I won anything.' Brenda drew into herself. She looked thinner again and Chrissie felt there was something recent, an illness or a hysterectomy. 'I'd say he loves chocolate.'

'I do love chocolate,' Greg said.

'I don't mind the odd square. That there's excessive.'

'I might be getting two Easter eggs this year,' he said. 'Last year a lady in the hotel gave me an egg when I finished my breakfast.'

'Did she?'

'In Devon. Just a creme egg.'

'Let's see how you get on with your breakfast here.'

The boy moved across the hall, touched the gold wrapping paper.

'There's so many baby ones.'

'C'mon Greg.' Chrissie put her hand out for the keys and Brenda passed them over.

'Have you eaten?' she asked suddenly.

'Stopped for a takeaway.'

'Good. I left a few sandwiches up in your room. Tea, coffee. I'd no idea what time you'd get in. I have to go out tonight, fiftieth wedding anniversary.'

'I thought we'd go the hospital this evening,' Chrissie said.

'No, sure Daddy's with her constantly. I'll be taking him to ten o'clock mass in the morning. You can go in then.'

'Right.'

In the bedroom, Chrissie unpacked their things while Greg sat on the bed watching TV.

'Do I look like her?' she asked him while the ads were on.

He kept his eyes on the screen, picking his way around a ham sandwich. 'If you're blind, everyone looks the same. But they feel different.'

Greg couldn't sleep, so eventually Chrissie got into his bed beside him. Halfway through a nature programme, he was snoring in the crook of her arm. She stayed there a bit longer, trying to use her phone with her free hand. She had the TV muted but at one stage she glanced at the screen; it was filled with a close-up of a giraffe's eye, soft and brown with these incredible eyelashes. It was the gentlest thing she'd seen in ages. Unblinking, it held her gaze, and she felt herself flooding with sadness. Seeping from her chest into her shoulders, weighing down her arms. She switched the TV off and might have started at the black screen for a few minutes. Back in her own bed she started a new comedy series on Netflix but the funny had gone out of it by the second episode, even with a large mug of duty-free red.

During the night a sound broke into her sleep, an irregular banging. She went over to the window to see what it was. Rain was sheeting down. A room at right angles to her own glowed bluish from a TV, maybe a computer screen. That must be the family quarters. Probably Michael up watching porn. She waited by her window. It took three more bangs before she located it; a black box hanging loosely off the satellite dish. It caught each gust of wind and hit the metal rod.

Although the noise still edged into her sleep, it wasn't as disturbing now that she'd married the sound to the source.

The next morning she woke abruptly, feeling watched. It was Greg, staring at her over the rim of his book. Stretching across to rub his shoulder, her hand brushed off the padded headboard. She was surprised by the sensation.

'I don't know if I could stomach a big breakfast at all,' she said.

'I'm getting a chocolate duck after my breakfast.'

'She never said that.'

'She did, she said if I eat all the breakfast.'

He reached across, raking his fingernails down her arm.

'Stop that.'

'I don't have to have a shower, do I?'

'Not if you don't want.'

When they went down, Chrissie opened the kitchen door. Fat was spitting in the pan, eggshells scattered on the counter. No sign of Brenda or anyone else. Greg stuck his head in, then moved off to study the wall map again. She had a quick look around; magnets on the fridge door from various destinations; Lanzarote was a big hit, Croatia a close second. Receipts and coupons. Then she spied the old dresser from home over by the back door. And ranged across the top shelf, there they were. The glass animals.

Her collection. Well, hers and Mammy's. How had they ended up here? The penguin with his polka-dot tie; the dancing horse; a blue hedgehog smoking a pipe; puppy twins and other dogs; the octopus with diamond eyes; top -hat-and-tails-robin beside the winking wagtail. Brenda's favourite, the frog playing a banjo, right up the front. Each only as big as your thumb. They gave her a rush of panic, a flashback to the old kitchen. Back to her last night with these little creatures silent in the background, watching. Now here they perched, happy out with their new station in life. The ease with which they carried on belonging here; she felt like they were mocking her.

Greg called out from the hall, 'Mum, I'm hungry.'

The dining room was also empty. There were enough tables for maybe fifteen people but only three were set: two singles, one already used, and a double.

Brenda appeared through another door.

'You're up now.'

'Yes,' Chrissie answered. 'How was the party?'

'I only went to pay my respects. Couldn't stop thinking of Mammy, what she's going through.'

Greg had taken all the condiments out of a glass bowl and was arranging them around the table by size; sugars, salt, mayonnaise, jams.

'Tea or coffee?' Brenda said.

'Tea for me please.'

With a nod of the head toward the sideboard, Brenda said, 'There's Coco Pops or Rice Krispies for himself.'

'Thanks,' mother and son answered together. When she was gone Greg held up the raspberry jam packet. 'Can I have this one?'

'Okay, use a teaspoon.'

Brenda came back in with a laminated menu, words printed over a sun setting across Galway Bay. Chrissie asked for the scrambled eggs and smoked salmon.

'What about himself?'

'I'll have that too,' he said.

'He'll hardly eat smoked salmon.'

'I will. I love it.'

Brenda leaned back into herself. 'Mine'd spit that back at you, they've that little interest in food.'

'He's a good appetite,' Chrissie said.

Greg looked at his mother. 'Can I have a sausage as well?'

Brenda stood there, staring at the two of them.

'If there's one on the go?' Chrissie asked.

'Up to you.'

'Yippee, a sausage please.'

While they waited, Chrissie walked over to look out the back window. Ordinary enough garden, with some class of hutches, maybe small bird coops, tucked in at the end. The thought of little birds returned the glass collection to her. Until she'd seen them, all lined up on the dresser, they had been completely absent from her memory. Not just an absence, it was as if they'd never existed. If she hadn't ended up here, in Brenda's house, they might never have come back into being. To not even know what it is you've lost. How had she not managed to hold onto these things, which had seemed so precious and constant?

Brenda pushed open the door with her back and turned in with two plates. Both were piled with scrambled eggs, a thick slice of smoked salmon across the top. She placed one in front of Greg and served Chrissie the other. Chrissie's piece of fish curled up at the end. The plates were identical except for the sausage on Greg's plate.

'Now,' Brenda said. 'I'll get some ketchup.'

Greg got stuck in. He dipped a big piece of salmon in the eggy pile. Chrissie saw what was coming. He wouldn't be able to finish it; even an adult couldn't clear that plate.

'I'd love a taste of that.' She reached across and sliced off half the sausage.

A woman came in and seated herself with her back to Chrissie. Brenda went over to her new guest and chatted. She returned to Chrissie and Greg with ketchup.

'You must have used half a dozen eggs,' Chrissie said. 'He'll never finish that.'

'I can eat it.' Greg voice was muffled, his mouth full.

'Haven't we all heard about his great appetite?' Brenda said. 'We'd never touch fish. Liam is all up on diets.'

With that she launched into Liam's food theories. He must've cobbled them together at some long-distance drivers' café, or dredged them up from the far reaches of the internet. Chrissie sat sipping tea, just to be doing something, as Brenda told her that Liam said people are allowing themselves to be duped, eating the least intelligent fish, and any species senseless enough to be domesticated or trapped. Cows, sheep. Sprat. The only fish he'd eat, if he had to, would be dolphin or whale. Smaller animals have faster heartbeats, quicker brains. He was breeding more intelligent strains of guinea pigs out the back. To eat. And hamsters.

'Hamsters?' Chrissie asked. 'They're so tiny. How could you even kill them humanely?'

Straight away, she wished she'd said nothing, for Greg's sake.

'He does. He gets Mike to give him a hand. What they do is—'

'Better eat this before it gets cold,' Chrissie interrupted. She started slicing through yellow lumps and Brenda moved off.

Greg was going at it with such speed that the feeling of fullness came upon him suddenly.

'Mum,' he whispered. 'I can't eat any more.'

'Leave what you don't want on the plate.'

His voice was shaky. 'I won't get the chocolate.'

'She was never going to give it to you.'

'She was. One of the little ducks.'

'We've a champion eater,' Brenda announced as she transferred milk from a carton into a jug and delivered it to her other guest. 'All the way from England.'

Greg malingered, piling the food closer together then spreading it out thinly. He ate a small piece of the salmon, pushed the rest under the eggs. Chrissie went to take the remainder of the sausage. She was going to wrap it up in a napkin. Pointless. She left it in the dish with the toast. This action seemed to revive Greg and he had another go, putting a tiny forkful into his mouth. But he couldn't swallow. A final gag and it was over.

Brenda came back in, a stack of plates in her hands.

'Finished? I'll clear these so.'

Greg stared across at Chrissie, making tiny 'no' shakes of his head, but she said sure go ahead.

'Eyes bigger than his belly,' Brenda said. 'Isn't that always the way?'

As soon as they got to the bedroom, he let himself cry. Chrissie reached over but he pushed her away. 'I wasn't finished.'

He snuggled back under the duvet as she went around the room, picking up their things, packing up.

'A dolphin's not a fish. It's a mammal, isn't it?' she asked him, but he wouldn't answer.

During the ads, he muted the TV and said, 'You always say, "You never know".'

'Don't start.'

'So you didn't know if I was going to finish it or not. Why did you give me all the jam?'

He made a face at her and it was an effort not to reach over and shake every morsel of jam and egg back out of him. He'd hold on to this, no two ways. She took the control out of his hand and switched off the TV and told him it was not her fault. It was his choice, his alone and he'd better not hang her out to dry to some girlfriend or therapist in years to come. This was no picnic for anybody.

When she had everything in the room sorted, Chrissie walked him out to the car first. She strapped him in his seat before she went back and knocked on the kitchen door. No answer. She waited a minute, then called out, 'We're going now.'

Brenda came in the back door drying her hands.

'We're heading over to the hospital now,' Chrissie said.

'Just ask at the front desk, they'll direct you to the ICU. No children allowed in.'

'I wasn't going to bring him in.'

'I was just on the phone to Daddy. He's a few messages to get after mass before we head over.'

'Does he know we're here? What did he say?'

Brenda folded the tea towel until it was the size of her fist.

'Mammy's the priority right now. It's hardly the time for anything else.'

'Our flight's not till this evening. Though we'll need to leave early enough. So we'll see you at the hospital?'

'Right so.' Brenda seemed to brighten up. 'I've a crowd of Americans coming in tonight.'

As Chrissie reversed onto the road, Brenda stepped out the front door and followed them down the drive. Chrissie waited, thinking she wanted to say goodbye to them properly. No. She went to the wooden sign, switched it to *No Vacancies* and turned back into the house.

They were on the road maybe ten minutes when Greg began to yawn continuously, drawing in great swathes of air.

'You ok?'

'Feel a bit sick. My feet are sweating.'

'Take your shoes off.' She checked his face in the mirror; the colour had drained out of him.

'Can you stop now?' he said faintly.

'Do you think it was the salmon? It smelt very strong.'

'Don't say it. Makes me worser.'

'Take this.'

Fair dues to him, he got most of it in the milkshake container. The car filled with the stench. Chrissie rolled down the front windows and a blast of cold air hit her in the face. The shock was welcome. She swung a sharp left off the main road. Spotting a gate into a field on the other side, she veered across and pulled in.

When she opened his door he handed her the cup of sick. Nothing for it only to drop it over the gate. Half-lifting him out, making sure his mouth was pointing away, she stood him on the verge.

'Why didn't you stop?' he said.

'I was trying to.'

'I'm sorry.'

'For what? Lots of people get car sick.'

The blood was returning to his cheeks and he was taking steady breaths. She rolled his sweatshirt over his head and freshened his face with a wet wipe.

Somehow the whole episode perked her up; she'd been barely managing since leaving Brenda's. The thought of seeing her mother one last time, unconscious, shrunken, but still able to hear—that was one thing. But Brenda's carry-on and Daddy, that was another thing altogether.

'We can hardly go to see your granny right now, can we?' she said.

'Why not?'

'Because they don't want sick children in the hospital, that's why. It's very dangerous.'

'Will we go back to Aunty Brenda's?'

'No. We'll think about going to the hospital later.'

They settled back in the car and continued up the side road, windows open. She came to a T-junction; instead of taking the right into Galway she followed a sign for *An Spidéal*.

'Imagine I only saw the sea for the first time when I was your age. We went to a beach out here.'

She had grown up in Galway, but inland, near the Roscommon border. It was Mammy's cousin Fidelma, down from Donegal with a man in a blue car, who took them to the seaside. Fidelma tried to get Mammy to go too but she needed to get tea for the men in the yard, for Daddy. Then Brenda wanted to stay with Mammy and it was just Chrissie and the twins.

When they got there, Fidelma put a blanket on the sand, rolled up a towel for a pillow and lay flat, like she was in bed, not paying any attention to the sea or the children. It was late afternoon and other people were packing up to go.

Chrissie's brothers couldn't believe how the water went on and on. Fidelma's man rolled up his cuffs and paddled. The children kicked big arcs of water and he splashed them back, getting dark marks on his trousers. What they couldn't get over was that this was still Galway. 'Where are we?' her brothers asked the man. 'You're in Galway,' he said. 'This is all Galway, you ninnies.' That night in bed Chrissie puzzled over this; could it be true they'd spent that brilliant afternoon in the same county as Daddy's boggy fields and ditches?

'Will we see a drowning forest?' Greg asked. 'Or dead people?'

'What? No, that fella was talking a load of nonsense. There'll be sand. For a sandcastle.'

'I'm going to find a starfish,' Greg said. 'I might find a second one and put them together in their own rock pool.'

'It's a perfect day for starfish.'

A sign for *An Trá* directed them to a car park with a smattering of vehicles. Once they got out, Chrissie knew it wasn't a perfect day for anything. It was windy, they had no bucket and spade, no food. Even with coats on, they'd barely last half an hour.

Climbing down the grassy slope from the tarmac, it became clear this was no sandy beach, just a shoreline of large boulders, debris. Chaotic-looking. She remembered something from last night's news about the winds causing damage to the prom. This was more of it.

Greg clambered over the rocks towards the waves. 'This is amazing.'

'What?'

'It's like the moon. We can build a moon castle.'

She found a large flat boulder, dried it off with tissues, sat and faced into the grey sea. Greg's face was bright and happy. Rucksack on his back, he looked like the explorer he imagined himself to be.

'Leave your bag here, Greg.'

'No, it's fine.'

She stood, took it off him and put it beside her own handbag. He shook his head and came over, closed his hand around the rucksack straps. Then he thought better of it and busied himself, selecting certain stones, rejecting others, bringing the chosen ones back to form a pile nearby.

Her phone rang; Brenda's number flashed up on the screen. She let it ring out; it rang back straight away. She switched it to silent. Now she had taken away her sister's chance to say whatever it was she was going to say; that was a start. She imagined Brenda looking out her bay window over the low wall at the dreary seascape. She wouldn't hear the satellite dish above her, loosening itself inch by inch, until one day it would pull away completely and crash down. Chrissie was sure this would happen. She was sure too, that she would call Brenda back at some stage, have it out with her. She had to get the words right in her head first.

Greg pressed something into her hand. A mermaid's purse.

'I'm getting decorations for the castle, Mum. You look too.'

She wasn't inclined to move off her rock but taking a quick look around her she spotted a pink clam-like shell wedged against her shoe. It reminded her of a child's ear. So delicate. How had it not been ground to pieces by the force of the waves?

She wrapped it in a bit of tissue to put in Greg's bag, a surprise for later. But something stuffed in his rucksack blocked her hand. She pulled out the TV remote control. Greg stood off a bit, watching her.

'I forgot I put it in,' he said. 'Because I didn't know we were leaving.'

'Why did you take this?'

'By mistake. I don't know why.'

'But it's not ours. '

'I wanted one.'

'You don't have a TV.'

'I wanted to have one in my bedroom.'

She spoke to Greg about stealing things. He must've sensed it was half-hearted so he listened without protest.

'Do we have to give it back?' he asked.

They might leave it at the hospital, she said, for Brenda to get later. Or post it to her. Greg went back to building his castle but the rocks were too smooth; the wall kept collapsing.

'It's never going to work,' he said. 'And there's no rock pools here.'

'Why don't we build a cairn? It's an old Irish thing.'

She described it as best she could remember from her schooldays. He set to the task immediately, combing the beach.

Once he was off she pointed the remote at the sea, clicking the on/off button. Her clicking fell into a rhythm that matched the waves. She increased the volume and listened harder to the breeze swirling around, the thud of the sea breaking on the shore. Then she copped herself on. Using the control, she gouged out a hollow in the stones, put the device in and covered it. Amen to that.

They worked away on the cairn, building up layer after layer. When Greg went down to the water to get some small stones for the top, her phone rang. Brenda again, probably noticed the bloody remote was gone. Well, her

Americans would just have to get up off their fat arses to change the channel. Big deal. The sun had grown stronger and Chrissie turned her face to it as she listened to her sister's message.

She passed. Where were you? We were in D.I.D. Electric when they rang. Daddy needed a new kettle. She passed at twenty-five past ten. By herself. Where are you?

Chrissie took a breath. *Where were you?* Where am I? *She passed.* All she could think of was a kidney stone. Passing through; a painful exit. She re-joined Greg at the cairn. He had collected a stash of seaweed and washed-out plastic scraps. They added these on as decoration.

She got her handbag, took out a tiny dancing horse.

Greg stared at her. 'I saw that in Aunty Brenda's. You stole her pony.'

'I was bringing it to the hospital to show Mammy.' She stood the horse on top of the stones, its glass hooves snatching at the air. 'That was Aunty Brenda ringing to say I was to keep it.'

'Glass is actually made from sand,' Greg said.

'That's right,' she said. 'Sooner or later this little horse will be sand again.'

'Mum, that will never happen,' he said, a high note of shock in his voice.

She knew this was the moment where she should say of course you're right, it will never happen. That's what he needed.

Although their stone cairn was well above the tideline, Chrissie knew it would be swept away later. The whole pile would be flattened by waves, their stones shifted up and down the shore. The remote control would float out a distance before sinking. It might get wedged in a barnacled crevice, a resting place until the next tide moved it on again. The glass horse, smashed into smaller and smaller pieces.

She reached into her bag and produced a frog. A banjo-playing frog. 'Look who's here, Greg. All set to chase the waves with our little dancing horse.'

Doon Cottage

Cashel, Connemara, September 2019

The signal disappeared at the start of the second week,
and with it pictures, muffled sounds of a world
getting on without us perfectly well, or descending
to hell in a handcart, depending on your politics.
The engineer shook his head, in sorrow more than
fat chance of a solution. Lightning strikes, fractured mast,
Paul Henry's mountains between us.

It left a window out onto sea and rock,
faint specks enlarged by binocular to blubber and fur,
big eyes rounded on us, adjusting focus, screen format,
as we performed an episode of their favourite serial.
Tiring of that, we took to the car, turned a bend,
passed a satellite dish moored in low-tide, pointed seawards,
tracking the flight of a red admiral who showed no sign
of turning back as it skirted crest after briny crest,
land receding, leaving behind a testcard of heather and broom.

Nessa O'Mahony

'Wasn't It Herself Told Me?'
Irish English Dialect in Galway
Stan Carey

In Eilís Dillon's novel *The Bitter Glass*, set in west County Galway during the Irish Civil War, there is a line of dialogue that is quietly extraordinary in showing some of the turns the English language has taken in Ireland: 'Wasn't it herself told me ye were coming today. . . '

Few Irish people would bat an eyelid at this—or pause to deconstruct it, such is the story's momentum. And it borders on cryptic for readers uninitiated in Irish English dialect; certainly its nuances and cadences are likely to be lost en route. So humour me while I marvel at some of its features.

1. *Herself* as an unbound reflexive pronoun—not bound to a *she* before it, as in standardised English. This use of *herself* is not just grammatically unusual: it connotes familiarity and respect, so it doesn't simply replace *she*, *her*, or *she herself*. In Ireland's historical shift from Irish to English, the fact that the rhythm of *sí féin* was preserved in *herself*, not in *she herself*, may have motivated its unbound use. (This kind of prosodic matching may also have led to the stereotyped *at all at all*, after the Irish *ar chor ar bith*.)

2. Clefting for topicalisation. When we say things like *It's inside they are*, instead of the more linear *They're inside*, we unconsciously extract an element, move it to the front after a dummy *it*, and put the rest in a subordinate clause. This highlights the element and gives the line a distinctive rhythm. Clefting is not unique to Irish English, but we are particularly fond of it.

3. *Ye* as second person plural. An array of *ye* and *youse* forms are so established in Irish English that we inflect and affix them in every imaginable

way: *yeers, yeez'd, youse'll, yehs've, yizzer*—all prompting red squiggles in my word processor till I put *smacht* on its dictionary. *Ye* is favoured in the west: 'Did ye practise yere piano pieces?' writes Galway native Mary Costello in her story 'You Fill Up My Senses'. Thanks to *ye* and friends, I don't feel deprived of American *y'all*, not to mention *yinz*.

4. Subject contact clause. The relative pronoun (*who* or *that*) that we expect before *told me* is dropped, strengthening the colloquial effect. This is an old pattern in English that persists in regional dialects, including some Irish English ones. 'There was a young doctor in the hospital asked me did I need a tranquilliser,' Mary Beckett writes in 'A Belfast Woman'. She also Irishly inverts the embedded question: *asked me did I need*, not *asked me if/whether I needed*.

We can repeat the omission, telescoping the syntax. Kevin Barry does this in *City of Bohane*: 'Was it Dick had the daughter married the fella of the Delaceys?' To some ears this will sound as Irish as it gets—but it occurs also in Australian, African American, and Canadian English varieties. Margaret Atwood has a character in 'Polarities' say, 'there's another boy wants it says he'll paint it himself'. Dialects converge and cross-pollinate; it's in their combined features that we discern their special flavour.

People do language much as finches fly or trees leaf: it's in our nature. Talking is an intimate expression of our identity as complex creatures with ideas, emotions, memories, and attachments. It reveals aspects not just of our personality but of places we've spent time in and people we've spent it with. (This is all true of sign languages too, but the focus here is on speech.)

Language, conventional wisdom tells us, is for communicating information. But it has many other functions. We use it to express emotion, entertain people (including ourselves), persuade people, show our individuality, negotiate social status, and maintain relations. A lot of this happens below our awareness—language has effects we can't always anticipate or control, setting off cascades of association in listeners' minds.

Language won't develop in a social vacuum. It emerges in a group and comes to signal our identity as part of that group. In childhood we learn to talk like those around us—family, carers, peers—but in a unique way: an idiolect. Families may have a familect. Zoom out and we find a dialect—the variety of language spoken by a community, generally defined geographically or socially. Dialect includes grammar, vocabulary, accent, and usage.

Picture a line across Ireland from Sligo through Leitrim and Cavan over to Louth. Below it, for most people, *scone* rhymes with *phone*; above it, with *gone*. Near the line, usage is more mixed. The line is an isogloss, like a weather-map isobar but showing where a linguistic feature stops or changes. There's one along the old Iron Curtain: in what was West Germany a pancake is a *Pfannkuchen*; east, it's an *Eierkuchen* ('egg cake'). A bundle of isoglosses together marks a rough dialect boundary, but it's seldom tidy. Dialects bleed into one another, complicated by geography, politics, and human interaction.

I grew up in Mayo with a Galway address. It was an early lesson in natural borders: my local post office was over the bridge. As an island Ireland has never been especially isolated, though, and many trademark features of our dialect show up in Scotland, England, Australia, Canada, America, and elsewhere. Some came from Irish before being exported; some we borrowed from Scots or regional or archaic English. 'Faith, and I'll send him packing,' Shakespeare wrote in *Henry IV, Part 1*, 'Myself, he and my sister' in *The Comedy of Errors*. Irish English is a complicated mosaic of influences, not all of them obvious.

For its size, Ireland has rich dialectal diversity. Listen to speakers from Dublin, Cavan, Donegal, Antrim, Mayo, Limerick, Waterford, and Westmeath and you'll hear a wealth of contrast; even neighbouring dialects, like Cork and Kerry, can diverge to the point of caricature. Some people say they can distinguish between accents from either end of a village or parish, Henry Higgins–style. Generalisation becomes necessary, but it can overshoot. In 2014, when YouGov asked British people what accents they found attractive, 'Southern Irish' topped the poll (followed by Received Pronunciation, Welsh, and Yorkshire). Ask anyone in Ireland what a 'Southern Irish' accent is, and they'll wonder which one—it seems hopelessly vague.

Geography offers a useful analogy. Different regions of Ireland have distinctive landscapes, yet it makes sense sometimes to refer to 'the Irish landscape': it has unifying traits. Similarly there is merit to the idea of Irish English as a dialect. Linguistically Ireland has many shared features, even more so when the Republic alone is in the frame. Any local dialect on the island will have properties that mark it as Irish English, though their frequency and proportion will vary from one place or speaker to the next.

So it is with Galway. Its dialects are close in many ways to those spoken anywhere west of the Shannon, where Irish lingered longer and had more effect on the English that largely, and violently, supplanted it. But the county's size and topographical range mean there are considerable differences in local speech as we travel from the towns and farmlands of the east—virtually the midlands—through the city and westward to Connemara and the islands, where in many households Irish prevails.

Contact between languages is a driving force in language change. From the early 17th century 'many Irish speakers began to communicate with English speakers by grafting English words and structures onto the stem of their Celtic language', Loreto Todd writes in *Green English*. In this way there emerged 'a form of English that reflected Irish influence at every linguistic level'—sound, syntax, rhythm, idiom, vocabulary. Galway's Gaeltacht and distance from Dublin and Ulster meant that influence was relatively strong here.

Irish is the source, for example, of our subordinating *and*: 'He was in a wild state yesterday and he leaving the house' (Jennifer Johnston, *Shadows on Our Skin*); 'How would I hear it and I down in the calefactory room taking the stems off berries?' (Brian Moore, *Catholics*). It's a simple, subtle thing, nonstandard but perfectly ordinary to an Irish English speaker, part of what lends the dialect 'the novelty and vigor of the hybrid', in Séamas Moylan's phrase.

Another structure bestowed by Irish is the after-perfect, so named because it uses *after* to form the perfect tense, usually in reporting something recent and of high informational value—hence its other name, the hot news perfect. Since Irish lacks a verb for *have*, a literal translation of the perfect tense ('I have eaten') was not possible, so we transposed Irish phrases like *tar éis* and *i ndiaidh* and ended up with 'I'm after eating'. P.W. Joyce, in *English As We Speak It In Ireland*, said the after-perfect is 'universal in Ireland, even among the higher and educated classes', but that English people would not understand it.

Modern research confirms its ambiguity. One study asked native Irish English and British English speakers the meaning of the line *I'm after getting a cup of tea*. Nearly all the Irish understood it as 'just got a cup'; most of the British interpreted it as a wish for tea. Centuries ago, curiously, the after-perfect generally applied to future events: *will be after going* meant *will go*. That the shift to past reference matched similar change in Irish underscores the two languages' close interaction.

What we did with habitual aspect is equally striking. The distinction between *tá mé* 'I am' and *bíonn mé* 'I (habitually) am' was so integral to native expression that our ancestors remoulded English multiple times to retain it, perhaps helped by convergence with Scots and English dialects. There is *do be* ('The people do be full of stories of all the cures she did' —Lady Gregory, *Visions and Beliefs in the West of Ireland*), *do* by itself ('I'm not so old as you do hear them say' —J.M. Synge, *The Well of the Saints*), *-s* on a verb in first person ('I gets tired'), and the northern *be's* ('But sure plenty dogs be's that way' — Robert Bernen, 'Brock'). *Do be* and *be's* are quintessentially Irish, but you'll also hear them in Newfoundland, an imprint of emigration.

The Irish relationship with time shows a certain contrary pliability: saying you'll be ready in five minutes is like a tease for philosophers. This warp has entered our idiom. When we say someone *is here with years*, we forgo *has been* to create a hyper-extended present tense (alongside nonstandard *with*, from Irish *le*). *Never*, meanwhile, can have radically short time reference: *She never rang yesterday evening.* This line, used in Raymond Hickey's *Survey of Irish English Usage*, was accepted most (91%) in Galway.

Grammatically we do many things differently for assorted linguistic and historical reasons. We can use *them* as a demonstrative pronoun (*He loves them trees*), drop *to* after verbs that normally mandate it (*I used allow them stay*), and make generous use of the definite article: *She likes the maths. We do have the chats.* We can metathesize *modern* into *modren*, and we'd be fierce fond of the conditional, by which I mean we are.

Thanks to Irish, we do quare things with prepositions: *Is it yourself that's in it? That dog has the garden destroyed on me.* We have something called the statal or resultative perfect, a widespread but little-noticed feature: *You've it ruined* in place of *You've ruined it.* This can be useful semantically: Hickey notes that *Have you read* Ulysses? means 'Have you ever read *Ulysses*?', while *Have you* Ulysses *read?* means 'Have you finished reading *Ulysses*?'

Irish manifests in Irish English more obviously in the form of words adopted for their particular meaning, sound, style, or connotations: *acushla, amadán, asthore, bannock, blather, boreen, boxty, céilí, colleen, cruiskeen, culchie, currach, dudeen, fooster, glug, gob, gom, grig, kreel, mallafooster, mavourneen, meas, pishogue, plámás, praties, pus, skelp, sleeveen, smacht, spalpeen.* Other loanwords have archaic English or Germanic origins, such as *crack, hames, yoke,* and *delph,* from the name of a Dutch town.

The suffix *-een*, from Irish *-ín*, is highly productive and has been smuggled into standardised English through the likes of *poteen, shebeen,* and *smithereens.*

The few Gaelic loanwords to join it there tend to have their spelling codified: *banshee, brogue, clan, drumlin, galore, shamrock, tory, twig* ('understand, realise'), sometimes with small variation: *whiskey/whisky*. For other words, the options can be prodigious: the sceptical interjection *mar dhea* has been anglicised as *moryah, maryeah, mara-ya, mauryah, maureeyah, moya, muryaa*, etc.

Irish expressions that were habitual among older, agricultural generations can lose favour among the city-based youth, dropped with the customs and contexts that carried them. Some regret the gradual swing from rural idiom with its deep Irish symbiosis towards a more homogeneous, supraregional variety. But people may lose their ancestral tongue 'yet cling to its patterning for centuries', Loreto Todd has written. The channel stays open in both directions, allowing for translingual mixing like the marvellous word *ráiméising*—found in both literature (Lisa McInerney's *The Blood Miracles*, for one) and Dáil debates.

One person's regionalism or colloquialism is another's slang, whose vexed taxonomy reflects its slippery status. When I was in secondary school in north County Galway, *brown* meant angry, *gomey* was uncool, and to *wheel* someone was to wind them up: *I'm only wheelin' ya*. Slang is occasionally annexed by the mainstream, but most holds its aura of impropriety or faddishness.

Slang can fade, linger, or mutate. *Sound*, a common adjective in Irish English (*She's sound out*), gained the sense *thanks*: the Róisín Dubh pub had a sign saying 'No shifting at the bar please—sound :)'. They must've had mouldy buffs with a rake of pints on them atin' the face offa beoirs. Hup ya savage! That word *beoir* (*beure, buor*, etc.) is unusual in coming from Shelta, Travellers' argot.

Irish English abounds in these signature terms in every grammatical category. Take its adjectives, many of which convey broken, drunken, exhausted, or other subpar states: *arseways, banjaxed, bockety, buckled, bullin', fluthered, killed, knackered, ossified, plastered, polluted, thick, twisted, wrecked. Class, grand,* and *mighty* buck the trend, while *pure* and *fierce* can intensify anything, producing such improbable combinations as *fierce gentle* and *pure filth*.

Idioms are often counterintuitive, especially when they hinge on irony. If you tell me *Would you stop, go away outta that!*, I'll do neither. Much depends on context and shared understanding, and a phrase can flip from warm to withering with the slightest inflection: *I will, yeah* is seldom to be taken at face value. *Sham*, in the west, is not the negative word it is elsewhere but a friendly term of address.

Another such term, *horse*, is for people known well, *horsebox* doubly so. If you know someone genealogically, you *know the seed and breed of them*. These and other phrases, like *Shtall the digger* and *How's she cuttin'?*—a welcome revision of *How're they hangin'?*—are echoes of farming in our vernacular.

Saying goodbye, *Good luck* can be smushed to *G'luck* for casual effect. The same economisation turns *young fellas* into *youngflas*—that you might see sparching (dossing at the Spanish Arch), keeping sketch for the shades if they've smoke on them (watching for the guards if they're carrying marijuana). Not that efficiency is the main driver of Irish speech: Why say *Listen* when you can say *C'mere till I tell ya*, or *No* when you can say *Musha indeed now and I am not*.

Musha (from Irish *muise*), like its cousins *wisha, arrah, erra,* and *yerra*, and some special uses of *now, so, sure, then,* and *well,* are what linguists call pragmatic or discourse markers (or even discourse-pragmatic markers). These words, which show great geographical variety, help us manage and frame our conversations. Sometimes only a *Sure lookit* or an *Arrah now* will do, with their lifetimes of accumulated implication.

Dialects delight me so much that I'm taken aback when they incur scorn, which they routinely do, being a convenient proxy for racism, classism, xenophobia, and other prejudices. The shame can be internalised. Centuries after Jonathan Swift sneered at the 'odious sounds' of people around Galway, children in one village school in the west who wrote *do be* or *I done it* had the offending text cut from their copybooks with a scissors and were made to bury it outside in a hole in the ground. Digital technologies with their normative algorithms— voice assistants stumped by local accents, interfaces that reject diacritics like the *síneadh fada*—fuel the myth that nonstandard dialects are substandard or unworthy.

Usage snobs believe standardised English to be the most correct and logical dialect (though they don't tend to even see it as a dialect). This kind of *seafóid* (nonsense) stems from linguistic ignorance and unexamined ideology. Dialects differ in their global utility, but none is ultimately more logical or valid than any other: each serves its users' needs. The prestige of standardised English comes not from linguistic virtue but from historical happenstance and the power concentrated by the rise of print, wealth, and imperialism.

Amn't is a fun counterexample. Because it's more logical than *aren't*—amn't I right?—children often produce it naturally till they're taught otherwise. For an Irish person the difference between *amn't* and *aren't*, trivial on the face of it, can conjure a legacy of stigma and alienation. Eavan Boland, in 'An Irish Childhood in England: 1951', wrote of leaving her homeland at six years old,

> when all of England to an Irish child
> was nothing more than what you'd lost and how:
> was the teacher in the London convent who,
> when I produced 'I amn't' in the classroom
> turned and said—'You're not in Ireland now.'

Accents are the most conspicuous part of a dialect, and how we perceive them can be highly subjective. The Galway accent is 'a posh Mayo one' according to someone I know; it's the other way around according to another. Niall Tóibín considered it 'the nicest and softest' accent in Ireland. Accents differ especially in their vowels, and Irish English vowels draw heavily on Irish Gaelic ones. And we don't just alter them: we can add them to words like *girl* and *film* and remove them from words like *poem* and *general*.

In some cases it's a throwback. Pronouncing *-ea-* as *-ae-* (as in 'too clane to be dacent', in Alice Taylor's *Quench the Lamp*) is a Middle English practice conserved in some Irish English dialects. This pronunciation, preserved in names like Yeats and Keane (in the west but not the south), was once mainstream but now marks regional speech or is used to affect a rustic manner.

This is something we commonly do, code-switching for effect: *old one* becomes 'oul wan', *kettle* 'kittle', *poisoned* 'pizened'. We say there's *atin' and dhrinkin'* in Guinness because *eating and drinking* is too prim for the role we're performing. A Galway friend tells me *I seent it* ('I saw it') is used by youngflas aping older generations to take the piss or 'exaggerate how Galway they are'. All speakers of Irish English, Raymond Hickey observes, 'know what features can be donned to impart a popular touch'.

Come Sahurday you'd right to head wesht, take a gandher at the Bens where you've not been with yonks. Let you round up the feens and d'care but ye'd have mighty divilment with a gang in it and a hape o' hang sangwiches—you made a hames of the last plan and they givin' out yards since. If the weather is cat sure what harm, gallivanting up them hills you'd be like Lord Muck.

Robert Lloyd Praeger, in *The Way That I Went*, describes the rural west as a magic region 'to which one's errant thoughts recurrently stray, and which remains a lodestar to people of many lands'. This grows truer with each year's passing and its influx of people and languages. But still every field and hill has an old name that fastens the land to our mental maps, though the names can wither with time or translation: 'Irish placenames,' wrote Tim Robinson, 'dry out when anglicized, like twigs snapped off from a tree.' The roots, to endure, need tending.

Galway city, bustling hub and passageway, continues to be a vital conduit between west and east and a centre of gravity for stories and histories from settlers and visitors from all directions. Galway's dialects, like Irish Englishes generally, are vigorous, mutable, and many-sided. They will no more stay still than the salmon leaping up Aasleagh Falls or the Corrib rushing under Wolfe Tone Bridge.

Dóthain

Ní theastaíonn uaimse
ach mo dhóthain
mar lón,
don chodladh suaimhneach,
greim ar bord
agus deoch le n-ól
is gan deoir anuas
sa ngeimhreadh

    ach

cén chaoi gur eol
do dhuine a dhóthain?
Nó an ionann dóthain
is fuílleach?
Nó ar mhair aon neach
ar an domhan seo fós
a d'aithin a dhóthain
go díreach?

Joe Steve Ó Neachtain (1942-2020)

Ba mhór an feall litríocht na Gaillimhe a cheiliúradh gan an ghlúin a fheacadh do Joe Steve Ó Neachtain. Táimid buíoch dá fhoilsitheoir Micheál Ó Conghaile as cead a thabhairt dúinn an dán seo leis a chur i gcló (as *An Dé Deiridh*, Cló Iar-Chonnacht, 2008) agus do David Wheatley as é a aistriú.

Fill

All I expect
is my fill
to sustain me,
for a sound night's sleep,
a table in reach,
drink on tap
and no leaking drop
in the winter

    but

how is a body
to know its limit?
Are enough and
plenty the same thing?
Or has anyone yet
lived watching
the glass fill who
knew to say 'when'?

David Wheatley a d'aistrigh

It would be impossible to celebrate Galway's literature without honouring Joe Steve Ó Neachtain. The editors are grateful to his publisher Micheál Ó Conghaile for permitting us to reproduce this poem (from *An Dé Deiridh*, Cló Iar-Chonnacht, 2008) and to David Wheatley for his translation.

I want to become a punk at 40

Béibhinn says she is the lone punk of Gort town. Looking at her,
I want to draw thick black lines under my eyes and layer mascara on my lashes.
I want to attack a packet of safety pins and make piercings about my body.
I want to splurge on platform high-laced boots, a leather jacket with spikes,
belts, a choker, and I want fucking chains.

I want to stick The Clash in my ears, hop on the 2.40 to Gort,
stride up Bridge Street, knock fists with Béibhinn's friend Mike,
that skinhead, and tip on up to find our tribe.

On the train, myself and Béibinn will redefine radical thinking.
At Ceannt Station, we will scrawl our best words in purple lipstick on toilet walls.
I will scream radical thoughts at the top of my lungs on a soapbox on Shop Street.
The blood of my home piercings will get infected and I won't care.

The Valium is ineffectual.

I will be a punk and pretty, oh so pretty.

Joanne McCarthy

The Billionaire Kevin Carty Photographed With Fifty-Nine Of His Sixty Dressage Warhorses

Andrew Meehan

The billionaire Kevin Carty, with any amount of cars and drivers at his beck and call, is having himself flown into Knock. A convoy then of horse-boxes to Glenamaddy where, in the Cartys' back field, the animals will be photographed in their finery.

(Which has to be among his more romantic ideas).

And nice on occasion, in the midst of a journey homeward, to treat yourself. A bit of hush for flossing the gums, talcing the feet.

The billionaire Kevin Carty slips out of his new shoes; their name being somewhat beyond him. As soon as he's on the phone to ask what they're called—'loafers and/or moccasins'—the second in command stalks out of the cockpit. The new pilot goes stone mad whenever anyone takes calls. But it's not the new pilot's plane, he doesn't own it, he didn't buy it. It's the billionaire Kevin Carty's plane.

A Cessna Citation, his shapely golden teardrop. If he'd any sense he'd have bought two. Nor has he the ankles for loafers and/or moccasins but who's going to tell him no?

A few handy words are exchanged and as he stows away his phone, the billionaire Kevin Carty falls quickly into indignation and into shame. The ice is melting in his Bacardi and undoubtedly he is alive to any humiliation going. There is now every chance of the shakes, the same twitching he gets in dreams. In a horse they'd call it trembling—you have to squint to catch it, a reflex to call upon all your awe. For how can something like a sculpture be all feeling? But it would seem so, Kevin. The shadows they cast make him think of twirling ribbons. And how often does he have access to that kind of language?

He only buys horses because his wife loves them. And whatever she loves he hates.

When they met she liked to remark that he made odd demands of a masseuse. But how was she to know that Japanese women rubbing softened butter into his back was just something the then multimillionaire Kevin Carty enjoyed?

—*Buerre de Normandie*, he said. The best. The salt exfoliates and the butter nourishes.

He put it all down to her habit of appearing just when he was about to total himself off his roof-terrace and consequently the rest came sweetly. She became established in his brain with outré forms of meditation. Beyond explaining the meaning of *enjo-kōsai* his horizons expanded in nightclubs where ozoney drinks came in frozen bottles. For her he ate fish that would electrocute you before sending you for a lovely night's sleep. Morale hit a record high. Then there was the other thing: gimmicky sex, contortions that would have astounded The Ross Sisters themselves.

One morning he tipped her with a cheque for ten thousand pounds, following this with an unintentionally mean-mouthed kiss on the hand (the happiest moment of his life, perhaps its only happy moment), following this with many dauntingly-spiced Bloody Marys, following this with lunch itself: an entire rigor-mortised pike and a menacing amount of well-done beef accompanied by wines that, like everything else he drank, were sound-tracked by his appreciative snorts. She looked grateful when it was all over; which was the very moment the billionaire Kevin Carty, in an awful panic, asked Jitsuko Tanaka to marry him.

This morning was bad, for him and for her. Last night was bad. And yesterday morning was bad.

He could have had breakfast sent up, but likes to get a good look at the comings and goings in the lobby. Customs, and him the customs officer.

The maître d'—the absolute worst cunt going—danced them to a table in the conservatory. Usually the billionaire Kevin Carty has no issue with making his needs clear; instead he sat facing away from the view, hanging baskets and all. Over a green milkshake he told them all how he had once been offered the opportunity to buy a share (a few floors anyhow) in this hotel, which at the time was sore in need of something drastic to happen to it. How, when others had rolled over in front of the trucks during the recession, he'd gone into overdrive. And does he bring any of that bank-talk into the house? It was the maître d's fault he was talking about it now.

He pointed to his preferred table by the fire. The maître d' was pious on the billionaire Kevin Carty's behalf. Come back tomorrow and you will be looked after. That's what was said and that's what was heard.

An old Arab lady was sitting at the table the billionaire Kevin Carty knew was his. The woman and her granddaughter were horsing into cheese omelettes and one waitress was making a show of fetching hot chocolate and all that for the little girl. There was a balloon tied to the cruet set. A balloon. Didn't the maître d' gallop about the place lighting candles and setting tables? And didn't the billionaire Kevin Carty suggest that he was happy to wait until the Arabs were finished? If they could bring him a nice cup of hot coffee, he would stay where he was and wait. And did it make a blind bit of difference? Another hot chocolate was offered—the first one hadn't been touched—and the old woman asked then that the milk be warmed a small bit more. The billionaire Kevin Carty hated and loved this person—so relaxed that she could have gone soundly to sleep at her stolen table. When they were finished she took her time undoing the balloon and another minute or two to tie it to her granddaughter's finger. The balloon collided with his head as they passed.

Ten horse trucks lined up in the car park. With them comes the suggestion that the Aga Khan himself is having the tea at Knock Airport. Or perhaps it is something else better than the Aga Khan, and more religious.

With all this talk of horses, the billionaire Kevin Carty has almost forgotten about the hares. He's counting on seeing them in the back field, tearing up to you as if for a dare, settling in then for the country chronicle. Litanies on the seasons, the slow seasons, the being alone, quite alone, and, yes, happenings in the sky, and disturbances in the ground.

The plan nevertheless is to motor broadly south-east through the county. There's a car to meet them, a child could suckle on the upholstery. But if the billionaire Kevin Carty had been home lately, he'd have known a Bentley would be too much for the road. The car almost finds a ditch and doesn't he hate the certainties of ditches?

He hates the fields too, the bales, the sheds, their roofs, the gates, the ruins, and the way the new houses spite the old. He's a wild hatred for school still, the uniforms, girls and boys in colours of dried blood and skidmark. And as much as he hates the variegated badnesses in the frocked clergy, their specific and tender savagery, he sees that in himself and hates it all the more.

The billionaire Kevin Carty ducks every time the car passes under a dishevelled tree. From nightmares the overhanging branches are grabbing at him. Through the window he gulps rusty air; it travels, he feels it and sits straighter at the thought of his horsey playthings, all knowing, wary and delicate and, it only occurs to him now, most certainly ill-equipped for the bogs of north Galway.

Quick to run out of words to describe the land, the distinguishing features are no more comprehensible than bruise or tumour.

—The fields, according to the billionaire Kevin Carty's wife, have the look of being darned.

To her questions he says childhood was to do with nothing other than discomfort. And coal.

He sees himself but not very well, the small bones leaping under his skin. The pain of being poor as strong as sciatica. On he goes about his sister then, meaning within meaning, like a love-letter. She nearly died of polio, then nearly died from a dedicated diet of frankfurters and supermarket rum. Neither got her in the end. Wits about her long enough to tell the doctors to go fuck themselves, displaying the same attitude to sickness as she had to health: belligerent indifference followed by belligerent supplication.

His mind empties—flights, Cessnas, wives, butter—and before the driver can come to a halt, the billionaire Kevin Carty springs out in a cloud of talc and it's coming, it's there, only he, a crow with a belly full of rat poison, can feel it.

—The cunt, he says. The colossal cunt.

It's not right that the billionaire Kevin Carty's wife should see him like this, it's not right that she should go through any of that.

—Perhaps she's knocking it down to rebuild?

—It's just the kind of thing she would do, start demolishing a fucking house without a word to anyone.

—She's piling up all the bricks.

—Likes to do things by hand.

—Weathered bricks, she says.

—Pretty penny.

*

The photographer is dressed like a hobo. And doesn't appear to have much in the way of enthusiasm about the light.

—The light is a bit milky, he says.

Sure, who can work with milky light?

There are any number of cameras available to him, but it's more in the photographer's line to be putting on ChapStick. And he's not long in asking for a go in the Bentley.

A warning mist hangs at ankle level.

And an important, story-time feeling is starting in on the billionaire Kevin Carty. He imagines hares, he imagines them coming into the hotel in the morning, all the way into the penthouse, and up on to the quilt with them for a chinwag. His head is working evilly, for truly over that wall is the hollow part of him, the ambitious part of him, and the persistence of the breeze carries with it the plain facts and watery truths of the years. And the worried infant within scurries. The indeterminate smell of shit could be his own.

There is very little the billionaire Kevin Carty remembers of his sister; arty type and law unto herself, sitting down to a dinner at two in the morning. Is that her shape now in the mirroring on the field's surface, the water visible in small tides of dark blue and darker grey?

He is as well writing a cheque and having the whole place tarmacked. No good way of expressing any of it except to say, —Let's do the photograph down there.

—In that field? says the photographer.

—That field, yes.

—It's a swamp.

—Where are you from? That's a bog.

He turns on his loafers and/or moccasins. When he reaches the Bentley, the billionaire Kevin Carty's sister is there sizing it up. Bellied like a starving Biafran. The stitched cranium and the handy big hole in the throat. And she must have treated herself to some new tools ('for my art!'), specifically the hammer she is holding. At least it's not a shotgun.

—What's that for?

—I've been hanging pictures.

There is nothing in her chalky mouth and pterodactyl skin to make him believe she has become any more knowledgeable about interior decoration.

—Would you mind putting that away? It's making me nervous.

—What's with the horses?

—What's with bulldozing half the house? Saving on the hoovering?

Hardly one of your modern women, she says, —Hoover's broken, will you buy me a new one?

—Go on, how much is a new hoover?

—A hundred euro.

—I'll buy you one

—Hundred euro.

—I'll have one sent on, a Dyson.

—Rather have the money.

The billionaire Kevin Carty can hear the words and, even though she wouldn't have the strength to swat a fly, he can feel their force as they are flung back at him.

A movement in the head takes him over the back wall and into the path of the hares—and if you go along the hare way of looking at things, fucking anything is possible, do you see what I'm saying, Kevin, anything. Depends on what you mean by anything. Horses! Whistling as they walk, the taunt of the behind calling to mind the cheerfulness of a dirty dream. And who here is to say you can't ride a horse, as in ride the hole off one? Oh, the billionaire Kevin Carty is right up to date with himself now. He's looking to talk to hares, he's imagining reefing it into poor defenceless animals.

—It's good see you travelling light.

—We're just taking a few photographs.

—It's we, is it? And where are we going to be doing that?

—Not by the house, obviously. It won't take long.

—It'll take no time at all because it doesn't suit. My, what's the word, my itinerary is full.

—Nobody's asking you to do anything. You're not going to be in any photographs. It's just me and the horses.

—Racehorses?

—Wait 'til you see them, they hardly move.

—What do they do then?

—Do you ever listen to the harp? Watching dressage is like listening to the harp. But tiring if you're the one doing it.

What's left of the Carty house has the sure aura of a CND poster, wet wool. Vapours that would put you in the ground. The billionaire Kevin Carty goes to wash his hands, and what greets him—dusk shapes—is so insistent and, in the way that it seems to be happening to someone else, may as well be news. In all good conscience, it is the powders of Mother's Day and by that he means 4711 and the sentiments of talc.

A cornflake box on the kitchen embers. The floors are bare, but something in the walls he takes to—for he recognises its shade, the mellow notes of curry out of a jar. But it'll be easier to get by without commentary. The billionaire Kevin Carty's sister is delving into drawers and coming up with condiments unforeseen. And this is more than he has counted on for the occasion.

Pawing through a cut loaf, she says, —I suppose you want something other than bread.

The voice is hers but with the offer of hospitality it is not easily recognisable. It's just that she is normally wary around guests, the whole family are.

There'll be no eggs and bacon, but she comes up with apple sauce to go with cheese on toast. For after, they turn to the ceremony of choc ices defrosted on the mantelpiece.

—What shall we talk about now? she says, I don't have much more to say about horses.

—I'll speak.

—I don't like the sound of this now. I'm belting around getting this place sorted out. And it's not even a question of asking your opinion. Your opinion doesn't fucking come into it. You're the one with the dancing horses.

—There's something I want to say.

—Go on.

His voice cracks as he says, —Will you come and stay with us?

The request seems to leave the billionaire Kevin Carty's sister faint. For a finish it looks like she is about to slide under the table.

—I'm waiting for the punch-line.

—I want to you to come to my house. I've been to yours.

At first he is vague but when he has finished his ice cream, the billionaire Kevin Carty becomes brave. He suggests dates. He should stop there but he carries on, asking all the questions in the world about buses and trains and, as all this is being said, his sister doesn't shift position once but freezes where she is, her face shining in surprise or doubt—for it's a given that she will not leave here unless she has to.

The photographer has set up spotlights. And in the glare the billionaire Kevin Carty's wife is presiding over an animal riot. Exit stage left the last remaining sparrows of Glenamaddy. Hares the size of horses are boxing unmistakably, the horses themselves with breath universally held. Some, as they are being led from the trucks, are trying to back up the ramps.

There's a certain pleasure to be had in smoochy talk, but no amount of it will soothe them. For they won't be wrangled, they won't be roped. The brave soul that has reached the field is lathered and winded, anxiety pouring out and into the ground where it will stay.

All the billionaire Kevin Carty can think of is getting the photograph done and being a bit quick about it. He can't imagine the consequences if they don't, for now the photographer—who deserves everything he gets—gets laid out by a Holsteiner that's normally as timid as a toy. Now it's caught in the ground, blasting around like a spastic. It could be having a fit. The front end is wheeling, the back leg bending into all the way into a bow before snapping handily as a wishbone.

Imagine it: a poor horse folding itself up in apology, death its only thought.

And the billionaire Kevin Carty is thinking, are we safe here, am I safe here? This is all very moody and introspective, until from the wheeling horse he gets an awful crack in the chest. The sweat is out through him, he can see his own collarbone. No one knows what to do, the sissy photographer doesn't know what to do, the billionaire Kevin Carty's wife doesn't know what to do. She inclines her face. It sounds like she's asking him where he wants to have breakfast, whereupon a fair amount of the sensation flows out of him entirely. There are convulsions now. What else would you call them? A hare, one of the elders, runs up to him, and the billionaire Kevin Carty knows why and there are mixed feelings, but truly he is grateful and then there is an awful spacing out.

The maître d' is waking him for breakfast and after being the first to arrive in the dining room he's eating all his cereal and licking the bowl. A hare, up on his hind legs, is having a healthy green milkshake for himself. But the billionaire Kevin Carty is at this moment answerable to no one. The maître d' is asking who in this room has ever mastered Mandarin, who has filed patents for renewable energy? When others are cutting it out altogether, the billionaire Kevin Carty has stepped up his charitable work and the Happy Heart Fund and Irish Modernist Association don't know how lucky they are, he might have to row back a small bit on all the munificence, which will give them all a belt. But what is in it for him? He knows what is in for them, but what is in it for him? With granddaughter in tow, the old lady appears to pay her respects. There's a balloon for you, Kevin. And soon they are all marvelling at the homework he does before meetings, how he knows his way better than anyone around the like of forfeiture notices and covenant breaches. It's the younger ones, the sarky pricks in cheap suits, who come in unprepared. But he'll go through them all like a locomotive. He'll grind them into feed for the animals. He'll listen to the screams and move on. For the billionaire Kevin Carty isn't going to be talked down to by anyone and that is the end of the story.

Exposure Therapy

Cloud Café Guy
IT Building
NUI Galway

My Love,

Frankly, I'm insulted.

So I think what's brought me to writing this letter, more than anything, is how you keep letting me down even in my most vulnerable states. On those foggy Galway mornings when I've realigned my spine after a short night on a friend's couch, I arrive at your counter, hungover and bleary-eyed. And what do you have to offer me? Half-shot coffees and pre-made sandwiches that always, *always* have tomatoes in them. I hate tomatoes. You *know* I hate tomatoes. I have to pull each one out like a salivating vegetable tongue, and you never seem to care. I shouldn't have to be pulling out tomatoes, drunk or sober. And you, though it pains me to say it, have become a tomato in my soul.

You've never asked my name, nor my course, not even commented on the weather. In fairness, I don't know your course either, but it's not for want of trying. If you'll direct your attention to my suggestion card, as you hopefully already have, nametags would really make the Instagram research a lot swifter. It's sad really that someone could be so oblivious, that the best thing in their life is strutting by twice daily, bundled in jumpers with laptops and handbags swinging off her, throwing back lattés like they're going out of fashion. It's like every time I order, you forget who I am. I'm not just that awkward pack mule with a brown coat and a wonky ponytail. I'm a vanilla latté and occasional mocha.

Am I addicted to the caffeine or the rush of adrenaline? You used to keep me up all night. What's *happened* to us? It's like it's become a job to you and the steaminess has run out. We went from *grande* to just *grand*. It's not as if there's nothing to talk about either. I even go to the trouble of bringing a reusable travel mug—bamboo—sexy, right? But do you say a word about it? No. You just look at me indifferent and drone, 'That's €2.50, please.' But that's not what I need to hear from you. Our relationship costs me. Don't think for a second that it doesn't. I've examined the figures and had it not been for you, I would have saved up the price of a George Clooney Nespresso dispenser months ago. What Else™ can I do to make this work?

It's turned toxic. I'm afraid to trouble you, I accept whatever you give me—full fat milk being on one occasion. (For the record, my lactose-intolerant stomach has been disapproving of you since the beginning.)

I've heard you've been serving other customers. And, yeah, I think that's pretty low. So I've started seeing other baristas. There's a ride in Starbucks who's always trying to find out my name. I'm still playing it coy, and have yet to tell him, the flirt.

Yours,

Vanilla Latté/Occasional Mocha

Katie O'Sullivan

The Trees, They Do Be Tall

Would you mind, just, you know…

Oh sorry, a ghrá,
I never rea-li-sed,
twisting the fingers off o' you, I was,

you shoulda said…
you do love the dancin'
… you're deadly, do you know that?

I'm deadly alright.
… do you not mind dancin'
with a woman a head taller than you?

No bother in the world
getting to the top o' a tall tree, darlin',
when you do lay it on the flat of its back.

Do you know, now, they're that tight,
I'll never manage to get them trousers
off o' me on my own tonight

… without the bit o' help?
You'll have to come home with me, do!

Or you'll let me stay,
go on, say I can stay.

Won't I only hug you and hold you
and kiss you and love you
the entire long night?

Wouldn't it be a lovely sight,
all the same,
the pair of us,

scrambling about,
looking for your shoes
under the springs o' my bed?

Aideen Henry

Balm for the Halfpenny Place

Alan McMonagle

I have been living in an amusement park for four maybe five weeks now. I eat here. I sleep here. I even manage to pick up some work upon accidentally striking up conversation with the owner while idling on the roadside wall one particularly balmy evening. Every morning I cross the road and take a dip in the sea. Sip coffee at the promenade kiosk. When I'm especially hungry I nab some coins from the daily takings and nip up to Strawberry Fields for a Hero. I seldom know the time of day, the day of the week, what is happening either side of the bay-view in front of me. I have everything and nothing. I should be the happiest twenty-one-year-old alive.

I get along with the owner of the amusement park, my boss. He's an out-of-towner who shows up every summer and opens up the hurdy-gurdies, the giant slide, the merry-go-rounds, the win-a-prize stalls and donkey derby. There's a shooting gallery, too, for fans of pellet guns, and this is where I sleep. I work as security. The nightshift. I begin at ten o'clock and last until I start to nod off. My boss doesn't know I am living on campus. Evenings, he turns up a little after nine, spends an hour or so gathering his daily takings into a number of large coin buckets, which he has me leave locked inside the Nut Hut. He's very impressed I am never late for work.

At night I patrol the grounds. For the first hour or so I watch people walk the prom. End-of-day strollers, busy bees out to cram in a bit of healthy living, by-themselves types with dogs on leads, the occasional photographer in search of a heartbreaking sundown. After dark I see giddy youngsters of my own age on their way to the clubs. Several hours later I see them again, staggering home. After that it's nearly always quiet. Upon completion of my patrol, I let myself into the Nut Hut, plunge my hand into one of the coin buckets and pocket a fistful. Then I make for the shooting gallery, and the mattress-bed liberated from a conveniently located skip.

Sometimes I sit up all night and read. Sometimes my friend Freeney turns up and tries his luck with the pellet gun. Sometimes it rains and sometimes the wind blows in off the sea and sometimes the night sky is a disarray of stars. Sometimes O'Mara—retired policeman, amateur mystic and self-anointed guardian angel—swings by in his car and we go for a slow drive along the coast road. Four maybe five miles out, he stops the car at a random verge, cuts the engine and stares into the darkness. At some point he leans forward, grips the steering wheel and shakes his head. 'The halfpenny place,' he says. 'We need to look out for people in the halfpenny place.' Then he restarts the engine, and we turn around and drive slowly back. So far I haven't asked him if there is anyone in particular he is looking out for and he hasn't felt the urge to enlighten me. We seldom say much to each other beyond hello and goodnight.

Sometimes I don't feel like patrolling the grounds or sitting by myself within the drab confines of the shooting gallery. Instead I go to a nightclub. Within spitting distance I am spoilt for choice. There is Rumours, which attracts all the teenagers. There is CJ's, which the locals seem to go for. The Oasis lures an eclectic assortment of holidaymakers, the newly employed, headbangers, and students who have stuck around for the summer—most likely because they have flunked exams and need to sit repeats. Beside the Oasis stands the Warwick, and this is where the interesting people stray towards. It is also where the best music is played. Friday nights, in particular. So to the Warwick is where I go.

The other Friday the songs were especially good. The DJ played 'Planet Claire' by the B52s. 'Fisherman's Blues' by The Waterboys. 'Boys Don't Cry' by The Cure. Until the death I was slinging it good-oh on the dance floor. The DJ finished with 'My Baby Just Cares For Me' by Nina Simone. On each of the several occasions I have been to the Warwick he's finished with this song. Every time, the tune's jaunty piano intro simultaneously picks me up and drops me down. Up because of its fun and reassuring melody. Down because it is the last song and end-of-night beckons.

I owe money everywhere. I owe my landlord three months rent on the place I have without notice vacated. I owe my former housemates for a variety of small loans doled out unflinchingly to me at crucial junctures over the past eighteen months. Some they have written off, on account of my exhausting unreliability. Some they seem to have forgotten about, and I haven't been bothered reminding them. I owe an ex-girlfriend. I have unpaid bills. I owe the owner of the corner shop I haven't dared step inside since legging it from the house I was co-renting. I have a credit union loan I have been reneging on. I have a middling-to-decent size gambling debt after an all-night card game I should never have gotten involved in. (I wouldn't bluff my way past a dummy in a shop window.)

'You need to be careful,' Freeney tells me when he shows up for a turn with the pellet gun. 'People are on the lookout for you.' He doesn't tell me which people or where they are looking or if he has deigned to provide any clues as to my whereabouts. Instead, he switches subject and tells me he's had enough and has decided to leg it the hell out of here once and for all. 'I have it narrowed down to three places,' he says when I ask where will he go. 'France, Spain or Italy,' he says, and looks triumphantly at me. He then says he is going to find out some things before deciding. Money things. Food and drink things. Language things. 'Actually, I have started learning the languages,' he says. 'Whichever one comes easiest will help influence my final decision. I want to be able to talk to people when I am there.' 'What people?' I ask. 'The woman who gives me a job. The woman who serves me a beer. The woman who shows me the way home after a night out.' 'Is it only women you intend talking to?' I ask him. 'I'm fed up talking to men,' he says, and grips the rifle, takes steady aim. 'When are you planning to go?' I ask. 'End of summer,' he says, and fires off a few rounds, tut-tutting after a nonchalant perusal of his efforts. Then, because he has gotten it inside his head that my current living situation has cut me off entirely from the outside world, he offers me snippets of local news. Crusties are bathing in the church grotto at the Claddagh. There are rumours of a live sex show happening somewhere in the Liosban Industrial Estate. Oh, and it turns out that the bishop is a daddy, has been for the better part of twenty years—they are calling it the Immaculate Deception. Then he tells me when he next speaks to me it will be in a different language.

I see my ex-girlfriend on the prom. She is by herself. I watch her for a few minutes, contemplate crossing the road and inviting her up to Strawberry Fields for a smoothie and some shredded beef. 'On me,' I say, upon acting on my urge and hailing her to stop. She gives me one of those looks that necessitates further insistence on my part. 'Honestly. My shout.' 'Pull the other one,' she says, 'it plays "Jingle Bells".' She broke it off not long after the night I let myself into the house she shares with four trainee nurses. She was on night duty and I forgot to tell the trainees I would be swinging by. Another thing was that I had no key to get in. So I smashed a window after hopping the back wall. The nurses had the boys in blue at the house before I reached the bedroom. I could tell they really wanted to let me have it. I could tell the trainees were not at all averse to the idea. The boys in blue could tell I had a few drinks in me. They let me know what they thought I deserved and so I invited them to do their worst. I owe my ex-girlfriend a considerable amount. She has paid off some of my gambling debt. This was after I'd blown an initial sum she handed over to me for the same purpose, following a succession of other sums I had somehow coaxed out of her in order to cover my buy-in stakes to card games I could not resist. She said my freaking out her housemates was the final straw. I am not at all surprised she now considers Christmas tunes a viable way of communicating with me. After the Jingle Bells taunt I am resolved to repay her every penny.

Over the next few nights I patrol the amusement park, raid the coin buckets, and my resolution grows far and wide. I will repay my former housemates. Sort out my back rent. Look after the bills I have for so long neglected. I will call the credit union, try to make an arrangement.

At the Warwick that Friday I crazy-leg my way through 'Gone Daddy Gone' by The Violent Femmes. 'LA Woman' by The Doors. 'I Feel Good' by James Brown. 'Baby Please Don't Go' by Them. For a few minutes at the bar I chat to a bunch of summer students. Once they discover that they are in the wrong venue they move swiftly en masse out of there. For another few minutes I chat to a trio of young women from Bilbao. 'My friend wants to go to Spain to talk to women,' I tell them. They too decide to move on to the next available nightspot.

A third of a bucket elicits enough coins to cover my unpaid bills. The bank cashes me up, and I am able to make the payments through the post office at the top of the street. A further half-bucket takes care of my housemates. I count out the individual amounts, tuck the cash inside personalised envelopes, pass them to Freeney and tell him to stick them through the relevant letterboxes. I have no reason to believe he won't take a dip himself. I include a note of apology to each of the individuals concerned. *Dear John/Paul/Mark/Declan, enclosed herewith is the sum of money I owe you, some of which you know about, some of which you have probably forgotten about, some of which you definitely do not know about. Please accept my apologies. Dave.*

Sometimes I walk to the end of the prom, continuing as far as the diving platform. It rises twenty maybe twenty-five feet into the air, juts out over the water, and it's so quiet in the middle of the night that standing at the very edge of the platform I can form what passes for a plausible thought or two: stay away from card games, and: what am I doing in this town? Sometimes I walk the other way, back towards the harbour. The lights of the Long Walk blur in the distance. Those of fishing villages across the bay. Going in this direction helps me form another plausible thought: stay away from card games.

Afternoons, my boss has someone come and take the coin buckets to the bank, and every night by close of business they are spilling over again. He has no idea how much money he is taking in. 'Some day I must find out,' he says to me, chuckling. 'You're doing a good job,' he says next. 'Here. Consider it a bonus.' And he leaves an envelope on the counter alongside the pellet gun.

Come Friday, as a reward to myself for paying off my bills and repaying the longstanding personal loans, I throw myself about the dance floor to 'This Charming Man' by The Smiths. 'The Passenger' by Iggy Pop. 'Tainted Love' by Soft Cell. During an especially apoplectic series of movements to the closing chant of 'Brewing Up A Storm' by The Stunning I clatter into a circle of tattooed skinheads, and after an uncertain moment manage to wrangle my way out of a tricky situation by buying several rounds of ciders and shots. By the time 'My Baby Just Cares For Me' comes on they have accepted me into their mosh-pit dance circle.

A few weeks pass and I manage to siphon off both the back rent I owe and the bulk of my credit union loan. I phone my landlord to let him know, firstly apologising for my irresponsibility, and eventually insisting that I will call in person with the sum owing, when he seems reluctant to believe what he is hearing. On his doorstep he twice counts every bit of it and then closes his door on me without saying a word. En route to the credit union, I step inside the corner shop. I am already halfway down the central aisle by the time it occurs to me I have neglected to do anything about the debt owing here—a sizable account run up over the course of ten or twelve months. Luckily, Richie, the owner, is not on the premises and I continue as far as the counter. I am in need of a little sugar after the weekend's dancing. I feel like a Mars bar. Maybe some Taytos for my salt-deprived system. I root in my front and back pockets for change to pay. By the time I have left the shop and turned the corner I no longer have the cash intended for the credit union. Back to the shop I go. Ask the girl. Yeah, there was some cash. A tidy sum. An old lady picked it up off the floor. Oh, the relief. But the old lady said it was hers. The shop girl is so kind. She has a theory the old lady is fond of a flutter. One-armed bandits. She suggests we try the arcades. She even locks up the shop and comes with me. We go up and down the street three times. Scour the arcades. Every nook and cranny. We even try the bingo hall. But there is no sign of the opportunistic pensioner. By the time we are finished our search, the clouds have blown in and the heavens have opened. Sometimes I get caught in these heavy downpours and sometimes I am unlucky with money.

True to his word, Freeney starts speaking to me in Italian. Correction. Tries to speak to me in Italian. 'I can't my head around it,' he says, eventually. 'I just can't.' 'So I'm guessing that rules out Rome and Venice,' I tell him, and he shakes his head sadly. 'I wouldn't mind but I've gotten to like pasta,' he says. 'And I really wanted to see the Bridge of Sighs. Did you know it was the last view of Venice convicts had before their imprisonment?' 'No, I did not know that,' I tell him, but he is in no need of an answer. He has fumbled through another few phrases and he becomes so frustrated that he grabs the pellet gun and yanks it away from the chain attaching it to the counter. Before he leaves I give him the envelope of cash my boss had given me and ask him to pass it on to the card sharks as part payment on what I owe them. He then disappears, but not before informing me that local nudists have turned up at City Hall demanding a clothing-free stretch of beach. The rumours about the live sex show in Liosban have grown arms, legs and other body parts. Oh, and there was a bomb scare last night. 'I was abroad in the toilets of Tigh Neachtain's,' Freeney says, 'and when I landed back inside the bar everyone was gone, bar-staff and all.' 'What did you do?' 'I sat up at the bar and practised my Italian.'

Later, I patrol the grounds with the pellet gun, bridging the gun across the broad of my back. I pause from time to time, hook my arms around butt and barrel, brood, and then situate myself in some faraway locale. The black hills of Dakota. A one-horse town in Arizona. A high plain in Wyoming. Outlaw country. All I need to complete the transformation is a wide-brim hat. Spur boots. And a neckerchief. I plunder the buckets and come morning I make for the bank, determined to cash in the coins and then pay off my corner-shop debt. The beggar outside Spar has other ideas. 'Spare some change, brother,' he says, eyeballing me for effect. Of course, brother. Plenty more where this came from. I dump the lot in the cap laid out on the path in front of him.

I see my ex-girlfriend on the prom again. This time I offer her an à la carte dinner in The Galleon. Window table. Chilled wine. No strings. When she politely declines I try to press upon her a bundle of cash that comprises my first few weeks wages. 'Where did you get it?' she wants to know. I tell her I am trying to be a better person. I tell her I am working and point over to the amusement park. Security. 'Security in an amusement park,' she repeats back to me. 'Now, that's funny.' She bats away the cash bundle and mockingly warns me not to be late for work.

In The Galleon I order enough for two, do not shy away from the selection of desserts, tip the waitress exorbitantly. On my way back to the amusement park, in the window of a charity shop, I notice a mannequin, naked except for a waistcoat and wide-brim Stetson. 'How much?' I ask, having stepped inside. 'Don't suppose you have any neckerchiefs?' She does. 'What about boots? I'm thinking leather. With spurs.' 'We have buckles.' 'Close enough,' I say, and happily pay way over and above the asking price.

That night, clobbered up and arms hooked around the gun, I strike out. Soon, I have arrived at the town with no name. Straight to the saloon, parting the swing doors, tipping my hat to the corset-wrapped, red-lipped barmaid. There's a badass sitting at the poker table. I take aim and give it to him right between the eyes. A collective gasp reverberates, the relief palpable. I am the still-waters-run-deep hero. The barkeep lets me run up a no-limit tab. Red-lips plants one on my dusty cheekbone. At some point in the night I actually hear some rustling near the ice-cream shack. It's a pair of teenagers. Boy and girl. 'Give us a 99 and we'll leave you alone,' offers the boy, big in front of the girl. 'How about I offer you both barrels of this,' I say, and level the pellet gun at him. He turns and legs it out of there, with not a thought for the girl he was so keen to impress. 'Let me see if I can power up this bad boy,' I say, and minutes later we are both enjoying a 99.

'You'd better be careful,' Freeney says, taking aim with the gun. 'If they report that they had a rifle pointed at them you will be in trouble.' 'I made her a 99,' I tell him. 'That will get you in more trouble.' He squeezes out a few pellets. Then he speaks some French. It is early days but already he has decided that it is easier than Italian. 'So you might get to see the Eiffel Tower and Napoleon,' I tell him. He nods without much enthusiasm, then goes on to express, in broken French, his concerns about the food. Frogs' legs. Raw meat.

Snails, for crying out loud. 'How am I supposed to make conversation with a woman over a plate of snails?' Then he tells me an activist has locked himself inside a cage in Eyre Square because he doesn't like the way chickens are being treated. Ten million's worth of cannabis has been discovered on a boat out in Ballyconneely Harbour. A lad called Ming wants to legalise every bit of it. 'Ming?' I say. 'Yes,' Freeney says. 'Ming the Merciless.' Oh, and he almost forgot. The card sharks are very grateful for the payment; when do they get some more? I pass Freeney the bundle of cash my ex-girlfriend didn't want. He takes a peak, whistles, and assures me he is the only person who knows where I am. Then he grabs the pellet gun and speaks some more French. His accent sounds like the real deal, but there is reluctance in his delivery. His aim is not improving.

O'Mara swings by and we take our slow spin out the coast road. We go a little a further this time, and it occurs to me that we might be heading out to cannabis-infested Ballyconneely, but after eight or nine miles he stops the car at a bend in the road, passes a few minutes gripping the steering wheel and staring into the darkness. Then he turns on the CD player. It's a song I don't know. A language I don't recognise. 'Portuguese,' I hear O'Mara say after a couple of verses. His eyes have glistened over. 'Balm for those in the halfpenny place.'

A couple of weeks later, due in no small measure to the appearance of extra coin buckets, once again I have enough to take care of the credit union. This time it goes without a hitch. The manager is so impressed he even waives the last tranche of accruing interest. Richie from the corner shop is similarly delighted. And later that same evening, before he goes home, my boss sticks his head inside the shooting gallery. 'I heard you chased off some troublemakers,' he says, reaching a hand inside his jacket pocket. 'Wish there were more like you.' And he leaves another envelope on the counter.

So pleased with myself am I that come Friday night I freak my ecstatic little head off to 'Blister In The Sun' by The Violent Femmes. 'Take A Walk On The Wild Side' by Lou Reed. 'Love Will Tear Us Apart' by Joy Division. From their customary perch beneath the rainbow arch at the top of the floor, some of the interesting people applaud my dance floor antics. I beckon them onto the floor alongside me but they wave me away. By the time 'My Baby Just Cares For Me' has piano-hopped to its inevitable conclusion I am the only one left on the floor.

When I see her on the prom again I offer my ex-girlfriend a weekend away at a luxury hotel of her choosing. Penthouse suite. Twenty-four-hour room service. Spa beauty treatment. It's all yours, I tell her, all you have to do is pick where and when. With nothing further to say I shove the envelope of cash at her. 'Please. I'm working. I'm earning a living. I have paid off everyone—you are the last,' I tell her. 'Please take it.' She has no interest in the envelope, not even the appearance of my boss, taking some sea air, can sway her. 'Ah, no wonder you are happy in your work,' he says, barely breaking stride while smiling from me to my ex-girlfriend. 'Hang on to this one,' he tells her. 'He's a winner.' She eyes me for another incredulous moment, then walks on.

I am following her with my eyes when I sense them, hovering. Three. Maybe four. Then the voices. *Hi Dave. Been a while. We hear you're a big shot in the amusement park. What's in the envelope, big shot? Is that for us? It is?* And then lots of theatrical gratitude when they have relieved me of the envelope I would have handed over regardless. They have started to move off when their spokesman pauses. Turns around. *Oh, Dave. There's a game happening Saturday night. A biggie. Come along. There's always a place at the table for someone like you.*

Freeney is now speaking Spanish and quite fluidly too. He seems as amazed as I am. 'I can't explain it,' he says, in Spanish. 'It just comes out. And I can read it too. I read yesterday's edition of *El País*. The news in Spain! My tutor reckons I could be fluent in a year. She is adamant I keep going. Damn! I should have tried Spanish to begin with. Think of all the time and effort I would have saved.' 'So,' I reply, 'you are going to see the running of the bulls. You will walk the way of St James. You will sleep your way through hothouse afternoons and go on food crawls.' In beautiful Spanish he congratulates me. 'For what,' I ask him. 'For paying everybody back. You have wiped the slate clean. You can start over again.' Then he tells me a Garda sergeant is telling buskers on Shop Street they can play but only if they perform six original songs. The nudists are due any day now, watch out! And there is something about hell breaking loose at Claddagh Pier after the Crusties were caught trying to lob a swan into a cooking pot. They can toilet and bathe and cavort in the grotto to their hearts' content, but don't touch the swans. I am no longer listening, don't even correct him on the inaccuracy of his claim on my behalf, that there is still the matter of the sum owing to my ex-girlfriend. Mostly, I am no longer listening because I have started to think about Saturday night, about that card game I have been invited to.

*

Sometimes I think of my ex-girlfriend and me dancing together. She is a really great dancer. I loved when she stepped in close, clasped her arms around my neck and I could bask in the tang of her lightly perspiring skin. Sometimes I think if I say her name out loud often enough she will appear alongside me in this cement-wall shack I now call home. Sometimes I think if I whisper her name a single time I will splinter into a million pieces.

O'Mara drives us further than before out the coast road. Just when I begin to think that this is it, we are not stopping this time, he pulls over, gets out of the car and disappears over the ridge leading down to the water. I reach over and turn on the CD player. The same singer, the same plaintive melody, the same beautifully indecipherable voice. A pleading voice that, in time to come, I will associate with the Conamara dark, a voice trapped in a place I will never know in daylight. By the time O'Mara has reappeared, dripping wet, I am trying not to think about Saturday's card game. 'I made an offering to the halfpenny place,' O'Mara says, on the drive back. I wish he had said something sooner. I could have made an offering too.

That Friday I see her in the Warwick and I'm lunatic on the dance floor. Raw and wild and dancing spasmodic. I close my eyes and slam into others and invade space and am unyielding to anyone who has the nerve to nudge me back. Eventually someone taps me on the shoulder. Without opening my eyes I tell myself it's my ex-girlfriend, on the dance floor with me. She puts her finger on my lips, don't speak, and without a word passing between us, we are dancing dizzy to some of her favourite songs. 'Get On Up' by James Brown. 'Moondance' by Van Morrison. And the next song. And the one after that. To the extent that by the time 'My Baby Just Cares For Me' comes around the floor is wheeling about me, hurdy-gurdy style, and I am lost in the sea of possibilities. I will get her something new to wear. No. I should buy her a nice car. That's something I remember her saying she would one day like. I'll see her on the prom and roll up alongside her in the gleaming, open-top Mini, dangle the keys at her, all yours. I'll have her speed us off to the other side of the country and the cruise liner that awaits us. Anywhere you want, I tell her. Spain. France. Italy. New York. Sydney. Rio de Janeiro. We'll sail away forever and a day, I tell her. We'll check out the wonders of the world. We could take a walk together along the Great Wall of China, I hear her say. 'Yes we will,' I cry out, crazy-legged and gung-ho. 'Yes we will yes we will yes we will.' And I'm dancing happy for the duration of Nina's reassuring piano. Dancing happy back to my cement-wall abode. I'm still at it as I take my place at the card table the following night, and on I go, footloose and oblivious, all the way to the moment exactly one week from now and my boss discovers the loser he's had working for him all this time.

Rain Lyric

after Denise Riley

Landscape   combing   my reflection   in the rain-
                                                streaked   window
        charcoal tears   passing a- - - -cross
                    the calming   swish of leaves
                the glass an empty   meeting place
                    washed grey   with concrete
                        matter   *hey that's*
                            my face
                            in the
                            fall-
                            ing rain
                                flitting by   three engines roaring
                                            unisono
                                    as three hearts
        rrrrrrattling   t—rrrracings   b—rrrragging
                                        in my ears
                                        I am, I am, I am
                                                here
                                                portered by
                                                a-lone
                                                a-lass a-
                                                long the M6
                                                iamb-freeeeee
                held   in   *hearing   creatures   skating   in*
            this   porous
                container
            where   we fry   for   more   air
                                    and   carve   our way   out
                of the stuffed turkey to tinned cranberry sauce!
        always cutting   in-to   ourselves   where lyric tugs   for re-alignment

                    I I.   *le pas, en-core*

and for stringent accuracy to spite transparent odds where
subject and / or object are one and / or k-not in the same end

it is here we make odd and's meet because
if I were to tell you now that the bleeding's
stopped—*we followed the carver through to the edge*
see—that lyric's just a motor running any
way—through me, in me, to you, across
our traces in a GoBus window, facing the left—
would ye hear me out here in the clear or give
    in to the mist where ye miss yourself bleating out
        my clarion calls somewhere down a staggering
            line of shrubs and shrugs? You know it rains true
          in Galway just like this when it doesn't align itself
        too neatly round the edges but curls itself right
            round your tongue. You don't want my fogbows in a-
          jar on Prospect Hill cradling the Rhatigan crane, so
I give you a splash of rain in a bowl of light. Now lyric truth's
set, in motion—*my motion's spelled with an E though*
at the start right where green spills into amarillo—
        if you rub it, it's vanilla!—*ink's ebbing*—see,
           you cannot capture it evenly even now when
looking out again for yourself in the window seat because
        it's never this straight-forward once you
let your heartstrings sound in another s-hell: k-not
until they come in swiftly tailored with the rain re-
tailored again coming in with the rain and ring true
straight from my mouth. In-two. Yours. Sincerely,

Tiana M. Fischer

Hell in Connacht

It can feel like hell as you stumble
from a pub onto Shop Street, pissed
out of your head; a one-way sign
suddenly striking you as the sign
you've been waiting for, as you shamble
past a half-dressed young one evicted
from Heaven—Cinderella carrying
her own impossible shoes.

Mothers locked in hell as they wait
for sons and daughters to come home;
patrollers on the Claddagh keeping
an eye on those eyeing the water.
But the craic was mighty and if there's
one less of us tomorrow night sure
there'll be ten more the next.

Moya Roddy

Pilgrimage, *or* The Liminal Situation of a Connemara Erratic
Aoife Casby

Didn't used to think much about smell until all I could think about was not smelling. Smell isn't something you usually consider in landscape.

When they took Jesus from the tomb, was his body putrefying? Putrefaction is the fifth stage of death.

Things I know now: cadaverine and putrescine will remind you of rotting flesh. Can you remember when you last smelled that? Skatole. Think nappies; the bathroom after a stranger. Dogs. The stuff we do in private. The odour of decay, waste from our guts. Indole has a mustier, mothball-like thing going on. Granny's wardrobe. Hydrogen sulphide is the smell of hell; lewd, nasty eggs. Methanethiol will bring you to cold corridors in ill-heated blocks of flats. That leftover cling of boiled and rotten cabbage, the smell of hunger and dead novels. Dimethyl disulphide and trisulfide. Foul. Garlic that has sat in water and its own juice for too long. It hates itself.

The plan was to head west towards the islands, the arse-end of the Gaeltacht. Pete, Baggy, Alan, Brian, Maze, Anthony, Lucas, me, the guy that we didn't know, who was a friend of Baggy's. That was the first surprise. Baggy shot out of his car, late, and I could feel the hackles rise, just a touch of *what the fuck*, when we saw the hulk of a man getting out of the passenger seat. August.

'Hello, you fookers', and from that initial meeting in the car-park, it was us and him. Or maybe us and them, he and Baggy.

'Don't be a pack of cunts, lads, the car takes nine,' said Baggy as soon as he registered the reaction.

'Just saying man, you shoulda said,' said Brian. Brian liked certainty. He'd be the type to dislike August on principle but his reaction was infectious and we gave half-raised waves and curt nods instead of handshakes.

'I can't understand a word the fucker's saying,' Lucas said and clapped a hand across August's back. August turned quickly and the movement seemed a little off, like he was going to lay him out.

'Ah man,' said Lucas.

'You have to listen to understand,' said August, divining something. There was a strange comfort in the used cigarette smell of his breath but it was hard to crawl into his sound, all front of the mouth, trippy *rrrr*s, the trace of muddy snow off them, something unknowable. Baggy liked him though.

After years in London and Bahrain, Baggy'd come home, had met August through some site where the eastern European electrician had been advertising his skills. Made August chief electrician in his little company. August. Six foot three, muscle-bound and he didn't blink. Really.

'Lads, August here is great craic,' Baggy said as if reading from his cv. 'This man, could charm birds outta trees or the knickers off a nun. He is, me oul' muckers, great with the ladies... '

'All right,' Pete said, but Baggy cut him off with a loud

'*Aaaaaand*... the best part is, you won't believe, I mean, you won't... '

And all the time August was eyeing us, unflinching, unblinking.

'... credit it... He works as a clown in the fucking hospital. Can you believe that?' Baggy said.

And yes we could.

His new best friend was a clown.

There are people who spend their whole lives surrounding themselves with the thing they fear, carrying their own cross. This was not Baggy. He spent his life afraid of being surprised by clowns. The fear of clowns isn't something that appeared or developed in him. It simply was. He came into the world fully formed with it. A psychic trace cultivated over generations, right down the years, into his being. There was a clown with numbered buttons on the wall of our baby infants classroom. Baggy puked. At five. Over the years his responses ranged through not being able to draw pictures of a clown, to a puff-chested backing away, unable to talk, an abrupt paling, sweat, an awakening of shake and tremor. Baggy had many a white-out at a circus poster. There was a time when you could see the pale come up on him and you sensed a clown in the vicinity. He had radar for it, an inbuilt clown sense. But he did improve. Tolerance. Ribbing. Whatever. Maybe the lads on the building sites forced him to address it, but he did some sort of dealing with it. The puking and shaking stopped; the fight or flight became less unwieldy; positively almost manageable.

The second surprise was the face-painter. Lucas had booked her to paint us after breakfast. He was all tense and eager as he handed out the red noses. The face-painter (Maya) sat us around the benched table outside the cafe and loaded her equipment and a large mirror in a worktop on wheels that she unfolded. A genius piece of equipment. She took the first grubby dish of paint and opened it, made a face and said,

'Christ, that has the whiff of a bad egg off of it,' then picked up another.

Nine. That's a lot of men to mask, a lot of white face make-up. That's a lot of clowns.

'I'm not sure about this,' said Maze. 'I mean, why?'

'Because it's funny,' said Lucas in his flat way.

'That a reason?' asked Maze.

'I don't know,' said Baggy, but sat down in front of Maya.

'Be calm,' said August.

The transformation from man into clown was unnerving. The abrupt facelessness. It was difficult to tell us apart until we stood up and, still, then. Black diamonds out of which our eyes stared, gruesome red smirks and the dishonest white skin that took all personality away and made sketchy hedgehogs of stubble and beard. If there was anything left on our faces, it was resentment. August had no red nose.

Alan distributed eight red curly wigs. August didn't get one.

The hills across the gun-metal water in Clare were pouting against a peculiar sky.

Baggy's day, the fact of his birthday and the fact he'd never married, never had a stag or wedding and just wanted to have a marker, a get together for getting older. The hill walk had begun as a joke but the idea fell into that silence where everyone is deciding whether or not it's workable because really we weren't those sort of friends. Us. Life's disasters spread across us fairly evenly. Anthony, man-cancer and the aftershock of that. I was divorced. Brian, the estranged father of twins. Maze was orphaned, angry and rudderless since his mid-teens. Lucas was single, an attentive uncle with a chip on his shoulder. Alan, an unreadable father of one. Peter, a married dad of two. A litany of the fathered, fathers and the fatherless. I was a cultural geographer with an interest in the social, looking for a landscape that knew me, a map that could give me some answers. We all need something.

We got into the car. Maze slid the door shut with a bang. Nine variously apprehensive clowns. I was driving, my rear-view mirror a strange flowerbed of clowny carmine and uneasy grimaces.

'So, what is something you are obsessed with?' August said to Brian.

'I'm not obsessed with anything, what do you mean?'

'We all have the obsessions.'

'No, we fucking don't,' said Brian.

'Are you married?' August asked, and rubbed his own bare ring finger but, with him, the gesture seemed kind of rude, or like a challenge. Brian was the wrong person to ask this. August was hitting the nail on the head. Like he saw us. Or was mocking us.

'So, you married?' August prodded.

'None of your business,' said Brian.

'You're mad,' said Alan, very annoyed. I could see his face and he and the angry clown were one. 'No need to be so fucking whatever. Chill the fuck out.'

'Shut up,' said Baggy.

'No,' August said. 'No. He's mad.'

I wasn't sure if August was trying to be argumentative. I could see his clown face shiver in the rear-view mirror, unbearable to read, and I felt our sudden, awkward oneness and the horror of that. The men we were, disappearing, humour continued to deteriorate. Alan was fighting for control, cracking his knuckles and shifting in the seat beside me as if he wanted to escape, smelling like a fox, earthy and wild. And finally he let loose.

'You cunt,' said Alan.

'Fooker calling me mad,' said August.

Maze released a gaudy laugh. 'Jesus, relax, he didn't do anything.'

'Are you calling me a fucking liar?' August said and I was thinking, who? Is who?

'You call me liar,' said August again, real quiet like. Just looking straight ahead. 'Be afraid of a mask.'

'For Christ's sake,' said Baggy into the silence. But we were all wondering.

'Roll over fucking Macnas,' said Pete from the back, 'we are a parade the likes of which of you've never seen before.' I felt the fields and trees whizzing by, indecipherable.

The clown had already begun to gobble up Pete.

I put the radio on and the awful virtue of stay-at-home Ireland reviewing our situation was a small interruption into which we grunted and snorted until,

'I want a cigarette,' said August, pulling the plastic off a new box.

'I could do with a smoke too,' said Alan, real quiet like.

'No smoking in the car,' I said.

Maze, last in and last to take his seat, had been crossing himself like an expert at every graveyard, roadside shrine and church we passed. 'Relax, we'll pull over, lads, we'll pull over,' he said, nodding at me.

'Ah, the clean air of miles from Galway,' said Brian, as if a soft word could clear the atmosphere. 'God be with the days.' He was remembering something he evidently wasn't going to share.

A few minutes later we pulled into a green patch on the side of the road near a river. The clouds had evened out and were manifesting menace against the Connemara blue. It should have been windy and cold, but it wasn't.

A disharmony of mute clowns, boots on the rubber floor, the hoarseness of dragging a coffin from a hearse, gravel, passive grumbles and hollow knocks. Maze fell as he exited. I sat leaning into the steering wheel, wishing things were different. Baggy had always wanted to be one of us but he wasn't. There was no way to explain it. An accident of place of birth. He just wasn't like us but we tolerated him. Now we were all clowns and I don't know what that meant. The optimism in the planning phase of this hill-climb business had vanished, replaced with a ferrety anxiety. August and Anthony took off their boots and socks and put their feet into the cold water.

The second stop was uneventful except for nasty individualism released by the atrocious painted smiles. Our inane talk was more lads uncensoring their deeper thoughts. 'It's okay for you…' type stuff. Years-old jealousies. Arguing about time and wasting it. Luck and the distribution of it. Except August. He sat and watched. Heard everything. And when he went over a ditch to take a piss, excusing himself in a very polite way, Maze said,

'For fuck's sake, Baggy, what's the story with this fella?'

'Ah Maze,' said Brian.

'Seriously. He's a downer. Nuns and knickers my arse. He's about as much fun as... '

'Let it go,' said Baggy. Nice and simple. He didn't look around.

It was especially hard to tell Brian and Baggy apart. They were both stocky, shaggy brown hair, denims, white T-shirts. With the red noses and make-up they merged into one another.

'Fuck ye,' said Maze.

On the way back to the car, Lucas, in another attempt at solidarity, put his arm around August's shoulder and said,

'You're a quare one you, c'mon, tell us your story, there's more to you than meets the eye. Baggy says you have a way with the women.'

Lucas winked at us and as soon as he did, August said, 'Fook you too,' and threw the friendly arm from his shoulder, spinning Lucas into the side of the car.

There was a quick scramble and Brian and Maze squared up to August, shoving, shouting, trying to pin him down in an erratic overreaction, but Baggy was quick to split them up using a dynamic list of expletives. It happened really fast. I could hear Lucas's angry breathing re-open the silence between us. I wanted to take off the paint and nose, the itchy wig. The clown's voice inside me told me to keep quiet.

Alan took out a map and the unfolding paper crackled uneasily in his hands. The maps on phones were slow to load and Maze said he remembered a lay-by in a particular place. I could not have told them then that the language of the curves of the Connemara Gaeltacht had something to say.

'I'd love to be down in the pub just watching the football,' said Brian.

The radio was annoyingly intermittent. Baggy suggested a song and after an embarrassed quiet I swear the only thing us bunch of clowns could come up with was 'How Great Thou Art'. A bloody hymn. Belting out a religious song as we rolled over the narrow bridges across towards Cnoc Leitir Mór was eerie, but the strangeness of it covered up the tension for a bit. August sang too. I don't know why, but I was surprised he knew the words. I could see him in the rear-view mirror. His big red mouth word-perfect in a way the rest of us were not.

The third stop was where we reckoned we were going to start walking. We pulled into the gravelly lay-by and moved slowly out of the car. There was a hint of the southern hemisphere in the breeze and it mumbling to itself, judging; that feeling of being watched. Just as soon as the nine of us were outside, a man emerged from the heather, whistling loudly. The sound made us all turn at once and I caught the expression on the man's face as it changed from vaguely contented to shock and fear in an instant. He did a double take and stepped backwards, soundless, looking as if his soul was screaming *Ohhhh, fuck,* and as he did Baggy, Maze, Alan and Anthony, out of nowhere, seemed to move as one and stepped towards him, hands in the air, howling variations of 'run ya fucker'. The startled man turned and fled and the four lads ran after him.

'What the fuck?' said Lucas.

'Masks,' August said. 'Masks. They think they are having fun.'

'Fun? Jaysus,' said Brian, 'they'll scare the life outta the young fella.'

I walked over the edge of the mound of gravel down towards where the men had disappeared. It was amazing how quickly they covered distance, how small they appeared in a few seconds. I watched but couldn't make out what was going on.

All along the bottom lip of the great rough hillside were blackberry brambles knitted with wool from oblivious sheep, mouldy oozing fruit that escaped rats and smaller creatures, nervous birds, torn things, gaunt rises.

The land here is difficult to get into. Watery, detached, peninsular. We had passed houses that looked like they belonged, houses that didn't and water that had the aspect of an overlord about it, and in between the water and the houses and all their bits (tractors, sheds, boats, quays, bridges, monkey puzzle trees) there is the bog, stone, over-worked blessed wells, heather, and on a day like today, the alarming cobalt sky. There are odd bushes on these islands and messianic Scots pines, bare trunks with a toss of determination in green, the hand of man about them.

Granite protruded through the growth and after a few spongy steps I turned back. Brian was watching me. I sat on the ground against the side of the car. Listened to his breathing. We spent years not being close, then put on a mask and it's like that physical distance dissolves. I wanted to hug him.

'Look at that,' he said, and pointed to a bicycle with panniers tucked just behind the small ditch.

I went to the rise again to see if I could spot the young fella who I assumed was the owner of the bicycle which Brian, Lucas and Pete had begun to examine.

August came and stood beside me.

The three at the bike opened the panniers and started to pull out the contents.

'What the fuck lads?' I called.

'Chill out. Just looking,' said Lucas, 'and look at this.' He held up a small case on a chain, a funky locket. 'There's a little lump o' hash here.'

'For fuck's sake,' I said, 'put his stuff back.'

But Pete wordlessly continued to remove clothing, a notebook, shoes, a sleeping bag, utensils, some battered books, and gave a little harrumph of triumph when he came across a repair kit. He opened it and removed the small wrenches and with precise movements began to dismantle the bicycle.

'Why is there no trace of men in a lot of this?' asked August as if he had divined my calling. 'What did men do here?' He indicated the nauseating expanse in front of us.

'Lucky lads lived elsewhere,' I sighed and lied. I didn't tell him how they knew rain, how they mined and walked and farmed and fished. How they hunted and ran. How they told stories, were fluent in the name of every living thing in every square inch. How they would not have been scared of the dark, or masks, or the landscape and the way it could suck you into its innards and make you disappear. How they could navigate the land in all seasons by the smell of the gorse, the heather, the animals.

August laughed.

'What are your friends doing to the Spanish lad?' he said.

'Spanish?'

'Yes. He was Spanish. I saw it in his eyes.'

Was?

Then out of nowhere Lucas, who was busy following all of Pete's diabolic movements but had obviously been listening, said, 'I've never been to Spain. I'd like to do that walk.' His clown face was so sad just then; the eyes.

There was a meaty, short silence.

'The camino,' I said.

'Yeah,' said Brian. 'Sunshine, empty roads, silence, peace, no responsibility.'

'Like here,' I laughed, but I was uneasy.

He shrugged and got up from the ground. His earlier anger seemed to have died out and as he passed by us I got a strong smell of oniony sweat. He stopped for a moment to look out over the unfolding landscape, then turned and I followed him back down the little rise. August stayed standing, watching. Pete continued to dismantle the bicycle, and Brian circled back to resume taking each piece from him as he removed it, placing it on the ground.

'I'm going over. Your mad friends,' said August.

'What are you saying?' said Lucas. 'It's not a good idea to go there. Leave them to it.'

'Mad. Bad. Should have listened to me,' said August.

'Listen to what?' said Lucas.

'Be calm. Be afraid of mask.' He gestured his thumb to where Pete was slowly bending metal, manifesting his soul as if it had exploded about him, then disappeared over the rise in the direction the men had chased the young Spanish man.

'Scaring the fuck outta the young fella,' said Brian. 'That's all. But still, Baggy's not right. He's too fucking trying-to-please or something. And August, I'm telling you… Something's going to happen down there.'

Brian left the bicycle and pulled the red nose from his face and flung it across the ground.

'What are they going to do to him? Why haven't they come back?' he continued. 'Fucking clowns.'

His wig was halfway down his forehead. The red plastic nose idled across the ground in the low breeze. I watched it while he walked away. I could hear an odd shout in the distance and went, again, to stand on the rock to see could I spot anything in this ice-scoured place. A red car passed by. Then Brian was beside me again.

'August,' he said. 'Listen, whatever was going on with the lads, he's going to turn it into something. We shouldn't have let him go. He's been talking in fucking haikus like a Zen master or something.'

I made a list in my head of the things I knew should be out there, layered over years under the feet of the men. Sundew. Butterwort traps. Meadow vetchling. The raw jawbones of ferns, heather, brittle and dark, flowers like little girls, heads bent and if you listen closely you'll hear little breaths of music, tiny songs.

'I don't understand what's going on,' I said.

'That fella, August. I don't think that tourist is coming back,' he said.

'Jesus,' I said. 'Baggy, he'd be happier drinking a slow pint in Neachtain's, not saying much.'

'Clowns aren't supposed to cry, are they?' said Brian, and he walked away towards the van. Lucas was on the ground against the van, red curls glinting, his nose in his hand.

'What's it all about? When you are faced with yourself. We don't know how to talk to each other anymore,' I said, mainly to myself. I was suddenly overwhelmed by it all. Something similar had happened to Brian.

I thought about all the things I wanted to be true; to be irrefutably fact; the ones that were impossible; the impossible fact of friendship. There was nothing to say to Brian. I didn't know him. All these years and I never listened to him and for that matter, he had never listened to me. And all the things I knew were true: every blade of grass was hiding a history. A drop of blood. Of sweat. A hidden hair, a thread from a jacket. A button from a clown. In some ways fear is easier to see when you have face paint on, the muscles on your forehead wrinkle and twitch. Fear is unmasked. Like these hills. Brian was slumped against the rear wheel of the car looking up at the sky. I went to him and put my hand on his arm and he moved so quickly and with such violence, I wanted to cry. He banged his head against the side of the car and shouted. And shouted.

He didn't stop.

He screamed and shouted over and over and over for his mother.

Pete never stopped what he was doing to the bicycle. Lucas simply moved his nose from one hand to the other, juggling it with the Spanish lad's stash box.

I summoned a roar for Pete to stop. It was as if he were devouring a corpse the way they he was separating the pieces of the Spanish man's existence.

'How d'you think he'll feel when he sees his stuff like this? How will he get home?' I said. Pete ignored me. I laughed again.

Lucas took a deep pull from a joint he had skinned up, trying to hold the noisy inhalations in his lungs but he started to cough and curse.

From one second to the next, our selves are irretrievable. Like trying to hold onto a beautiful image. That's what loneliness is. In all our togetherness and sparse knowledge of one another, we were devastatingly alone. We were not able to carry one another.

*

Pete didn't stop his work. Every now and then he wiped his face and red and white smeared his knuckles. I went again to see could I spot the running clowns and this time, in the distance I could make out men moving, sunlight obliterating and clarifying them as they merged into one another. There were two dots of red blazing on the ground, abandoned wigs I supposed, midway between me and the blur of figures. One, at least, still wore a wig on his head. I couldn't tell them apart, who they were, or how many they were in their strange dance beyond the shadow of the glacial erratic, a huge sad rock positioned on the near horizon like a full-stop on the sentence of the land; sun burst from between sluggish clouds and a rainbow appeared. I swear, it was as if God himself was visiting down on us. I smiled under my clown smile. I'd no hope of hearing what they were saying, but it looked like an argument.

But now I could hear Pete. He was crying. Great snots smearing his clown face. I saw a shadow, a flicker in the way he was stirring his head and tugging his elbows into his stomach, gestures of self-protection.

I stood there considering how it might look from the point of view of the Spanish lad were he ever to return. I imagined him stumbling and falling, disappearing into the sweet coconut smell of the last gorse. It started to rain. Lucas took another drag and turned his face to the blood-warm drops but almost as soon as it started, the clouds moved away and the sky took on a gruesome pallor again.

Pete had spread out all of the belongings and pieces of the bicycle in a fan spreading out metres from the mound of gravel. He sobbed, cutting a tire with a penknife into rubber strips.

'Poor little Spanish boy is never going to see his daddy again,' said Lucas.

'Stop, stop,' I pleaded, but spoke into unhearing.

Pete continued to cut and cry. Brian was silent now and re-joined Pete in arranging the parts of the bicycle in a wrecked fractal, searching for a pattern, as if they were playing some sort of strategy game, manifesting normality. Each piece Brian picked, he brought to his nose and sniffed it as if he were meeting it for the first time, then placing or replacing it. All those tiny bits.

I sat down beside Lucas and watched the men, the dying sky. There was a type of spare cloudiness fringing the brutal blue of September, light like the inside of an oyster, the sense of the not-far-away or not-long-disappeared sea. Here.

August reappeared carrying Baggy as if he were a small child and cradled him, thighs across his forearms. Baggy had naturally put his arm around August's back and turned his head into August's chest, tucked under the ruined clown face and I swear, August lowered his head and kissed Baggy on the crown.

Brian ran past them, composed himself on top of the rise.

August divested himself of Baggy gently, placing him on the ground but still holding him. I went and stood beside Brian, scanned the littlest ridges. After all the centuries the land itself still hadn't settled. It was weary. Filled with parabolic and diabolic symmetries. I saw the fields and the way the sun chuckled or scowled over the lines it made of distance; how fences and walls behaved; how the land was telling us how to be. I knew that lakes could tell time, and now, looking out at the remnants of men among these clowns and the land gobbling them up, not only them, but their essences, I was dumb. We hadn't a clue. The heathers had made worms of our brains; conjured a spell that allowed the masks to work their magic.

August though. He'd managed to remove his face-paint. This puzzled me until I rationalised that yes, he's an expert, he's a hospital clown, he knows how to get rid of this stuff. He alone seemed to be content in this place of our pilgrimage. This place with that snarl of crippled bramble, the complication of heather, carnivorous flowers, the sun blearing beyond that erratic rock as if it were trying to eat its way through. The angelic grasses, crawling, kneeling at the side of the road; frayed leaves; the unravelling, undug hills. Devout montbretia. The clouds fall. The light falls. The earth falls. Maybe it was because the air was cleaner, lighter; maybe it was the light, leaving, returning, the cloud dance. My skin felt as if it truly were holding me together. I saw the whole map of me for one sorry instant.

Brian was breathing deeply beside me. Lucas had wandered over to join us. August was on his knees still holding Baggy.

Because there are things unsaid. Because we have relationships with our fathers. Because we don't. Because we don't know how to express distress. Because we are.

'He fell, blood. See.' August lifted Baggy's head and I could see the matted hair. 'Why is he crying?' He nodded at Pete. 'Fooking mad lads, like I said.'

'Werzh Maze?' Baggy slurred. 'Werez Maze, mad bashtherd.'

'Where's Maze?' I said. 'And Alan and Anthony? Where are they?'

'And the Spanish lad?' said Brian. 'Did ye kill him?' in such a flat voice.

'No good, no good,' Baggy said, low and wheezy. I couldn't make out if the red on his mouth was blood or smeared makeup. His eyes were closed.

'Who reared him?' he said. 'Who reared him? Daddy? Daddy?'

He kept asking.

I was waiting for the Spanish lad to come leaping over the rise, a cheeky Lazarus. I was waiting for him to see his mutilated bicycle and belongings and stare at us in disgust. I was waiting for the lively smell of him.

'What the fuck? You kidding me?' he'd say and break into a laugh that came from centuries ago, another wisdom.

I wanted to laugh but the muscles, my lungs had forgotten how to do that.

'What's his name? What's his name? What's his name?' screamed Brian at August.

August stood, stared at Brian.

'I'm August,' he said loudly.

'No, no, no, not you,' whimpered Brian.

'August,' whispered Pete, and he looked at me with completely naked eyes, a young child shining out and I wanted to tell that child to go away, go away, go away and I felt hot tears falling from my chin.

I will forever wonder about the actuality of them being alive, or hovering there on the edge of life, just out of the frame, or truly dead. Down that hillside. Unburied. Unmarked. I find myself, again, thinking about how long it takes flesh to pull away from the bone, all that skin and sinew, the deliquescing blood, humours leaching out. Enzymes. All that smell and no man to feel it. I am obsessed with it. The scent of hell. Hair. The consideration of eyes. The eyelashes. Cartilage. Nails and teeth. Falling away from their roots, forcing a path through the heather and bracken. It's not my fault I'm a geographer. It's not my fault Baggy wasn't. Whose fault is it that none of us know who we are? Whose fault is it that our identities disintegrate?

God is a Surgeon or a Huntsman or a Wolf

The hand of God holds an apple &/
a paring knife/ skins Snow White's septic heart/
& it falls/ tulip petals onto bedsheets/

The hand of God carries a peach stone/
in a tight fist/ the holy corpse/
of an unholy thing/

The hand of God is a rusted pomegranate/
& I eat dry toast/ because here/ even the melting of butter/
is not an afforded dignity/

The hand of God delights/ in showing/ all the ways it/
owns my body/ before being allowed/ to touch it/

Before me/ the hand of God plays/
at putting down/
a rabid dog/ rabid woman/ a loose tongue/

The hand of God plucks/ a fruit plate from the/
orchard of my skin/ gorging on the taste of me/
with the juice fresh in his maw/

The hand of God/ outgrows its own golden orbit/
the only consequence/ of such gorgeous gluttony

Aimee Godfrey

A Hell Taxonomy (On *Doom*, 1993)

Róisín Kiberd

> Hell hath no limits, nor is circumscrib'd
> In one self place; for where we are is hell,
> And where hell is, there must we ever be.

Christopher Marlowe, *Doctor Faustus*

1. Irish Hell

Hell is in the midlands: Rathcroghan, the largest unexcavated royal site in Europe, a network of burial mounds and ringforts built over 5,500 years. It was once home to Medb, the warrior queen. It is also a door to the underworld.

Hell is in the north, at Saint Patrick's Purgatory, another ancient site, this time in Donegal. Where Rathcroghan is the domain of pagan gods, this is its Christian counterpart: a cave revealed to Patrick by Christ himself, offering a glimpse of the inferno. Patrick used it as an educational tool, for scaring the locals into converting.

Hell lives in Galway, or rather, a celebrated architect of hell. Romero Games, the video game company founded in 2015 by Brenda and John Romero, has its offices just off Eyre Square. John Romero has worked on over 130 games, has founded eight companies, and has won over 100 awards for his work as a game designer and programmer. He made his name in the early '90s as a founding member of id Software, the developers who gave the world the first-person shooter, the deathmatch, and the goriest, grisliest, most hellish games the world had ever seen.

At midnight on December 10th, 1993, after roughly one year of working with all the febrile enthusiasm of twenty-somethings fed on heavy metal, horror films and pizza, id Software released *Doom*, its genre-defining first-person shooter. You play as the 'space marine' Doomguy, a tough, nameless motherfucker with a shotgun and a pixelated brush cut. Sent to Mars as punishment for insubordination, he faces down legions of demons before it's revealed that, through experimentation with teleports, scientists have accidentally opened a portal to hell, and the demons have overrun Earth.

Doom raised the bar, not only for gameplay, but for gore. It birthed a new kind of moral panic; rich in blood, guts and satanic imagery, critics labelled it a 'mass murder simulator'. Both of the Columbine shooters were *Doom* fans (in a video made on the day of his killing spree, Eric Harris even claimed 'It's going to be like fucking *Doom*'). Media outlets treated the game as dangerous—one paper even claimed it could 'widen the hole in any kid's soul'—while then-President Bill Clinton used his weekly radio address to highlight *Doom*'s role in 'a culture that too often glorifies violence.' In 2001, id Software was even named in a lawsuit filed by families of Columbine victims, along with entertainment companies including Nintendo, Sega and Time Warner Inc. The case was eventually dismissed.

I'm fascinated by moral panics relating to media and art; they attribute a near-mystical power to their target, whether it's a book, a film, music (played backwards, preferably) or a video game. The larger the panic, the stronger this power becomes. Ultimately, moral panics highlight the transformative potential in art, one which we often overlook until it's seen to go wrong.

Doom was transformative in so many ways; it introduced a new form of gaming, unprecedented in its violence and its possibilities for customisation. Perhaps this is why religious organisations and politicians wished to censor it. 'They did criticise it,' said John Romero, speaking to me over Skype from the Galway offices of Romero Games, 'but we never paid attention to that, because, you know, everybody loved it.'

This is no exaggeration. *Doom* was a phenomenon, a moment in tech and gaming history on par with the launch of the iPhone, or Windows 95, but a lot more metal. The night *Doom* launched shops were mobbed, whole university computer networks broke down, and systems belonging to schools, corporations and even government facilities ground to a halt due to the number of people trying to play it. 'It was the most fun thing anyone had played,' said Romero. 'People were going out and buying computers just to play the game, and networking got massive, because the game supported it. '

Doom established a genre, a way of playing, and an aesthetic which endure to this day. New first-person shooters are released every year, their protagonists walking in the frenzied footsteps of Doomguy. There have been eight *Doom* sequels and four *Doom* spin-offs, and fans continue to convene for Deathmatch tournaments, where players battle each other in a bloody free-for-all.

Decades have passed, but *Doom* still feels current. It continues to attract players across generations, not only for its gameplay or its place in history, but because it taps into something eternal; our fear of—and fascination with—hell.

2.   A Map of Hell

There is a hell for almost every culture. Aztec hell contains jaguars and rivers of blood. Zoroastrianism details a 'House of Lies', while Jain cosmology features a hell built on seven levels—you won't have to stay there forever, but it may take several billion years to get out. In ancient Mesopotamia hell was dry and dusty, and the living poured libations on the ground for departed relatives to drink. In the Apocalypse of Paul, hell has rivers of fire, but also rivers of ice for the cold-hearted. Dante's hell is highly structured and delivered in cantos, with levels for those who indulged wrath, lust, greed and so on. The Christian hell is rich in imagery and specific detail; it's a hell made for artists, writers, and designers of video games.

In 2018, Pope Francis is said to have denied the existence of hell in an interview with Eugenio Scalfari, a journalist he has spoken with on several occasions. In response, the Vatican stated that Scalfari's article was not 'a faithful transcription of the words of the Holy Father'—a convenient claim, given that the interview was apparently held in private, and not recorded.

Even if hell has been cancelled, we will continue to visit it in video games, where each day new conscripts are lured to the inferno. On Steam, the online video game marketplace, a search for the term 'hell' gives 22,781 results, suggesting games like *Hell Blade*, *Hellbound* and *Waifu Hell*, a hentai game where you alternate between ogling and shooting at naked, levitating women.

Shortly before *Doom* was created, in late 1992, the id team was heavily involved in a *Dungeons & Dragons* campaign, with co-founder John Carmack acting as dungeon master. Romero tried to procure a magic sword and caused the earth to be overrun by demons, inspiring, quite suddenly, the premise for Carmack and Romero's next game. It's worth adding here that *Dungeons & Dragons* was itself the subject of a moral panic; in the early '80s it was sued by anti-occult group BADD, which stands for 'Bothered About Dungeons and Dragons'. BADD linked the game to 'blasphemy, suicide, assassination, insanity, sex perversion, homosexuality, prostitution, satanic-type rituals, gambling, barbarism, cannibalism' and other practices. The lawsuit was dismissed.

The id team worked with a copy of H.R. Giger's *Necronomicon* on the table in front of them, and the name, famously, came from a Tom Cruise line in *The Color of Money* ('What's in the case?' 'In here? Doom.'). 'When we made it, back then, we just started with a bunch of gruesome images,' said Romero. 'Blood lakes, twisted faces, all kinds of stuff we found unnerving. And then just a lot of burning stuff. Pentagrams, you know?'

The aesthetic influence of horror films—as well as their ghoulish humour and their spirit of low-budget audacity—is palpable in *Doom*, as in id Software's earlier classic, *Wolfenstein 3D*, and, later, the wildly successful *Quake*. 'Basically it was *Evil Dead*, and *Aliens*, and *Dungeons & Dragons* and heavy metal,' said Romero. 'It was all those things mixed together, with dark humour and a shotgun and chainsaws. We wanted it to be like in *Aliens*, with lots of stuff coming at you. Hordes of bad things! And that fear that you felt with *Alien*, because it's dark, and you don't know what's around the corner, but you hear the noises. . . '

Doom was built to showcase technologies that had never been used in games before. As designer, Romero played through each level repeatedly, refining it, until he had run through each one hundreds, even thousands of times. Carmack built an improved graphics engine, with binary space partitioning and texture-mapping; shadows deepened at a distance, ceilings slanted menacingly, and walls contained secrets and interactive panels. The design was murky, mutable and brilliantly sinister, lending a chiaroscuro horror to proceedings even before the monsters arrived.

Doom's other surprise was its subject matter, which turned out to be rooted in religious imagery as much as in science fiction. Romero said, 'The thing about *Doom* was that instead of humans meeting aliens in space, which is what you'd expect, you're meeting *hell* instead. . . It's as if hell really exists, and now it's something you actually have to deal with.' Romero cited H.P. Lovecraft as an influence—in fact the final boss of *Doom*'s follow-up, *Quake*, is the Hell-Mother, a direct import from Lovecraft's Cthulhu Mythos. 'It was always a question of doing something different, and interesting, that we hadn't seen before. *Quake* had a Lovecraft influence in terms of the feel of the game—that constant, unsettling feeling that something is wrong. It was hyper-violent, and anything could happen, so you had to stay on your toes.'

3.   Hell as Bestiary

I'll tell you about the imaginary beings you meet in hell. They move in ways unfamiliar to humans; scuttling, sailing through air, issuing squelching, moaning sounds which haunt you long after you take off your headphones. The creatures of *Doom* strain at the limits of '90s technology. They possess a physicality I find deeply unnerving.

The Imp, *Doom*'s most mundane enemy, is sludge-coloured and easily defeated. Its eyes blaze red, while its face is fixed in a strained rictus of shock.

The Mancubus is a mass of seething flesh, a slightly-more-mobile cousin to Jabba the Hutt. It has two flamethrowers for hands, and its death is spectacular; an implosion of blood and viscera, body collapsing, head exploding, green glowing eyeballs that fall to the floor.

The Cacodemon is *Doom*'s mascot; one-eyed, blazing red like an inflamed organ. It pulsates smugly in the air, spitting out flame balls. Its death is a lesson in occult anatomy; it spurts red blood when you shoot it, but bleeds blue goop when it finally dies.

The Pain Elemental: found in *Doom II*, the best-named creature has a single red eye, horns, an otherworldly croak, and futile little T-rex arms. Kill a Pain Elemental and it splits itself into three Lost Souls; floating skulls which blaze across the room.

The Spider Mastermind, leader of *Doom*'s battalion, is a kind of Krang 2.0 crossed with the robot from *Wild Wild West*. When you finally defeat it, its metal body breaks apart and only its leering teeth remain.

Musclebound, red, with the legs of a goat, the Baron of Hell emits a cosmic darkness. Sometimes I worry that if I look at one too long, I will become sexually attracted to it. The Hell Knight is a weaker, smaller relative of the Baron of Hell, while the Cyberdemon is its gigantic, Minautaur-like godfather.

The Arch Vile, lurching and spindly, is perhaps *Doom*'s eeriest creation due to how closely he resembles a human. Tall and bald and emaciated, his ribcage protrudes across his contorted back. Sometimes he throws up his arms, as if giving thanks for the chance to kill you.

Finally there's the Icon of Sin; the boss of bosses; a wall-mounted goat head. Projectiles emerge from its wound, a flash of rosy exposed brain. Its eyes are dead, its mouth smiling. It is sometimes referred to as 'Baphomet'. Approach the Icon of Sin, leap into its wound, and you'll find the game's true nemesis: an Easter egg, the ultimate Oz-behind-the-curtain moment in gaming. You'll see a familiar head impaled on a stick, speaking backwards in the game designer's own voice: 'To win the game, you must kill me, John Romero.'

You shoot him, but hasn't he already won?

4.   Hell as Other Players

Inspired by games like *Street Fighter II*, which the team played during breaks, Romero proposed the 'deathmatch' during *Doom*'s development. Up to four players could battle over a local network, or two could use a modem. 'This is the first game to really exploit the power of LANs and modems to their full potential,' id wrote in a *Doom* press release. 'In 1993, we fully expect to be the number one cause of decreased productivity in businesses around the world.'

Doom is also credited with popularising the mod, or 'modification', a customised version of a game created by its fans. Mods can add new levels, objects, weapons, settings or characters. Modding was—and remains today—a popular first step for future game designers.

During our conversation, Romero noted the difficulties that prevent modding communities from forming around games today. 'Now when you talk about any big game it's basically un-moddable,' he said, 'because the games are so complex.' The exception is if a company specifically wants to encourage mods: 'You have to deliberately open it up and let people in, and make specific tools to help them mod.'

Doom arrived at precisely the right time in history, a point when the hacker ethic crossed over into popular culture. The game was customisable from its inception. Soon there was *Doom Simpsons*, *Doom* in a shopping mall, and even *Marine Doom'*, created by and for the US Marine Corps as a training aid. Today, versions of *Doom* number in the tens of thousands. Recently there was *BorderDoom*, a mashup with *Borderlands*, the gory *Meatgrinder Co-op*, and *Brutal Minecraft*, which is as it sounds, a shoot-em-up set in the wholesome, pixel-bricked world of *Minecraft*.

In this sense, *Doom* keeps alive the DIY ethic of early gaming, an industry largely created by teenagers making games at home, the way Soundcloud rappers build careers from their laptops today. 'The entire industry was founded on indies,' Romero said, 'and it still *is* indies that are pushing the boundaries with new ideas.' Romero himself began by making such games; as a teenager in the '80s he sent homemade games to magazines, where they were printed as code (readers would type the entire programme into their computers in order to play them).

As well as mods and deathmatches, id Software gave the world another small yet crucial trope in modern gaming: the presence of a hand—the protagonist's hand, more often than not holding a weapon, and always positioned at the bottom of the screen. This hand first appeared not in *Doom*, or even in *Wolfenstein 3D*, but in its precursor, id's 1991 title *Catacomb 3D*, where you play as a high wizard battling skeletons and reapers with spells that shoot from your fingertips.

The hand came back for *Wolfenstein*, then for *Doom*, and later *Quake*, by which time it had become an industry norm. There's something richly symbolic about this hand. Instead of a figure like Virgil to guide you through the underworld, it invites you to guide yourself. Here are limitless levels of hell which you can build yourself; a customised hell, different for every player. Much like the plot of *Doom*, its creators opened a portal which seems likely never to close.

When I asked Romero how it feels to have created something potentially eternal, he compared it to something unexpected: exotica music, the genre created by composer Martin Denny in 1950s America. 'Martin Denny started to create this Hawaiian jazz-lounge music, but he added animal and bird noises to it,' said Romero. 'He created a whole band where people were making animal noises—because who can teach frogs to make sounds on command? The people who were in his band after they finished repeated that idea, and continued to make exotica in their own style.' Exotica's afterlife was earned through its inherent strangeness: 'It died out after some point, but it lasted for decades. That was very niche back then, whereas *Doom* is huge in gaming, and is still going strong twenty-six years later. With the new games coming out too, *Doom* will definitely see a fiftieth anniversary.'

5.   Production Hell

Often I suspect that the gruelling quality of certain games hints at the circumstances in which they were made. From documentaries, and from watching game designers have occasional Twitter breakdowns, I get a sense of the industry as vampiric, attracting talented young outcasts and draining them of life. Much like writers, game designers suffer for their art in deeply unglamorous ways: mood swings, instability, caffeine dependence, and fighting with co-workers (if you have them—another thing I notice is how lonely the process of making a game can be). Designers' work requires persistence in the face of hopelessness—in the face of releasing a title that might never be reviewed, and will sell on Steam for a median price of $5.99.

John Romero knows about production hell. Work was delayed for years on his game *Daikatana*, a first-person shooter set in futuristic Japan, ancient Greece, Norway in the Dark Ages and finally, a futuristic San Francisco. Ideas clashed, one game engine was swapped for another, and the company's office, an extravagant penthouse, caused problems when it turned out that light from the ceiling prevented employees from seeing their screens. After multiple missed launch dates, staff departures, an overrun budget and an infamous print ad which declared that 'John Romero's about to make you his bitch', *Daikatana* was released to poor reviews and angry players in the year 2000.

Even in the earlier days at id Software's office, 'Suite 666', the team seems to have worked in permanent crunch mode. Tony Kushner's book *Masters of Doom* reveals that their office was next to a dentist's; the sound of drills and, occasionally, screams drifted in through the wall, inspiring the demonic ambience of *Doom*. *Wolfenstein 3D* was made in roughly seven months, while *Doom* took just over a year. *Doom II* was released the following year, and two years after that id Software put out *Quake*. Each of these games were hugely successful and influential, and their teams faced conflict, tight deadlines, no sleep and a diet of pizza in order to pull this off.

'You put into the game what you're feeling,' said Romero. 'It's something I think a lot of people don't pay attention to. With *Quake*, the mood was that everyone was expecting to have put a game out already, but we weren't able to because the technology wasn't ready. People were creating things they'd then have to delete, or make massive changes to, because the engine wasn't finished. We didn't know it was going to take that long.' If the designer's mood can influence a game, then perhaps a game can influence its creators in turn. *Quake*, with its brutal gameplay and nightmarish tone, was the product of an arduous creative process: 'That disturbing, unsettling feeling in the game needed to happen, no matter how we were feeling. So that's what we made.'

Within the last three decades, the game industry has grown to a market value of roughly $148 billion, and game development has changed accordingly. *Assassin's Creed*, as one example, could have over a thousand people working on the game,' Romero said. 'It's massive. It's hard to have a really strong creative force driven into a game, to the heart of it, to make sure it stays true to its vision.'

It strikes me that the industry runs on extremes of over- and under-staffing, with larger titles sometimes bloated and over-financed, while indie games rely on one or two fanatically devoted creators to see them into the world. Perhaps this is why so many of the indie games that stand out to me are framed as a journey through the protagonist's fraying mind—titles like *The Beginner's Guide*, or *Braid*, or *Amnesia: The Dark Descent*, or even *Hotline Miami*, with its claustrophobic sleaze and hallucinatory violence.

I am, evidently, not the first person to romanticise the highs and lows of creative employment; as I write this, a TV show is in the works about the early days of id Software, based on *Masters of Doom*. I know it's wrong to valorise exhaustion, not least in the context of larger development companies, but there's something I admire deeply about people who make video games; a kind of madness, an alienation and desire to be heard, which I see in writers too. It's a job that's contradictory to its core, requiring independence of thought, coupled with an almost maniacal need to reach people. It requires control, purpose, dedication, and, finally, the ability to give your project away and see it reinterpreted by everyone else.

6.   Screen Hell

In recent years I've played several games set in the underworld. There's *Undertale*, which I never finished, a kind of anti-*Pokémon* where you're given the chance either to talk to monsters or fight them. *Pinstripe*, an indie game about a self-destructive former minister, is set in a hell that's snowbound and lonely, while in *Limbo*, by far my favourite, you play as a boy running through a forest in black and white, searching for his lost sister.

These are not violent games; they're more like meditations, dismantling the tropes of gaming to ask questions about agency and guilt. They treat the screen as a canvas for spiritual inquiry. They ask what it is about hell that keeps us coming back.

I started working on this essay in Berlin at the end of the summer, shortly before moving back to Dublin. I began with the very enjoyable research task of playing *Wolfenstein 3D*. What made the game more fun was my understanding that it was banned in the country where I was playing it; due to section 86a of Germany's criminal code, which forbids depictions of symbols linked with unconstitutional organisations (even if the point of the game is to mow down Nazis), *Wolfenstein* and its sequels were illegal. I was wrong: a 2018 court ruling granted 'case-by-case examinations' of controversial material, and *Wolfenstein*

3D was made legal. It's still great, for the record, but it was more fun when I thought it was banned.

I grew up in an Ireland slowly making peace with its urge to censor, allowing the public to draw its own conclusions on morality and art. In the '90s and early '00s almost all the banned books were allowed, but video shops had entire shelves of yellow-stickered 'extreme' films like *Baise-moi* or *A Clockwork Orange*, made all the more enticing by their warnings, which implied that you *could* watch them, but at a risk to your own integrity, and possibly your soul. Video games took this sense of agency and possibility even further, landing the player in the middle of the action and inviting them to kill or be killed, to resist or embrace their own damnation.

Another game I enjoy, *Hotline Miami*, famously asks 'Do you like hurting other people?' I don't. In fact, I spend a ridiculous amount of time, in everyday life, worrying about hurting people by accident. Yet I love first-person shooters, top-down shooters, games where I shoot zombies or mutants or fascists or pixelated monsters. I rely on them in times of stress, playing with such fanatical consistency that my coffee goes cold and I lose sleep and little animated guns flash behind my eyelids for hours after I stop playing. My Steam account is a home for my contradictions as a person, a place to indulge murderous impulses I lack outside the screen.

I suspect the majority of games hold a latent morality, a prospect *Doom* interrogates with grisly irreverence. Why does it pit technology against the demons of hell, as though they're forces as strong as each other? The default skill level in *Doom* is called 'Hurt Me Plenty'. Do I enjoy hurting other people? Do I enjoy hurting myself?

Or have I absorbed by osmosis a view from American headlines printed when I was a child: the belief that a game might be too dangerous to play, and can damage the soul of its player?

7.   Hell International

In Tartarus you don't die, because you're already dead. Instead you simply fail, again and again, at repetitive tasks, exhausting, futile, almost murderous in their mundanity. These are dark nursery rhymes, morality tales that lack an ending.

King Ixion is tied to a flaming wheel for lechery and the murder of his father-in-law. Sisyphus is made to push a boulder up a hill, which falls down again. The Danaides, husband-murderers of legend, are forced to carry water in a jug to a bath, but the jug is full of holes. King Tantalus, after murdering his son, is condemned to stand in water, starving and parched, under a branch bearing perfectly ripe fruit. Each time he reaches for fruit, the tree pulls it away, and when he stoops to drink the water it drains away too.

In Ireland, before de Valera, before Bishop John Charles McQuaid, before the British and before even Catholicism itself, our own pagan 'hell' was a place notable for its moral ambivalence. We didn't really have hell, just an all-purpose Otherworld, built without segregation.

In Celtic mythology, the Otherworld is not a place of punishment, but a land of happiness. It's elusive—'other', but never very far away. It's known by multiple names, in multiple permutations—Tír na nÓg, Mag Mell, Mag Cíuin and Hy-Brasil, the phantom island located in the mists to the west. In some myths it's even called Tír na mBeo, the 'Land of the Living'; its residents are not dead, but alive forever. The Celts ran into battle fearless, because they believed they would endure beyond death. Their Otherworld could even be accessed from our one; burial mounds, and openings such as the Cave of the Cats (Oweynagat) at Rathcroghan, allowed passage between the two worlds, at Samhain and at Bealtaine.

As a Catholic, however lapsed, I find it a challenge to imagine an afterlife without the prospect of damnation. It feels central to morality, and to our national identity, however far we progress from our roots. It's woven into our language; after Saint Patrick arrived we learned to threaten each other with curses. One goes 'Go n-ithe an cat thú is go n-ithe an diabhal an cat' ('May a cat eat you, and may the devil eat the cat'). Another is 'Go ndéana an diabhal dréimire de cnámh do dhroma ag piocadh úll i ngairdín Ifrinn' ('May the devil make a ladder of your backbone, so that he can pick apples in the garden of hell'). Finally, in the late twentieth century, the earnest discussion of hell became unfashionable, and we consigned it to video games.

Rathcroghan, the hell-gate in Roscommon, is a site older than the Egyptian pyramids. At face value the Cave of the Cats is an unprepossessing hole in the ground, but it's also a place of pilgrimage. On YouTube there are videos shot by tourists; the person holding the camera climbs down, through darkness, into an oblivion of stones. Each video ends with a return to the light; they always stop before they reach the Otherworld.

In legend the cave functions like a teleport; a cow is dragged in and emerges a short time later, one county over, from the Caves of Kesh. Then there are the monsters which emerge; the Ellen Trechen, three-headed and scaly; the werewolves; the swarms of red birds and feral swine that wither crops with their breath before vanishing. There are the giant wildcats, which give the cave its name, and the Morrigan, goddess of war and fate, who sometimes takes the form of a crow. In legend the Morrigan emerges from the cave in a chariot pulled by a one-legged horse, a detail which strikes me as extremely metal.

I imagine the Celts and their baffled Christian successors repeating stories about a cave in the midlands simply to amuse themselves, and not guessing these stories would endure for over a thousand years. The cow-teleportation and the three-headed beasts remind me of games we play today; they prove that we keep the bad things close—but not *too* close—because it makes life more exciting.

8. 'In Hell is All Manner of Delight'

The above line is spoken by Lucifer in *Doctor Faustus*, Christopher Marlowe's 1592 play. I keep returning to *Faustus*, in part because it does something hundreds of video games and horror films like to believe they invented; it implicates the viewer, by delivering moral damnation as entertainment. *Faustus* makes a pact with the devil in return for magical powers and knowledge; consequently, he brings these wonders to the stage for us to enjoy. It's only at the end, when Faustus is dragged off the stage to hell, that we have second thoughts.

Another reason to love Faustus is that, centuries before headlines about games, critics claimed Marlowe's play had driven some of its audience members mad. There was even a suggestion that real demons appeared on the stage, 'to the great amazement of both actors and spectators', breaking the fourth wall by revealing the play itself to be a summoning ritual.

In *Doom* you go into every level expecting to die, again and again, but you keep playing. Unlike the calculated addiction tactics used by games today— the loot crates, the dark patterns and behavioural design—*Doom*'s approach was relatively straightforward. Romero and his team wanted to make a game so fun that you couldn't stop playing it.

Perhaps the danger critics saw in *Doom* was not that its players would be sent to hell, but that it might teach us to *love* hell. Perhaps we would become too powerful by playing; hell-bringers, gods of tiny, violent worlds.

Romero said, 'It's funny, with my son, when he was probably around eight years old we talked to him about hell, and he asked, "Why would you send a bad person to a place where only bad people are? Wouldn't that be awesome for them, like heaven for bad people?"'

It's tempting to claim that *Doom* exists because we transcended traditional morality, but then, what are we doing in playing it, but killing demons, and battling the armies of hell? Instead, *Doom* pays tribute to hell as a cultural phenomenon, a story which changes with every retelling, every player, every mod. Hell is a game we play with ourselves, and moral panics emerge when one hell-narrative falls away, and is replaced by another.

Create and destroy. Create, and *be* destroyed, then get up and create again.

Hell is eternal. 'Of course hell is eternal,' Romero said, laughing, 'because that's the whole idea of hell.' That final scene works as a sigil launched in the name of creativity. The demons are loose. Where will you go, now that hell is everywhere?

No Love Lost

Reared on stony ground where sparse flints of rationed love shave off and drop for you to find

Words

          fall and sprout

                    in cracks

                              made by others

Anne Mulkeen Murray

This is I

I come from the dead, a long line of wombs.
Born between two graveyards, stretched like wings
over our hill, rolling fields, church, the Angelus bell
my brother rang every evening at six o'clock.

I come from crows, swallows, hazelnuts, woods,
daily routine collecting eggs, pitted potatoes. Yearly
cycles—saving hay, turf, picking apples in autumn.
I grew in rhythm with cows, harrow, and plough.

I come from feeding lambs, calves, weekly burials
behind our house, watched parishioners descend
into death; boulders with circular heads, carved
Celtic crosses noted their ending, my beginning.

I am from clay merged in grey landscape, sentinel
spirits, walls, ancient epitaphs carved into crypts.
Hours conversing with ghosts, stone language a circle,
square, growing in contradiction, pagan and christian.

I come from promises, relics, foraged bone, ancestors
in tombs. Latin letters on slabs sheeted my body,
this world, my safe place. I live in a land of plenty.
I come from the land of the dead.

Attracta Fahy

These Are The Tools God Gave Us

Mike McCormack

The upshot of that last job—along with the injuries myself and Welger sustained—was that all my tools were destroyed, all my tools and a full set of gauges badly burned out. I was sorting through them when Welger swung into the yard.

'How are they?' he called, climbing out of the van. 'Are they bad?'

'They're fucked,' I said, ruefully. 'Every one of them.'

Welger bent down and picked one up. It looked gentle and pliant in his large hand; you could feel the dying warmth of it. He held it to his ear for a moment and then laid it down.

'We used to drown bags of these in the tide when I was a child,' he said.

Something in me bristled. 'These gauges have a full pedigree,' I started. 'Lineal descendants of a German K9.'

'That means nothing to me,' Welger said.

'Beautiful pieces of work,' I insisted. Why was I going on like this? Welger was looking at me. 'There's a three-year waiting list for a full set of these,' I added, on a final angry note.

Welger stood up. 'I know a man who can fix them,' he said. 'Throw them in the back of the van, I'll run them over to him.'

'Will I fuck throw them in the back of the van. Those gauges are licensed to my name; they have to go to a registered lab for recalibration.'

Welger shook his head. 'If those gauges turn up on someone's workbench and they download the last readings off them, it will be a long time before you're issued with another set and that's as sure as you're standing there.'

He was telling the truth and I knew it. And it was a mark of how difficult that last job had been and the extent to which it had scrambled my own sense of the future that I had not foreseen this. And then Welger decided it for me completely.

'Please yourself,' he said, 'but I guarantee that if you turn those things into a registered lab you will be out of work for five years; that's how long it will take for you to get through the screening process and get a new set. They will know where we've been and what we've been doing and that'll be the end of it.'

I made no pretence of mulling it over any longer. I gathered them up and left them into the back of the van. Welger closed the door on them. 'That wasn't what brought me over,' he said.

I raised my hands. 'If it's money… '

'It's not money,' Welger said. 'Calm down, it's something else.' He put his hand up against the side of the van and closed his eyes. A dull note of empathy swung through me. I knew exactly what he was feeling. That awful tiredness that washed through my body periodically, leaving it parched and hollow, the trailing flare of fireworks behind the eyes for minutes at a time afterwards which made concentration so difficult.

'I've been on tough jobs in my time,' Welger continued, 'but these flashbacks are not like anything I've ever had before.'

'I know, I've been getting them too.'

A look of relief crossed Welger's face. 'And I can't tell the time from Adam,' he continued. 'It's all scrambled on me. What time is it now?'

'It's getting on to four o clock.'

Welger shook his head. 'That means nothing to me,' he said. 'You could be telling me anything. I can't tell the time, my sleep is fucked… '

'I know what you're saying, Welger, but there was always risk on that job.'

'This is different.'

'It's only been a few days. Give it a couple of weeks and see how it goes. There should be some improvement.'

Welger's spirits slumped further, a weight visibly sliding through him. A real friend would have been sorry that some of his own anxiety and worry had been soothed by his suffering. But I wasn't and that's the truth of it.

'Sound,' Welger said, heavily. 'Sound.' He climbed into the van. 'I'll drop those gauges off at the man and I'll get back to you when he's had a look at them.'

'There's no rush.'

He turned out the gate and sped up the coast road. And if you'd told me then that it would be a couple of months before I'd see him again I would have been relieved.

I gradually improved over the following weeks.

The dissonance between my inner clock and external time slowly meshed as my circadian rhythms fell to their proper hours. And with my sense of time becoming more accurate, my ribs and shoulder began to heal properly; bones knitting together and the bruising on my abdomen clearing also. Day by day I was harmonising with myself, returning to my proper being. Three weeks later I was almost back to myself completely. Yes, there was still a slight lag in my sleep and in my ability to register time, but I was confident now of myself getting stronger and better.

As the days shortened and the winter light closed in around the house, my focus shifted from my own injuries to taking care of my wife.

Ellie is a keener, a professional keener.

One of those women who cry out their praises of the dead, smoothing their passage to heaven and soothing the souls of the bereaved. Keener by trade, keener by spirit, keener by vocation. Martha, our daughter, says sometimes that she is more comfortable singing the praises of the dead than those of the living. Her most recent contract was the difficult one—a male clone in his early twenties whose brutal murder threatened to flare up and incite more violence.

Ellie was standing at the gable with a mug of coffee in her hand. Our plot of land ran from the main road down to the foreshore in the distance. December clouds piled overhead and she stood raw and windblown, perfectly cut out for this time and place.

But she looked tired also. You could see the fatigue in her face, the blue shadows beneath her features. I had seen this before but there was a malignant depth to this that was new.

'Winter's here,' I said. 'It's come in early.'

'I'm glad. I like the winter.' Ellie pulled her cardigan around her and turned her shoulder to the wind. 'The time of year for rest and sharpening our tools, getting ready for the spring.' She raised her hand to my face. 'You look better.'

'I'm okay, not so sore now. I got paid also, so that's good.'

'Yes, I got paid too. It came through last night.'

'Two pay cheques will carry us till spring.'

'Hopefully.'

'I saw the footage; you did a fine job.'

'Yes, I hope so.'

'It looked difficult, you must be tired.'

'I am tired, very tired. It took me an age to get my head around it. You literally don't know what note to strike, always that dissonance around clones, even when they're dead. And it leaves you drained.'

'I hate that you have to go off in the dark like that, and no idea where you're going.'

'It was the other side of the county. It took two and a half days, making sure I crossed no major roads. But I thought you were following me? You were supposed to be following me.'

'I was but the GPS was twitchy—you'd disappear for hours at a time and then pop back into focus, it was hard to keep track.'

Ellie leaned back against the wall with her eyes closed. Weak light lit up the shadows crawling beneath her skin—it would take weeks for her face to clear.

'I now know why so many keeners avoid doing clones. It's so gruelling, and some of them never recover their proper pitch afterwards.' And then she smiled. 'But I got a nice note from the mother; she was pleased with my work. It says something good about her that she took the time to write to me.'

'She looked heartbroken in the footage I saw.'

'Who wouldn't be? Her only child just setting out in life and then dying like that.'

Later that same evening we set a small fire at the bottom of the garden and burned all the clothes she had used on that last keen—the dress she had walked over a hundred kilometres in, the jacket, her underwear and socks, her old boots. We piled them up, doused them in petrol and then struck a match. The night closed in around us as we watched them burn and as the last flames were dying down Ellie used the spade to turn the charred remnants into the heart of the fire, ensuring there was nothing left but ashes; the last part of the keening ritual now fulfilled. As we raked the ashes into a pile, Martha came from the house, stripping her head-cam as she walked. She came up behind Ellie and put her arms around her, burying her face in the back of her neck. Ellie was neither startled nor moved. She ran her hand through Martha's hair.

'There's only one person in the world with hugs like that.'

And in that moment, standing over the ashes of my wife's clothes, I thought myself a lucky man. Not because these two women were everything I loved of this world, but because I would have no sorrow in seeing the rest of it go to hell.

We hunkered down for the winter, the three of us. Ellie took the van to the co-op and did a huge shop of everything we would need to carry us through the next ten weeks. Cupboards and shelves were stacked with tins and boxes, the freezer filled up. Luckily, our old house with all its rambling additions and conversions was big enough to give each of us our own space during the day, so that our coming together for an evening meal was something we looked forward to. It was easy to believe we were returning from greater distances than was actually the case, with news and greetings from afar.

Outside, the days shortened down to a couple of hours' daylight, while the wind kept up a steady pounding on the hipped roof. And for me that was the worst of it. I could cope with the grey light that leached the colour from everything and the driving rain that drew so much of its slashing venom from the sea. But the constant pounding wind, that's what grated on me, that's what deepened my anxiety and wore me down.

And there was no sign of Welger. December passed and no word and as the year turned I began to think it might be an idea to give him a call. No sooner had I formed the idea than he turned up on cue in the yard, turning his van through the gate. I watched him from the kitchen window. I expected him to jump out and come to the door with that shouldering gait of his, but he surprised me by doing the very opposite. He leaned forward with his head on the steering wheel for a long moment, a pose so at odds with everything I knew about him that I was immediately on my guard when he eventually did get out and made his way across the yard.

'Welger,' I said, 'the very man.'

'Can I come in?'

'Sure.'

He pushed past me and craned his neck up and down the hall. 'Is she in herself?'

'She is, but is it me or her you want?'

Welger looked agitated in a way I had never known him to be.

'We can talk in there,' I said, pointing to the utility room beside the kitchen.

He surged head down through the open door. Inside he pulled himself up to his full height and faced me.

'What the fuck is on those gauges?' he said suddenly, stepping towards me.

I put my hand out to keep him at a distance. Welger was scared, I saw that clearly now, and it spooked me to have him like this, most especially to have him like this in my own house. 'You know what's on those gauges,' I said. 'You know all that.'

'Do I fuck know all that,' Welger fired back. He prodded a finger. 'You're a fucking… ' His rage surfaced once more, preventing him from finishing the sentence. He stood there, prodding the air.

'Explain what you're talking about, Welger, or you'll have to go. You can't come into my house roaring and shouting like this. Tell me straight or get out.'

'The readings,' he spluttered. 'Those readings.'

'As far as I know, Welger, there's nothing on those gauges except what they read on that last job—you know, you were beside me when we took them. So what are you complaining about now? I don't understand.'

I had sympathy for Welger. It was clear he was completely overtaken by a mixture of rage and fear. And whatever attempt he'd made in the van to calm himself and meet me with a civil tongue had completely evaporated in the short distance to my door.

He drew a deep breath, hauling air into the depths of his chest. 'I gave those gauges to this man I know and he took a look at them and said no bother, he'd wipe and reset them. But it would take a while; he had a backlog of work on his bench. Sound, I said, there's no rush. He got back to me yesterday— or rather he turned up at my gate and fucked them across the grass to me. "What's wrong?" I asked. "Take them away from me," he said, "and don't ever bring them near me again. I have never seen readings like these." I tried to calm him down but that only made him worse. So then he showed me what he was talking about.' And now Welger looked at me with naked disbelief. 'I was there when you did that scrape—I have a clear memory of it. And those readings are there, one after another, all properly stacked and sieved, there's no problem with them. But beneath them there's a parallel reading, a different screed altogether.'

'You mean a ghost script.'

'Yes.'

'We know about ghost scripts,' I said. 'It's not unlikely that those gauges would pick up ambient readings, they are seriously sensitive.'

'Well, they're there, trailing on the backs of the primary readings. In all his years of reconditioning gauges he has never come across anything like them. Frankly, he nearly shit himself. He checked and double checked but there's no disputing them.' Welger ground to a halt, his anger and frustration spent. He raised his hand above his head and laid the palm against the wall.

'Ambient readings, Welger; they're a nuisance more than anything, they can be binned.'

'No they can't, not these, not what's on them.'

Welger's anger had not weakened him. He was now gathered to some purpose beyond rage; it hardened throughout his body and every line in his face.

'So how bad are those readings?'

'You know where we were, where we took those readings. They were always going to be bad, and they are. But the ambient readings are worse, way worse.'

I listened to him and I heard his words but they were not what Welger was saying and we both knew it. I waited for him to continue but he was saying no more.

'Say it out Welger,' I pushed.

'I don't have to say it out.'

A blunt surge of anger pushed through me. 'I don't have all fucking day to stand here listening to you mewling and puking, Welger. Say what's on your mind.' I was appalled at my own recklessness. If this encounter came to blows, there was only one way it would go. Welger leaned into me with his teeth bared.

'You don't need me to tell you what's on my mind, you know damn well. But you do need to know that you can go to hell, you and your gauges. Don't come around me or my family again, or you'll be meeting me at the door with my gun.' He went to walk away before turning back once more. 'And if there is anything decent in your black heart you will pack a bag tonight and leave your wife and child and fuck off out of their lives.'

He threw open the door and strode across the yard. I watched as he opened the back of the van and fired the bag of gauges on to the ground. He swung around the yard in a skid of muddy rainwater, and the van disappeared from sight at the top of the road.

*

'I thought I saw Welger today,' Ellie said, later that evening.

'Yes, that was him all right; a short visit.'

'What did he want? I'm always uneasy whenever he calls.'

'Not much, he just left back the set of gauges.'

'So they're all sorted.'

'No, they're not all sorted; he wasn't able to do anything with them.'

'So what are you going to do now?'

'I don't know for the moment. I have to think about it.'

Ellie looked pointedly at me. 'Don't tell me he left them in the house?'

'No, they're out in the shed.'

'Leave them there, they give me the creeps.'

'You and me both,' Martha said, as she sat into the table. 'They weird me out. I can never rid myself of the idea that they're watching me, even when they're in the next room.'

'You don't appreciate their artistry,' I said. 'That's what's wrong with you two.'

'Those things,' Ellie shuddered. 'They're neither dead nor alive.'

'Nor animal, vegetable or mineral.'

'Some unholy hybrid.'

'Some unholy hybrid, forged in hell.'

I raised my hands. 'Okay, I get it, they stay outside.'

And they did. After Welger left I had carried them to the shed and put them in the corner. And of course I took a last look at them, lying in the bottom of the bag, and as always I was both fascinated and repulsed. Such extraordinary instruments! Their steady pulse arcing across the organic and synthetic, their reach into depths that became more abstract the deeper they went. Lying there, it was impossible to see them as the point at which metaphysics and a rogue strain of biotech had their communion. My wonder was complete and I closed the bag over them before going back into the kitchen where Ellie was setting the table and lighting candles.

But sometimes now, waking in the middle of the night, I sense them through the walls and across the yard to their corner of the shed. And it frightens me to know that they are there, sharing this world with me and my loves, ticking away and gathering their horrible testimony. And that same fear brings with it the certain knowledge also that I can never be rid of them, and that one day they will surely testify against me, and that will be all.

The Unseeing

Too often I've tried to write to you from terminus to tell you about the sea I miss more than I imagined, my underestimated need for the showdown wet-in-your-bones miserable mornings, the groundless chats I could only half-see the point of, and largely took for granted. The small talk doesn't feel so small anymore. Where are the faces I'd avoid by left-turn under a roofed laneway, the city's streets an automatic navigation, the *hovryas* cast across the cobbles from out under the starboard of the umbrella, the just seeing people you might know, who might know you, who hear you without filtering by accent, the place that used to wreck my head (sometimes). My heart too big of a tare to go back to zero, and also too proud to pick up the phone and call, knowing that distance's irregular alerts and notifications causes worry, how a missed call or a message at a peculiar time can be seen, but I promise, sometimes it is just me, casting a hello, me looking out the window at the oak, listening for the evening train braking along Dekalb Avenue. I have no one to chat to, no plan to go out, no what-you-up-to friend here, just yet. We will be out of sync and schedule for a long time, little allowance for outpourings the way the

Too often I've tried to write to you from terminus to tell you how we've been too blinded by myth and forgot to see the human. Tell you how some mé féiners who came overseas, rose to overseers, took the bait for whiter than white, abused become abuser, and built an identity so I don't even have to open my mouth here to be protected in the eyes of the law, in the eyes of the structures. We allowed it to happen, to continue, these brutal expressions a new normal so we could keep building a begod Irishness that forsakes the worth of others. We worked so hard and succeeded. They are the celebrated diaspora, and we are the green to be gazed upon. We are surname, after surname dropped onto others, no choice but a drop of Irish here, a drop there. Too easy to say not my country, not my problem, not my history, not my story. Don't we get annoyed when people come to Ireland, and they refuse to see the disappeared, the mass burial sites near the N17, the illegitimate generation still being denied and denied? How Dáil Éireann picks and chooses what is remembered as Irish and exports it? How some who pick and choose to be Irish-American othered the bodies and put the highway over them, the dead covered over to make room for a progress for some? I often try to write to you from terminus but there's an asterisk at the corner of my mouth to not let on about the blue, the collar, the green, the black.

rain falls out of the sky when it has formed, and it falls on you if you can see it falling, and know it's raining if you can feel it wet on your shoulders. Otherwise, it is just weather in another place, out of radius. The isolation of a country within a country in isolation. All the talk on the socials of *when this is over* plans for closeness, nailing them to feeds and walls. Those far from structures know the when is never over when you're still a stranger in a country with different rules for different portions. Too often loneliness is boundless, and all there is, is rain, a constant. Even then, I know now that rain is seen differently depending on whose structure got put on you. The intermittent is never over. It is constant the need for the comfort of friends who you do not need to explain yourself to, and they are a cloud on the horizon too often held out far, far at sea for fear to write, out of pride. I swim to the other side in a dream, legs fading and arm too short to reach the ledge, I tread and dip and tread and dip until I see a figure calmly come over and ask, 'Can you get to the other side?' I will to keep my body going and to not let on.

Elaine Cosgrove

Where We Come From

Peter Murphy

Once you have given up the ghost, Henry Miller wrote, everything follows with dead certainty, even in the midst of chaos.

It was an otherwise innocuous Thursday afternoon when I took the daughters to Supermac's in Blackrock, and we squeezed between yellow plastic tables and chairs bolted to the floor and ordered ice-cream sundaes, and I forced myself to speak words I'd been putting off for a half a decade. From now on I would only see them at weekends. I wouldn't be there in the mornings to make their breakfasts or find their socks or help with homework or make dinner after school. The response was anger, dismay, tears. I wanted to vomit my ice-cream sundae all over those plastic yellow seats.

Not all depressions are the same. Some are chemical. Some present as fallout from long-term trauma. Some are natural reactions to loss or grief. All it takes is three or four concussions—a clusterfuck.

Rewind a bit. Late 2007. I'd sold my first book. The night the cheque cleared I took a Dart into town and went to a gig in the Academy and had a few drinks to celebrate. Afterwards, crossing the top of O'Connell Street, I was clipped by a car, hard enough to take the wing mirror off, hard enough to fall and crack the back of my head off the concrete. I staggered upright, wheezing and heaving air into my lungs, blurry shapes of people running towards me. My ribs felt like they'd been kicked by a horse. Later, in A&E, waiting to get X-rayed, I removed the silver metal cigarette case from my inside jacket pocket. It was dented almost in half. The case had acted as armour, keeping my lungs from being punctured by the ribs, probably the first time a person's life had been saved by cigarettes. I spent weeks swallowing painkillers and trying not to sneeze.

I was probably still suffering from concussion when I messaged the girl from Michigan with whom I'd been having a sort of online epistolary affair and told her I was coming to meet her within the month. One more step and I'd have been pureed all over the road. Hubert Selby Jr's words: *'Two things would happen right before I died: I would regret my entire life; I would want to live it over again.'* I booked the flight and packed a bag, and when the day came I flew from Dublin to Frankfurt, Frankfurt to Detroit. The Homeland Security officer at Detroit Metro asked uncomfortable questions about my business in the States. Alarms went off as I walked through the arrivals lounge and the girl rose from her seat and turned to meet me. A 6,000-mile blind date.

We tried to sustain the affair long-distance, but of course it couldn't hold. She was the saner one, kept breaking up with me, and I, desperate and needy, wouldn't take no for an answer. My life at home was an ungodly mire, and I clung to memories of bright, quiet mornings in her condo, the snow-covered hush of Michigan in winter, until eventually, exhausted, I conceded defeat. I was a man in the midst of a messy separation, snarled in legal proceedings, newly estranged from his daughters, preparing to mourn a mother whose mind was erasing itself. I was in no fit state to conduct any kind of relationship, never mind one that had to span the Atlantic.

Something in me sprained around that time. I feared that if I didn't make some sort of radical, fundamental change I might be headed for another trip to A&E. Weird Freudian impulses were at work, the kind of subconscious urges that might compel you into traffic because you couldn't stand your life. Joint custody meant finding a place I could have the girls at weekends—*access* they call it—but house rental in the city was out. I searched online, inching further south, Bray, Wicklow, Arklow, I kept going until I got to Gorey, then Enniscorthy, my hometown. It made sudden sense. The distance would serve as a buffer from marital fallout. I could commute for journalism assignments. I'd be near my mother in her final days. The daughters could get to know their uncles and aunt and cousins better.

I found a house about a mile outside of town, a semi-detached in a small development, a stream at the back. A twelve-month lease. I told almost no one, not even the girls. While they were away on holiday with their mother I hired a man with a van and moved everything I owned, which was mostly books.

*

Late Summer, 2008. Lady Gaga on the screen in every takeaway. The crash was imminent, a cold front moving in. The first crack appeared when the car dealership in Blackrock shut. Within a couple of weeks the huge glass display window had spiderwebbed and weeds were crawling through the pavement slabs in the front lot, an echo of Detroit in South Dublin. Soon those cracks metastasized and followed me south. My hometown began to take on the look of some forgotten Soviet Bloc outpost. New developments and housing estates were left desolate, ghosts the only residents. Migrant labourers returned home to Poland and Ukraine. Bankruptcies and closures: the pizza place, the cinema, Xtravision, victuallers' and butchers' shops, family-run businesses I remembered from childhood disappearing from the grid. Only pound shops left, knockdown shops, Oxfam, NCBI, the ISPCA, cancer charities.

Most days the streets were emptied out by six, the only evidence of night-life the showbands that seemed to re-emerge after a twenty-year hibernation to reclaim the deserted gastropubs and disco-bars. It didn't take long for the thin veneer of modernity to wear away and the country to start its slide back into the 1970s. Local radio droned Lottery numbers and death notices and the Angelus, country-and-Irish waltzes, awful mawkish stuff, baby-men bleating about leaving for America, missing Mammy and the misty hills of home. Nothing for teenagers to do but walk the length of the prom and back again, maybe loiter on the forecourt of the Applegreen and eat chips and spit.

I found comfort there, despite. The terrain was dream-familiar, smaller than I remembered, everything seemed affordable. I caught the train to the city when I had to and collected the girls at weekends. I steered clear of sad songs and gloomy movies. I took a lot of baths. Winter it out. Winter it out.

When it all goes quiet, that's when you have to watch it. The process is insidious. The slow fraying of the nerves. The black dog chews through wiring, disables the very mechanism that apprehends him. One moment you're walking up Castle Hill clutching books plundered from a second-hand shop, the next you feel something give in your throat and you have to duck into a lane and hide until the weeping jag has passed. Emotional incontinence, they call it. I'd find myself stalking the roads, four, five miles a day, engaged in frantic arguments, lodging objections with myself or the exes, the babble so loud in my head it spilled out my mouth. I was wired and wrung out and devoid of appetite.

Such was the climate in which I wrote my second book, the story of a haunted river, a novel about a suicide cycle, about a strange, craven man named Enoch O'Reilly. At night as I fell asleep the babble of the brook merged with the babble of my brain, the constant torrent of anxiety, neuroses, worry over the kids, guilt at not visiting my mother enough, obsessing after the girl from Michigan who had moved on and found another man. I became the Crazy Ex, entering her name into the search engine, clicking through twenty pages of results, re-entering the name in different configurations and doing it again, all the while simultaneously fixating on the book (the book, The Book, THE BOOK) and the divorce, the affidavits and the legal correspondence and the statements of means.

The babble reached maximum intensity somewhere around November of that year, my fortieth birthday. To mark the event I got the book cover tattooed on my shoulder. The burn of the needle felt like a bloodletting. I sensed the slow turning of a wheel. My mother passed on a May morning in 2009, and anticipatory grief became actual grief, real grief, and at last we could begin to mourn.

For a while then I lived with a woman who became my second wife and then my second ex-wife in a 400-year-old thatched farmhouse five miles from town. At night the silence was intense and the darkness almost total, but for the stars. One day in April a spark escaped the chimney flue and cooked the girders and the thatch began to smoke. Neighbours came from all around. Within minutes they had emptied the cottage of our belongings, but water damage from the fire brigade's hoses made it uninhabitable. I sat on the front lawn and took a swig from a bottle of Jack Daniels someone had placed on the grass, and I passed it to one of the firemen, a lad I'd been to school with, who took a nip and told me we were lucky, that if the fire had happened at night, three breaths of smoke and you don't wake up.

If Enniscorthy was the home I came from, then Wexford Town, twenty miles down the road, is the home I came to. I go mad in landlocked places. The sense of being trapped, of stagnation and decay. Towns or cities built on the sea suggest the possibility of embarkment, escape. In Wexford town there are open-mic nights in coffee shops and the pubs pipe their bar staff's playlists. There are food festivals and plays and concerts in the Arts Centre and the Opera House. Fishing boats and trawlers moored on the quay. It is a town full of musicians, painters, playwrights, filmmakers, photographers, writers and actors, but it can't be a European City of Culture because Wexford is not a city, it's a town; a big town, a port town, maybe a portal to another dimension, but still a town. That town nestles in a county. And in that county there are so many creative practitioners I can't even begin naming them for fear of the ones I'll forget, and besides, it would probably just read like a list of artists you've never heard of, because we live too far from media centres to be included in dispatches and broadcasts. That's not an anti-Dublin dig, it's just a fact that journalists and bloggers can no longer afford to spend money on travel and accommodation to cover this near-subversive cultural regeneration occurring in places like our county, and in Limerick, and Cork, and Derry, and Belfast, so it's incumbent upon us to make ourselves heard, to amplify those voices and promote galleries and gigs and theatre productions and independent book shops and publications that sprout like mushrooms every autumn. And yes, a virus killed this year's crop, but they'll grow back.

On a strangely still night during lockdown this summer, myself and my friend and collaborator Dan Comerford recorded a spoken-word video on Main Street in Wexford. It was a sort of love letter to the place that took me in when I was wretched, the place that allowed me to put shape and form on plans, dreams. I wrote it while I was writer-in-residence at Carlow College, St Patrick's. It shares its title with a poem from Annemarie Ní Churreáin's book, *Bloodroot*. If you want to, you can find it online.

Where we come from: Viking settlements, Norman colonies, Templar ruins, Catholic cathedrals, Protestant estates, Franciscan friaries and medieval castles with wi-fi aerials. Port towns, former garrisons, farmlands, fishing villages, one-shop Sat-Nav blips. Names like Caim, Killane, Killinick, Kilmore, Tacumshane, Carne—the rump of the country, the deep south-east, the coast roaring like a beast.

Where we come from, our ancestors were seafarers, tinsmiths, travellers, tillers of the land. Now we are historians, hurlers, nurses, clerks, musicians, fishermen, IT sorcerers. Folk who hate to be rushed. Folk who wouldn't see you stuck.

Where we come from, the land is beautiful, but there's darkness in the soil. A heaviness, a haunting here, a trauma that originates from way before the Famine and the Rising and the Civil War, before the druids and the bishops and the high priest caste of new technologies—a darkness rising in the bones like damp. Sometimes the suck of it seems inescapable.

And yet, when the sun comes up the boats go out. People rise and go to work. The landscape hums. The air is spiced with smoke. On this meridian the stars seem near. The sight would catch your heart.

Where we come from, the landscape doesn't care, it just endures. You can take leave any time, but you're fated always to return, for births or weddings, wakes or funerals, in a wooden box, or in your dreams—

this is your home.

Skinny Dipping

i.m. Laura Thornton

Remember that time after the pub we got our kit off
at Blackrock and ran lawlessly towards the water?
Until that night, Galway Bay had always been a
Foster & Allen song to be suffered on a Sunday,
an image printed on a tea-towel, or the face of a
dish on display in a room that nobody ever sat in.

I listened to the cadence of my heart calming down,
stared ahead and watched a trawler scraping itself
seaward. I was reminded of beach parties in the
mid-nineties, a couple of dozen mutineers waiting
for their fathers´ boats to steam out the harbour
so as not to meet them on the loaded road home.

Remember that night we shacked up in a French bistro
belting out Joni Mitchell songs on an out-of-tune
guitar? It got poetic after the third jug of Merlot—
you telling me how you've trouble describing apples
falling in darkness, or how the colour of footprints in
spilt red wine will depend on the surface of the floor.

Napkins, damp beer mats, a narrow scroll of till receipt—
I wrote them all down—every 3AM after-thought,
every viscous whisper. When I guided my chin over
your shoulder to cement the hug, I inhaled your jacket—
tobacco, the salt of a west coast winter; an inaudible image
of seagulls hovering in the breeze along the Long Walk.

Remember the morning you disappeared and I followed suit
as plumes of smoke left in the unscripted absence
dissolved into the wind ghosting along the promenade?
A room that nobody ever sat in was suddenly opened up,
neighbours were ushered in, condolences offered, sympathy
beaming from do-gooders with trays of tea and fancy biscuits.

I drifted from one room to the next, out the front door, down
D'Alton Drive, stumbled through Lenaboy Park and out
towards the water where I waded in waist-deep, fully-clothed
and thrashed at the surface, disturbing the reflection of clouds,
their illusion of this city as a home in which I have built
us an empire of memories, precious few of which were ours.

Neil McCarthy

What Was It Like There

Michael Phoenix

A barrel jellyfish was washed up on the top of Grattan Strand between the stone beach wall the high point of the evening tide and its body was the colour of the stones and the water it was the moon in the night sky upon the cold shore. Cars' light white headlights curled east and west the road behind the wall to Galway the city and Salthill village. As I walked towards the water as I left behind the hard sand the curling car lights the tilt of the beach began into the waves and when I ducked down when I dived in the waves washed me their colour atlantic and the moon was not the body of the beached jellyfish but something that pulled at the water around me this is a story about tidal force one day in Galway the summer two thousand eighteen.

When I had got out of the water had dried the cold the night air's weight from my chest and wiped the sand from my feet my ankles had gotten my shoes back on and was sure the keys to the 1970s apartment I let had not fallen, no, were still there in my trouser pocket beside the coins the ten euro note when I was back on land, when I had returned, the street lamps were burning matchstick white down the Salthill prom, they were leading the road back to Thursday night and town.

I crossed through the gap in the dry stone beach wall and began to walk away from the traffic. I turned down the Grattan Road and on the grass of the knuckle of the park named after Celia Griffen (who died in the famine aged six years old in 1847) passed the Famine Ship Memorial and coloured tents of couples come to Ireland roaming, those couples were then drinking glasses of Guinness in west-end pubs they were walking the bridge to Mutton Island to its viewpoint its lighthouse its water treatment plant and at the Gaelic pitches in the south park where I often stopped I stopped. The wind moved there as though it were something welcomed in by the creation of space behind the ball kicked the players racing the hurl where it dipped, by falls, there could not have been a windier pitch anywhere in Ireland and two women were out passing a sliothar that night.

It began to rain when I reached Nimmo's Pier and the drops fell fat towards the Claddagh where I rejoined the Grattan Road. I decided I would stop in town before the rest of the way the apartment and wait the rain out with a pint in a corner of the west-end where there might be someone I might know and, if not, from where I could look out through the window the rain running through the River Corrib (*An Ghaillimh*) and into the Atlantic. The blues and whites and blacks the navy of the night gave way as I pushed into the pub they were replaced with amber red and brown. Inside sounded accents from most of Ireland over and some French Italian Brazilian. In the end the rain came heavily it became a storm and for a long time did not clear so I stayed though she did not appear, I drank my pint, and when I left the water was running fast under Wolfe Tone Bridge.

Early the morning Galway, the hour of the seagulls, every day they woke me and I had long known they would I got up, got half changed, set myself down the stairs into the kitchen I put on the kettle, lifted one of the kitchen chairs out from around the kitchen table walked to the front door knocked it open and ran out into the day the chair thrown up above my head the coastal air striking my face, mad, and cried *don't misunderstand me you bloody birds get away go on get I am not as considerate not as empathetic as all that is my rubbish my neighbours rubbish not your breakfast go catch a fish for once would you and leave us down here be*

they did not argue with me, I was not worth it, there were bins half open weak plastic bin bags set out all over the neighbourhood and in some of them even the rests of white fish, it was a problem of our own making but I had done what I could that morning and the kettle was boiled.

I sat the chair in the courtyard to the side of the door and the drainpipe as the kitchen window went steaming over. I went in made tea and came back out among the wreckage of the rubbish to sit, drink it hot with milk, and forget another day about the seagulls and all the other things that came for me in the morning.

Time passed through the city. Articulated lorries came bouncing down the road behind the apartment building. They were the sign to go back in go get showered for things might happen again, and anyway, didn't I have to go to work wasn't it true that those kegs would not be lifted be rolled be pushed or dragged out of their room not got into their proper position by themselves it was Friday, meaning more the town for drinking. You have responsibilities to the place you have chosen to live and there are many ways in which somewhere might become your home.

I packed a quick bag left the tea-mug for the sink locked the PVC door behind me and went to get a fresh scone at the bakery on Middle St I would soon be eating it with a bit of raspberry jam in the sun alongside the Spanish Arch, there might even be in the harbour a hooker hoisting its sails.

But the bakery on Middle Street closed two years ago. It was replaced with a new version, with a Scandinavian design, and this is now what we know as the bakery on Middle Street. In a sense it has erased the old place. But maybe this all happened before. Maybe it is what happens again and again. On my way for my scone I passed tourists looking round the Latin Quarter amazed. There is a fine line between a city and what is being made of a city. The heart of the heart of the matter beats there, in the tension in between.

At the harbour there was no hooker no sails being hoisted but the sun climbing, and a few of us sat there drinking coffee eating our breakfasts in the chill of the day to come I hung my legs over the harbour wall and through the Corrib ran no trace of the storm the night before.

As I waited in front the chipped wooden door of the bar my place of work a chef a kitchen porter smoked in the narrow passage the restaurant beside *did you hear they've got the red flag flying the water at Blackrock today there's word of a lion's mane going around heard it's sent a few men over the university hospital and its panic down there the water* in Galway, that summer, news was forever going around and what was happening to anyone in the city was almost happening to you, there was a proximity in the city then that is uncommon. I said to the man who opened the bar door before we set to work *they're saying there's a lion's mane about down at Blackrock pool have you heard anything at all* and there was no doubting the sightings of the jellyfish for he had indeed heard tell of them there was a story going around the city that day it was being pulled by the moon.

The lion's mane jellyfish (*Cyanea capillata*—disputed), the largest known jellyfish in the world normally to be found in Northern Hemisphere oceans off the coast Ireland England eastern Canada or in waters Scandinavian they are boreal, dangerous. They grow to an estimated 2 metres in diameter and have between 70 and 150 tentacles which they trail 30 metres deep. They feed on small fish on other jellyfish and are themselves eaten by sea turtles and sea birds (guillemots). If they manage to avoid their predators they live only a year during which time they stay near the surface of the water and are carried, chaotically, by currents. Yearly, towards the end of summer into early autumn, when they are fully grown and at their heaviest, lion's manes are pushed towards the shores of the geography they drift off where they will eventually wash up and their lives will end.

We had rearranged the last of the kegs, the cold room was locked, the bars upstairs and down were stocked with beer wine whiskey and gin we had swept and mopped all of the floors had swept the smoking area of glass of cigarette butts of papers tobacco and had lifted the small plastic bags the resins of marijuana there was soap and rolls of paper in the male female and disabled toilets they were cleared and bleached the windows to the front we had well polished it had taken us the guts of three and half hours. As we went about the work we listened to a mix of heavy metal music from the main bar its speakers and the level of the music fell and rose as we moved about the bar. All kinds of thoughts pass through your mind before the shift is over.

When we had finished we stored the mops the mop buckets away, hung up the keys to the cold room the stock room the office, filled pint glasses with blackcurrant cordial ice and water from the taps behind the bar, turned the music off and went to sit on wooden pallets stacked on the flat of the bar's tar roof. A tributary of the Corrib ran behind the building the street. We drank our water. There was not a cloud, the sky.

Are you on a shift-split today? No, I was off. *Sweet. Doing anything tonight?* Not sure. *Some of the other staff are heading for pints.* I was thinking of walking out towards Blackrock, in my bag I had my things to swim. *To see the lion's mane?* Maybe. *Sure send us a text if you're about after.* Alright. *Good stuff. There're some tips sitting for you behind the bar by the way.* Is there much there? *Not really.* Okay, is your one heading tonight? *Yeah, she should be.*

I went out by the fire exit and turned left the street behind the bar along the olive-coloured tributary. Not far on I turned left again then right and with the fresh tips in my pocket took out *a bag of chips salt and vinegar* from the fish and chip shop. Sometimes that summer there was change in our pockets sometimes there was not rents have risen in Galway the four seasons of every year since 2012 and in the bar like almost all the bars we earned minimum wage (€9.55). Everybody knows this. I wrapped the chips up in their brown greaseproof bag and walked back the tributary. The water there was up the tide was almost in.

There was a line of people on the cross of the Corrib from Bridge Street. They were stood up on the curb from the busy road the toes of their shoes pressed against the stone wall of the bridge itself, looking towards the river, pointing. There was Irish Spanish German among them and them/they becomes us/we.

In the water below the bridge, an ordinary day, sea trout Atlantic salmon would drift, waiting to make a rush and jump the small falls of the weir up ahead. Once past the weir they would push further on through Lough Corrib to quiet turns in small inlets of the river where the females would bury their eggs with gravel. But that day was not an ordinary day the fish were not where they ought to have been. Two harbour seals had swum the river as the city had passed into the city's first high tide and had set about a hunt of the salmon and trout. As the fish raced and the seals fought after them, incredibly thick and powerful, we watched the river be split at its surface and just below by darts of silver charcoal and stone. There were fly fishermen along the path that ran the river up to the weir. They were hunched down on the balls of their feet their nets across their laps like rifles. *Someone might shoot them*, it was a young French man said this. *Someone ought to*, it was an Irish woman and as one of those fishermen did stand up and lift his rod his rifle, the rest of us we were silent, it was a complicated, amazing thing to see.

When the salmon the trout passed beneath us when the seals went under the bridge we ran to the other side of the road and the passing traffic was forced to a stop to let us follow the hunt and flight down the river to the harbour the ocean and whatever awaited them there. As we lost sight of the smooth backs of the seals I broke with the crowd turned off the bridge and made down the walkway back to the harbour to follow them out to sea.

As the seals disappeared in the waves beyond the pier I decided I would go to Blackrock before the change of the tide. I took my phone from my pocket before I set off, then closed it and put it back in my pocket. There were many people on the path that led the town away.

Tidal force is the change of the force of gravity over distance. It is one of the relationships between objects in the universe and is determined by three factors within the equation of gravitational force: (1) the strength of the unperturbed force of gravity acting between one body and another (determined by the mass of these bodies); (2) the extension of the examined body; (3) the distance between the two bodies. These factors form the symbolic reality of tidal force.

If a person approached a microscopic black hole (feet first), the black hole as a *thing out there having enormous mass* would create a gravitational force that would act upon the body of the person. The strength of this force would be felt differently upon the person's toes (where it would be almost unimaginably strong) and the top of their head (where it would be incredibly weaker) given the size of any person relative to the black hole (with its enormous mass). As the person approached the black hole this difference would cause them to greatly, terrifyingly stretch. This is the fantastic reality of tidal force.

The Earth's oceans are stretched in this way, albeit more gently, by the Moon and (to a lesser extent) by the Sun. This creates our local reality of tidal forces: tides. The Earth rotates on its axis every twenty-four hours (approximately) and so all places on Earth change their position relative to the Moon, which orbits the Earth at a much slower rate (every twenty-seven days), each day and at the edge of the Atlantic Ocean, Galway moves through two high tides in twenty-four hours, once when the moon is directly above the city, once when it is directly below. When the Sun Moon and Earth are aligned, which is also when we see new and full moons, the tidal forces generated by the Sun and the Moon on the Earth pull in the same direction and the tides the Earth moves into are at their largest. These are known as spring tides it was one of them that day and the ladder leading out of the water by the diving tower at Blackrock Beach only glimmered below the surface of the breaking sea.

A female lifeguard sat with her back against the stone wall that divided the water and the rock shore at Blackrock from the private land around it and the road it led off. She was in a red swimsuit and shorts and the sun fell over my shoulder onto the skin of her bare right arm and a shade of freckles forming there. There was a white and red megaphone on the ground at her side, a pair of binoculars, and above us a red flag flying from a tall, rusted iron pole. I thought I remembered her voice. *You could take a chance could swim but you would be better off without risking it there's a lion's mane true enough but though we think he's drifting out to sea again it's a while we haven't seen him so decide for yourself but no, do not chance it, they aren't to be messed with on such tides.* I felt the pack on my back my swimming togs my towel in it, I would go and have a look. *If you want. You'll recognise it and think it lonely.*

It was a strange thing to say, even in the summer in Galway.

Her eyes were a very pale blue, almost green.

As I walked towards the water, for the storm the night before, for the drink, the seagulls the morning, for the work in the pub and the sun on my shoulders I felt heavy, not tired, but as though I could sleep.

The lowest level of the concrete tower that rose out from the rock shore and over the water was submerged by the tide. The second level ran about ten feet above the water and along it there were people gathered, some in their swimming suits, looking out over the water and at the sky blue to the horizon. I passed by them and climbed the stairs.

The third level of the tower was another ten feet high. There the air was cooler. And although I would have liked it to be different there was not another person there.

I moved forward towards the platform's edge, the water, and looked out, first across the close surface of the ocean, then back from where I had come, to Salthill and Galway. I turned towards the rock shore and looked for the lifeguard, but she was gone.

There were many seagulls in the sky. They were out hunting. And somewhere in amongst the weight of the water that pushed along the coast were the seals from the river the trout and the salmon. I could not see the lion's mane and it may or may not have been there too, drifting or fighting against the tide. In Galway, the summer, watch how the present does rise and fall.

STINGING FLY PATRONS

Many thanks to:

Susan Armstrong
Maria Behan
Valerie Bistany
Jacqueline Brown
Trish Byrne
Brian Cliff
Edmond Condon
Evelyn Conlon
Sheila Crowley
Paul Curley
Kris Deffenbacher
Enrico Del Prete
Andrew Donovan
Gerry Dukes
Kieran Falconer
Ciara Ferguson
Stephen Grant
Brendan Hackett
Huang Haisu
Sean Hanrahan
Christine Dwyer Hickey
Dennis & Mimi Houlihan
Garry Hynes
Nuala Jackson
Charles Julienne
Jeremy Kavanagh
Geoffrey Keating
Jerry Kelleher
Jack Kelleher
Margaret Kelleher
Claire Keogh
Joe Lawlor
Irene Rose Ledger
Ilana Lifshitz
Lucy Luck
Petra McDonough

Jon McGregor
John McInerney
Maureen McLaughlin
Niall MacMonagle
Finbar McLoughlin
Maggie McLoughlin
Ama, Grace & Fraoch MacSweeney
Mary MacSweeney
Paddy & Moira MacSweeney
Anil Malhotra
Gerry Marmion
Ivan Mulcahy
Michael O'Connor
Ed O'Loughlin
Lucy Perrem
Maria Pierce
Peter J. Pitkin
George & Joan Preble
Fiona Ruff
Anne Ryan
Linda Ryan
Alf Scott
Ann Seery
Attique Shafiq
Eileen Sheridan
Alfie & Savannah Stephenson
Helena Texier
Olive Towey
John Vaughan
Debbi Voisey
Therese Walsh
Ruth Webster
The Blue Nib (Poetry Website)
Museum of Literature Ireland
Solas Nua

*We'd also like to thank those individuals who have expressed the preference
to remain anonymous.*

BECOME A PATRON ONLINE AT STINGINGFLY.ORG

Kevin Barry is the author of six books, most recently the story collection *That Old Country Music*. He also writes plays and screenplays, and is co-editor and publisher of the annual arts anthology *Winter Papers*. He lives in County Sligo.

Megan Buckley received her PhD from NUI Galway in 2013. Her work has been published in Irish and international journals. She works in educational publishing and as a freelance writer and editor.

Stan Carey is an editor and writer from the west of Ireland. He writes a column on language for *Macmillan Dictionary* and has also written for *The Guardian, History Today, Merriam-Webster, Slate, The Fortnightly Review*, and others.

Aoife Casby lives on the west coast of Ireland where she swims, grows potatoes and works as a writer, editor and visual artist. She completed a PhD in Goldsmiths in 2020. Her short fiction is widely published in literary magazines and journals.

Emily S. Cooper's work has been published widely in journals. Her debut pamphlet, *Glass*, will be published by Makina Books in 2021.

Gavin Corbett is from Dublin. Among his published works are three novels: *Innocence, This Is the Way* and *Green Glowing Skull*. He has been Arts Council writer-in-residence at both Trinity College Dublin and UCD.

Elaine Cosgrove is from the west of Ireland. Her debut book of poetry, *Transmissions*, is published by Dedalus Press. Elaine emigrated to Atlanta, Georgia in 2019.

Louis de Paor's most recent collections are *The brindled cat and the nightingale's tongue* (2014) and *Grá fiar* (2016). A new bilingual selection of his poems with translations by Biddy Jenkinson and Kevin Anderson will be published by Bloodaxe Books in 2022.

Annie Deppe's third book of poetry, *Night Collage*, is forthcoming from Arlen House. Her work has appeared in numerous journals and anthologies including *Poetry Ireland Review, Sojourners*, and *The Forward Book of Poetry, 2004*. She makes her home on the coast in Connemara.

Rob Doyle is the author of three internationally acclaimed books: *Threshold, This Is the Ritual*, and *Here Are the Young Men*, which has been adapted for film. He has written for *The New York Times, TLS, The Guardian*, et cetera, and edited the anthologies, *The Other Irish Tradition* and *In This Skull Hotel Where I Never Sleep*.

Attracta Fahy completed her MA in Writing at NUI Galway in 2017. She had a poem featured in New Irish Writing in *The Irish Times* in October 2019. She has been a Pushcart: Best of the Web nominee, and was shortlisted for the Over The Edge New Writer of the Year Award and Allingham Festival's poetry competition. Fly on the Wall Press published her chapbook, *Dinner in the Fields*, in March 2020.

Dean Fee has been published in *The Stinging Fly* and *The Dublin Review*. He participated in *The Stinging Fly*'s mentorship scheme in 2019 and is currently working on a novel.

Tiana M. Fischer was born in Gifhorn, Germany, in 1993, and re-born in Galway in 2017. When she doesn't moonlight as a writer of experimental verse, she researches and teaches obscure literature at NUI Galway.

Ella Gaynor is a recent graduate from NUI Galway's BA with Creative Writing. Her memoir 'On Swimming' was shortlisted in the Write by the Sea Literary Festival. Ella is currently working on a collection of short stories.

Aimee Godfrey is a disabled poet, whose work largely focuses on how disability intersects with and impacts on other facets of the human condition. Her work has previously been published by *Dodging the Rain*. She is working towards a first collection.

Aideen Henry is a physician living in Galway. She has published short fiction and poetry. Her collection of short stories, *Hugging Thistles*, was published by Arlen House. Her two collections of poetry, *Hands Moving at the Speed of Falling Snow* and *Slow Bruise*, were published by Salmon Poetry.

Fred Johnston received a Hennessy Literary Award in 1972 and, with Neil Jordan and Peter Sheridan, was co-founder of the Irish Writers' Co-operative (Co-Op Books). In 1986 he founded Galway's annual Cúirt festival. His most recent collection of poems is *Rogue States* (Salmon, 2019). He lives in Galway.

James Martyn Joyce is from Galway. Publications include: *Shedding Skin* (poetry, 2010); *What's Not Said* (short stories, 2012); and *Noir by Noir West* (short stories, as editor, 2014). His most recent collection of poetry, *Furey*, was published by Doire Press in 2018.

Róisín Kiberd is a writer from Dublin, currently living in Berlin. Her essays and journalism on technology and culture have been published in *The Dublin Review*, *The White Review, The Stinging Fly, The Guardian, Vice,* and others. Her first book, *The Disconnect*, will be published by Serpent's Tail in 2021.

Clara Kumagai is from Canada, Japan and Ireland. She writes fiction and non-fiction for children and adults, and currently lives in Tokyo.

Joanne McCarthy writes in Waterford, in both English and Irish. She is most recently published in *The Honest Ulsterman* and has work forthcoming in *The Stony Thursday Book* and the Ireland Chair of Poetry Anthology. She is founder and co-editor of *The Waxed Lemon*. Tweets @josieannarua

Neil McCarthy is a graduate of NUI Galway. His first book, *Stopgap Grace*, was published by Salmon Poetry in 2018 and subsequently shortlisted for the Shine Strong Award. He currently lives in Vienna.

Mike McCormack is the author of two collections of short stories and three novels. In 2016 *Solar Bones* won the Goldsmiths Prize and in 2018 it was awarded the International Dublin Literary Award. He is currently working on a collection of short stories and teaches creative writing at NUI Galway.

Afric McGlinchey is the author of two collections, *The lucky star of hidden things* and *Ghost of the Fisher Cat* (Salmon Poetry), which were translated into Italian and published by L'Arcolaio. A surrealist chapbook, *Invisible Insane* (SurVision) appeared in 2019. An auto-fictional memoir is forthcoming from Broken Sleep Books.

Alan McMonagle has written for radio and published two collections of short stories. *Ithaca*, his first novel, was published by Picador in 2017. His second novel, *Laura Cassidy's Walk Of Fame*, was published in March 2020.

Carolann Caviglia Madden is a University of Houston PhD candidate. Her work has appeared in *World Literature Today, Nimrod International Journal, Yalobusha Review, Public Poetry,* and elsewhere. Madden is a recent Fulbright recipient, Poetry Editor for *Gulf Coast,* and winner of the Inprint Verlaine Prize for Poetry. She currently lives in Galway.

Andrew Meehan's work has been published in *The Moth, Banshee* and *Winter Papers*. He has published two novels, *One Star Awake* (New Island Books, 2017), and *The Mystery Of Love* (Head of Zeus, 2020), and he teaches at the University of Strathclyde in Glasgow.

Geraldine Mitchell has three published poetry collections, her most recent being *Mountains for Breakfast* (2017). Her next collection is forthcoming from Arlen House. She is a Patrick Kavanagh Award winner and lives on the County Mayo coast, looking across the mouth of Killary Harbour to County Galway.

Cian Murphy was born in Cork and lives in London. His poems have most recently been published in *Poetry Ireland Review, Popshot* and *Strix*. He is a board member of the Bristol Poetry Institute.

Jade Murphy graduated from NUI Galway with a BA in Creative Writing, English and History. She is currently finishing her master's degree in Education and teaches in Salerno Jesus and Mary Secondary School in Salthill, Galway. Murphy writes both fiction and poetry. Her work has been featured in *Poetry Ireland Review.*

Peter Murphy is from Wexford. He has published two novels, *John the Revelator* and *Shall We Gather at the River* (Faber). His band recently released their debut album, *Cursed Murphy Versus the Resistance. The Hands of Franky Machine,* a 'movie for the ears' is available online.

Anne Mulkeen Murray is a retired Educational Psychologist who grew up on the Donegal/Derry border. Her family roots are in Connemara. She writes comedy scripts for radio, screenplays for film and television, and occasional poetry.

Kathleen Murray lives in Dublin. Her stories have appeared in anthologies such as *Davy Byrne Stories* (2009) and *All Over Ireland* (2015) and in journals including *The Stinging Fly, The Dublin Review* and Granta online.

Nuala O'Connor lives in County Galway. Her forthcoming fifth novel, *Nora,* is about Nora Barnacle, wife and muse to James Joyce; it appears in early 2021. Her chapbook of historical flash fiction, *Birdie,* was recently published by Arlen House. Nuala is editor of the flash e-zine, *Splonk.* www.nualaoconnor.com

Mary O'Donoghue's short stories have appeared in *The Stinging Fly, Granta, Banshee, Georgia Review, Guernica, Kenyon Review, The Dublin Review* and elsewhere. Originally from Clare, she lives in Tuscaloosa, Alabama and works in Boston, Massachusetts.

Nessa O'Mahony was born in Dublin. She is the recipient of three literature bursaries from the Arts Council of Ireland. She has published five books of poetry—*Bar Talk* (1999), *Trapping a Ghost* (2005), *In Sight of Home* (2009) and *Her Father's Daughter* (2014). *The Hollow Woman on the Island* was published by Salmon Poetry in 2019.

Scríbhneoir, aisteoir agus craoltóir mór le rá ba ea **Joe Steve Ó Neachtain**. **Joe Steve Ó Neachtain** was a renowned writer, actor and broadcaster.

Katelyn O'Neill is a student at NUI Galway, who spends her spare time reading, writing, and endlessly scrolling through TikTok. She is currently working on a first collection. Previous publications include *Burning Jade Magazine*.

Katie O'Sullivan is a Creative Writing student at NUI Galway. She has had poems published with *Dodging the Rain*, *Strukturriss*, NUIG's Writer's Society, *SIN* and *The Galway Review*. She is currently working towards her first collection.

Michael Phoenix is a writer and human rights researcher from Belfast. He is currently working on a novel.

Ruth Quinlan was selected for a Heinrich Böll Cottage Writer Residency in 2020 and the Cork Poetry Festival Introductions series. Previously, she was selected for the Poetry Ireland Introductions Series and an individual artist bursary by Galway City Council. She is co-editor of *Skylight 47*, the Galway-based poetry publication.

Liz Quirke is a writer and scholar from County Kerry. Salmon Poetry published her debut collection, *The Road, Slowly*, in 2018. She teaches on the MA in Writing at NUI Galway and is completing a PhD on Queer Kinship in Contemporary Poetry.

Moya Roddy's debut collection, *Out of the Ordinary*, was shortlisted for the Shine Strong Award. Her novel, *The Long Way Home*, was described in *The Irish Times* as 'simply brilliant'. *Other People*, a short-story collection, was nominated for the Frank O'Connor International Short Story Award.

Emer Rogers lives in Dublin but hails from County Limerick. She was a participant of The Stinging Fly's fiction workshop and has an MA in Creative Writing from University College Dublin. Her fiction has been previously published in *The Stinging Fly*. She is working on a collection of short stories.

Toh Hsien Min has authored four books of poetry, most recently *Dans quel sens tombent les feuilles* (Paris: Éditions Caractères, 2016). His work has also recently appeared in *Magma*, *PN Review* and *SAND Journal*. Hsien Min lives in Singapore, where he edits the *Quarterly Literary Review Singapore*.

Molly Twomey has been published in *Poetry Ireland Review*, *Banshee*, *The Irish Times*, *Crannóg*, and elsewhere. In 2019, she won the Padraic Colum Poetry Prize and was runner-up in The Waterford Poetry Prize. Selected for Words Ireland's Mentorship Programme 2020, she is currently under the guidance of Grace Wells.

Colin Walsh was named Hennessy New Irish Writer of the Year in 2019. In 2017 he won the RTÉ Francis MacManus Short Story Award. In 2020 he received a bursary from the Arts Council towards the completion of his first novel. He lives in Belgium. He is from Galway.

Is as Cill Mhantáin ó dhúchas é **David Wheatley**, ach é ag cur faoi le fada an lá anois in Albain. *The President of Planet Earth* (Carcanet) an leabhar is deanaí uaidh.
David Wheatley was born in Wicklow but he has been living in Scotland for many years. *The President of Planet Earth* (Carcanet) is his latest collection.